Oxford for the Under-Eights

A guide to Oxford for carers of young children

About this Book and NPN

Oxford for the Under-Eights attempts to guide parents, prospective parents and carers through the various facilities on offer in Oxford; from antenatal care to going to school and beyond. Subjects covered include healthcare, support services, recreational facilities, eating out and childcare. We have added an expanded index to make it even easier for you to find what you need quickly.

Many thanks to all of you who have made kind comments and suggested additions and alterations. We hope you will like this new updated and redesigned version. Most of the research for this edition was undertaken in 2003. Every attempt has been made to ensure that information is up-to-date and accurate at the time of going to press, but with a book of this type details are constantly changing so please forgive any errors and omissions.

Most of all, KEEP THE SUGGESTIONS COMING! Please use the form at the end of the book or contact Heather ☎ 249466 or Nichola ☎ 775832 or email oxfordforunder8s@oxoncis.org.uk

New Parent Network

We are an independent local, self-help, group/voluntary association of people who care for children. We particularly welcome new parents and parents who are new to Oxford. As well as providing information and support in the form of this book and regular magazines, we organise social and educational opportunities, including coffee groups in people's homes, early education groups, workshops, parties and pub evenings led by speakers on parenting issues.

Annual membership costs £6, which includes three magazines. To join, please use the form at the back of this book. For more information about the New Parent Network or its activities, please call either Heather ☎ 249466 or Nichola ☎ 775832.

Oxford for the Under-Eights

A guide to Oxford for carers of young children

NPN 2004

First published in Great Britain by New Parent Network 1990
Second edition 1993
Third edition 1996
Fourth edition 2000
This edition 2004

Text copyright © NPN 2004

ISBN 0-9544160-1-5

Illustrations © Val Norman (1996), Pauline Battigelli (2000)
Maps of Oxford © Heather Dalitz (2004)

Children's pictures by: Emily Bradbury, Francesca Burrell, Claudia Chalmers, Coral Flitney, Catherine Godfrey, Ruth Hamilton, Eloise Huxley, Chad Meadowcroft, Leon Quelch, Isadora Reeve, Louis Rogers, Georgia Saldanha, Ella Walmsley, Alexandra Waring Paynter, Hebe York
Illustrations © 2000, 2004 resides with the artists

Bus route maps courtesy of Oxford Bus Company and Stagecoach; many thanks to Rachel Wiggan for the map of East Oxford for asylum seekers

With contributions by: Catherine Burch, Kirsten Burrell, Martin Cattermole, Vicki Cullen, Heather Dalitz, Tracey Chantler, Lynne Gardham, David Hodges, Rachel Honey, Ann Horrell, Julia Horsnell, Liz MacKinnon, Nichola May, Jane Mouat Saldanha, Denise Salambasis, Paula Tebay, Kim Waring Paynter, Marilyn Watts, Caroline Whitfeld
Edited and Designed by Julia Bruce

Many thanks to everyone who provided us with information to produce this fifth edition.

The NPN is grateful to the Oxford City Divisional Liaison Panel and the Oxfordshire Children's Information Service for financial support.

Printed and bound by Parchment Oxford, Crescent Road, Oxford.

All rights reserved. Apart from fair dealing for the purpose of private study, research, criticism or review, as permitted under the Copyright Designs and Patents Act 1988, no part of this publication may be reproduced, stored in a retrieval system, or transmitted in any form or by any means, electronic, electrical, chemical, mechanical, optical, photocopying, recording or otherwise, without prior written permission. All enquiries should be addressed to:
New Parent Network c/o 67 Princes Street, Oxford OX4 1DE

The contents of this publication are believed to be correct at the time of printing. Nevertheless, *New Parent Network* cannot accept responsibility for errors and omissions, or for changes in the details given. Inclusion in this publication does not imply endorsement by *New Parent Network* of any services or information.

Contents

Oxford area map   inside front cover

Preface   vii
Signposts   viii

Chapter 1
Having a Baby in Oxford   1

Chapter 2
Your Child's Health   18

Chapter 3
Parental Support   39

Chapter 4
Meeting People   50

Chapter 5
Getting About   70

Chapter 6
Shopping   77

Chapter 7
Mail Order and Services   88

Chapter 8
Libraries   100

Chapter 9
For You   107

Chapter 10
Eating Out   115

Chapter 11
Out and About in Oxford   132

Chapter 12
Days Out   145

Chapter 13
Holiday Times   164

Chapter 14
Parties and Treats   174

Chapter 15
Activities for Kids   182

Chapter 16
Childcare   203

Chapter 17
Playgroups and Nursery Schools   210

Chapter 18
Off to School   218

Index   223

NPN membership form   241

Standing order mandate   243

Updates and improvements   245

Refugee resources map   247

Oxford city centre map   248

Oxford Bus Co. map   inside back cover

Stagecoach bus map   back cover

Keep the suggestions coming!

You can either use the form at the end of the book or contact NPN direct:
Heather ☎ 249466
Nichola ☎ 775832
oxfordforunder8s@oxoncis.org.uk

☎☎☎☎ A note about telephone numbers ☎☎☎☎

Telephone numbers are all Oxford (01865) unless otherwise stated.

Preface

Welcome to the fifth edition of *Oxford for the Under-Eights*. It is many years since a friend, Mary Cann, and I decided to put a booklet together giving information on what was available to parents in Oxford. Having had our first babies, we were fed up with how difficult is was to find out what was going on.

Those new babies are now strapping young men of 19, and over the intervening years there have been many new initiatives in the early years, both at national and local level. What started as a very slim booklet grew, thanks to the efforts of many, into a book.

How pleased I am to know that the guide is still going strong. As always it has been compiled and produced by people 'in the know': parents of young children. So, if you are pregnant, or have the care of a baby or young child, live in Oxford or visit regularly, this is very much the book for you.

I hope you enjoy this new edition and that it enables you and your children to make the most of Oxford.

Vicki Cullen
April 2004

FAMILIES OF VISITING WORKERS AT OXFORD UNIVERSITY

The Oxford University Newcomers Club holds informal coffee mornings at 13 Norham Gardens every Wednesday during term time and summer holidays, and has meetings for families with children aged 0-4 every Friday from 10.15 to 12 noon during term time. It offers help, advice, information and secondhand items for sale to wives, husbands and partners of visiting scholars and members of the University new to Oxford.

DISABLED AND SPECIAL NEEDS CHILDREN

A Local Guide for Parents of Disabled Children and Young People and those with Special Needs is available from the Childcare Development Team ☎ 875215 or the Oxfordshire Children's Information Service, ☎ 01993 886933, email enquiries@oxon-cis.org.uk. See also Chapter 2 - Your Child's Health under "Special Needs" for details of the more comprehensive "Green Pack"

FAMILIES WITH OLDER CHILDREN

See *Oxfordshire Survival: A guide for young people*, SLM Publishing, ☎ 395235. For information on Youth Centres, groups and activities for teenagers/young people contact the Oxfordshire Children's Information Service tel 01993 886933, email enquiries@oxoncis.org.uk or visit the Oxfordshire Youth Service website www.spired.com

ASYLUM SEEKERS

Visit Asylum Welcome at 276a Cowley Road, ☎ 722082, email asylum-welcome@supanet.com. The map on page 247 shows the locations of Asylum Welcome and the other major local facilities for refugees and asylum seekers (eg, advice, free English lessons, housing, schools, surgeries).

Chapter 1 - Having a Baby in Oxford

In this chapter we look at pregnancy and childbirth and the related facilities and support that you can expect to find in Oxford. The quality of care here is very high and there are a number of antenatal and birth options available to you.

PLANNING A PREGNANCY

Before getting pregnant you might like to have a chat with a health professional. Ask your doctor's receptionist for the name of your **health visitor** or **community midwife**, they will be able to give you information and advice. If you are new to Oxford and need to register with a doctor call **NHS Direct** on 0845 4647. NHS Direct can also offer advice on illnesses, conditions and treatments as well as complementary therapies and how to look after yourself.

If you are concerned that you might pass on some inherited disability to your baby, see your GP who should be able to advise you and, if appropriate, recommend genetic counselling. Alternatively, contact Lynne Bell, Level 2, John Radcliffe Women's Centre, ☎ 221716.

Tip: To help ensure a healthy pregnancy, check that you are immune to Rubella (German measles). If you are not, ask for a vaccination at least three months before you become pregnant. Women who contract Rubella in pregnancy run the risk of the baby developing abnormally. It is also recommended that you take a supplement of folic acid (a member of the vitamin B complex) before and during pregnancy, to reduce the risk of spina bifida.

Having a baby in Oxford

Fertility Problems

If you have been trying for a baby for over six months without success, you may have a fertility problem. You can ask your GP for a referral to the fertility clinic at the John Radcliffe Hospital ☎ 221622. Investigation of the problem will usually involve blood tests for women and sperm sampling for men. These diagnostic procedures are free on the NHS and, in most cases, will identify a likely cause of infertility.

Some treatments are available on the NHS, but if you need IVF you will be referred to the IVF unit at the JR ☎ 221900 and your treatment will be self-funded. This is not cheap! A cycle of IVF can cost more than £2,000. (Less complicated treatments are cheaper.) The unit has a voluntary group, Friends of IVF, which produces a newsletter, fundraises and operates a helpline. ☎ 221900 for details.

Fostering and Adoption

If you are considering fostering or adopting a child, contact the **Social and Health Care Directorate** of **Oxfordshire County Council** ☎ 815347 for an information booklet.

There are many myths about who can foster and adopt children; so please don't be put off by your preconceptions. The truth is that ordinary people, from all walks of life and all sections of society, are needed. You can be single or married; own your own home or be renting; with or without your own children; you may be in paid employment, in early retirement, or unemployed. Age is not in itself a barrier.

Once you apply to become a foster or adoptive parent, the Social & Health Care **Family Placement Team** will invite you to attend one of their information meetings and will provide preparation, training and continuing advice and support to ensure that this challenging experience is a very positive and rewarding one for both you and the child or children in your care.

Overseas adoption

It is also possible to adopt from abroad. The charity, Parents and Children Together (PACT) can advise on adoption generally and offer an overseas adoption service ☎ 0800 731 1845

IF YOU THINK YOU ARE PREGNANT

Emergency contraception

If you have unprotected sex, or your contraception fails and you do not wish to run the risk of becoming pregnant, your GP can prescribe the combined pill within 72 hours of intercourse. For those who cannot take the combined pill, there is now a new, but less effective, emergency contraceptive pill which has to be taken within 48 hours of intercourse. Alternatively, you could have a coil fitted within five days of intercourse.

Advice and guidance on contraception is available at the **Alec Turnbull**

Having a baby in Oxford

Family Planning Clinic, East Oxford Health Centre, Manzil Way, Cowley Road, ☎ 456666. The clinic also provides free contraceptive supplies, and information on sexually transmitted diseases. You can phone for advice or simply drop-in Mon–Fri 9.30–7.30 or on Saturdays between 9.30 and 12.00.

Pregnancy testing

Most chemists sell easy-to-use home pregnancy-testing kits. Alternatively, you can take a urine sample into a chemist advertising pregnancy tests or ask your doctor for a free pregnancy test. You can also get a test done at the Alec Turnbull Clinic (see above). There is a small charge unless you are on income support. You are given immediate results and the clinic will discuss the choices open to you if you are not happy about being pregnant.

Pregnant? Need advice?

Have a chat with your doctor or contact the following organisations:

*British Pregnancy Advisory Service
☎ 0845 7304030
Pregnancy testing, contraception, counselling and information about problem pregnancies, sterilisation and infertility.

*Oxford LIFE Pregnancy Centre
130 High Street, Oxford
☎ 202435
Offers practical help including free pregnancy tests, non-directive pregnancy/abortion counselling and counselling after abortion. Also offers help with housing before and after birth and a hospice for sick new-born babies.

If you have a miscarriage

Your GP or health visitor will be able to advise you on the medical aspects of your miscarriage but if you would like to talk to someone who has been through the same experience, contact:

*The Miscarriage Association
☎ 01924 200799 (9.00–4.00 Mon-Fri and 24-hour answerphone)

*Miscarriage Support Group
For advice and information
☎ Angela Taylor 432854

CHOICES OF ANTENATAL CARE

You can usually choose the sort of care you receive during your pregnancy. This may be completely 'community based' or shared between your GP and midwife and a hospital consultant. Remember, if your doctor does not provide the sort of care you would like, you can go to another doctor. If you want to know more about the different patterns of antenatal care available, ask your midwife, GP or the staff in the **Antenatal Clinic** of the hospital.

More information about antenatal care and tests, care in labour, postnatal care and the maternity hospital is avail-

Having a baby in Oxford

able in a booklet produced by the **Women's Centre** at the John Radcliffe Hospital. The following types of care are available.

Community-based care

This is available within Oxford if you have no serious health problems, are not taking regular medicine or have not had a major problem with an earlier pregnancy. Antenatal care is offered by your GP and community midwife at your local surgery or health centre.

You will get to know your community midwife through your GP and, if this is your first baby, she may visit you at home before your baby is due. When you go into labour you will be attended by a midwife from your community midwife's team. If your pregnancy is normal, you will not need to attend the hospital for any of the regular antenatal care, although you will be offered an ultrasound scan at the Women's Centre during your pregnancy, usually at around 19 or 20 weeks.

If you opt for a home birth you will be attended by a community midwife. Contact the **Community Midwives' Office** ☎ 221696.

Care outside the city

Community-based care is also offered outside the city. If no problems are anticipated, you could arrange to have your baby in one of the cottage hospitals. These are at Chipping Norton, Wallingford and Wantage. (Oxford residents can elect to go to Wallingford.) The standard of care in labour and postnatally is very high at these hospitals and they have been awarded **Baby Friendly** status by UNICEF in recognition of the support they give to breastfeeding mothers and their babies.

Hospital/consultant care

Under this option, most of your care is at the hospital under the direction of a consultant obstetrician. This will be recommended if your medical history suggests that you might have problems in pregnancy or labour.

The Silver Star team

If you have specific medical problems which develop during, or are affected by, pregnancy (e.g. pre-eclampsia) you will receive extra attention from the specialist Silver Star Team.

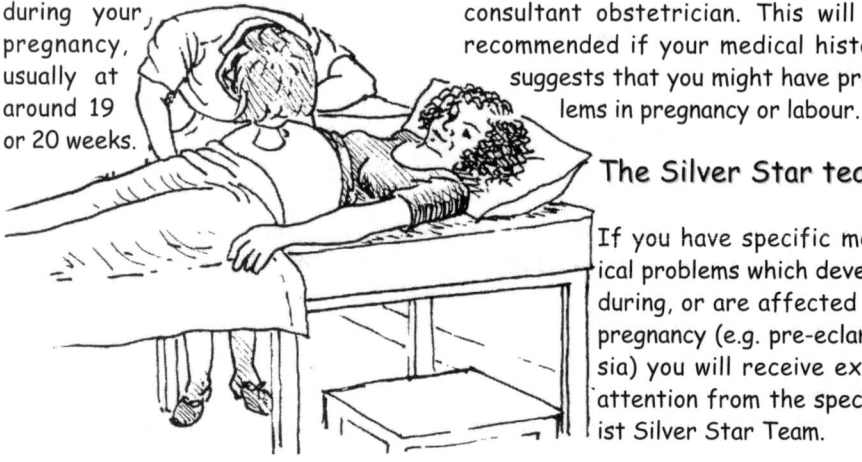

Having a baby in Oxford

The **Day Assessment Unit** is closely linked to the team and offers frequent and detailed checks on mothers' and babies' well-being if complications develop.

Hospital births

The Women's Centre is a separate block at the John Radcliffe Hospital which handles all maternity care. It houses the **Delivery Suite**, antenatal facilities – such as ultrasound scanning – and the maternity wards. The centre is very well staffed and equipped and the standard of care is high. The overall atmosphere is friendly and relatively informal. A birthing pool is available and the staff are trained in the use of some complementary medical techniques such as aromatherapy. There is a breastfeeding clinic on Level 5 which has a very high reputation. (See: *The JR Women's Centre* below)

Home births

If you would like to have your baby at home, you will need to talk to your midwife and/or GP. If your pregnancy has been normal, a home birth can usually be arranged. You can be referred to another GP practice if you feel that you are not being given appropriate information to enable you to make an informed choice about the place of birth. The supervisor of midwives at the Women's Centre will give you the necessary information and will support you in your choice. To talk to other mothers who have chosen a homebirth you can contact the **Homebirth Support Group**: ☎Oddny Bagguley 07881 624208

It is also possible to employ an **independent midwife** to provide your antenatal care and attend at your homebirth. These are midwives who have practised in the NHS and now offer a private service. Independent midwives usually provide all your antenatal care in your home, as well as attending the birth and visiting for up to a month afterwards. They can refer you for scans and other antenatal tests, which will normally be provided on the NHS in your local hospital. Many independent midwives can also attend your birth in hospital if a transfer becomes necessary, although this varies between areas. The fees may be from £1,500 to £4,000. **The Independent Midwives Association** has a list of independent midwives in the UK. *www.independentmidwives.org.uk*

A **doula** (pronounced "doola") is a professional labour supporter and/or postnatal helper. A labour doula provides advice and support and acts as your advocate during labour, while a postnatal doula visits you after the birth to help out and to support you with breastfeeding. ☎ Caroline Naish 361569 or look on the website: *www.doula.org.uk*

PREPARING FOR THE BIRTH

Your midwife and GP should give you advice and support during your antena-

Having a baby in Oxford

tal check-ups. They have information leaflets on a range of topics and will talk to you about issues like antenatal tests and your plans for feeding the baby. You may also find it useful, particularly if this is your first baby, to go along to some of the many antenatal classes available. As well as teaching skills and offering support, the classes provide an opportunity to meet other people who are expecting babies and often lasting friendships are formed.

• • • • • • • • • • • • • • • • • • • •

Tip: If you are a smoker, try to give up. For advice and encouragement contact Quitline on 020 7487 3000

• • • • • • • • • • • • • • • • • • • •

PARENTHOOD CLASSES

Antenatal classes usually run in the last weeks of pregnancy and can be divided into two groups: exercise based and factual. The factual classes aim to prepare you for birth and parenthood. Topics include labour and delivery, feeding, life with a new baby and how your partner can help. Women are encouraged to bring their partners to classes as much of the purpose is to discuss with each other your plans for the birth and care of the baby.

NHS Classes

These take place at the Women's Centre or your local clinic and are free. Those at the hospital are run by a midwife and an obstetric physiotherapist. They will familiarise you with the Delivery Suite and maternity wards at the hospital, lead discussions on health during pregnancy and answer any queries you may have about everything from diet, back pain and exercises, to the development of your baby and relaxation and pain relief during labour.

The course also offers advice on care of the newborn. It consists of five evening sessions starting at about 30 weeks of pregnancy. Your midwife will let you know when your most appropriate course starts at your local clinic.

One-day preparation classes are usually one Saturday a month. Phone for dates and details. Participants must attend the hospital tour beforehand (see below).

If you think the hospital classes may suit you, call the **parent education midwives** for details on ☎ 220458. You should book for these classes when you are about 22-24 weeks pregnant.

Having a baby in Oxford

The midwives also run refresher classes for those who have had a baby before and would like some updating and revision. The two-session course runs on Tuesday mornings; ☎ 220458 to book.

Pre-natal diagnosis run an early pregnancy class. You are invited to attend ideally between eight and ten weeks of pregnancy, but up to 16 weeks is fine. Sessions are held on the 3rd Tuesday of every month at the Women's Centre, from 7.00pm. All aspects of early pregnancy are discussed. Please phone 221716 to book a place.

Women's Centre tours

If you are considering a hospital birth at the John Radcliffe you may like to have a look around first. Tours take place on Tuesdays at 3.00 and Mondays and Thursdays at 6.00. Meet in the reception area on Level 2 at the Women's Centre; no need to book. ☎220458 for more details.

*Young Mums' Pregnancy Club
This is an informal opportunity to meet other young mothers, a midwife and a physiotherapist to chat about all aspects of pregnancy, labour and becoming a mother. You don't have to book, just turn up at the Parent Education Room at the Women's Centre on Wednesdays between 11.30 and 1.00. Bring anyone with you, including other children if you have them. There are refreshments and toys for toddlers. ☎ 220458 for details.

National Childbirth Trust

NCT classes seek to give impartial and comprehensive information in the informal and friendly setting of the teacher's home. As every birth is different they discuss all the possible courses labour may take, covering inductions and caesareans as well as drug-free deliveries. Plenty of time is also devoted to life after the birth, recovering, coping and caring for and feeding the baby. Classes are run in small groups ensuring that people are comfortable to ask questions and try out relaxation techniques. Many groups stay in touch and form a valuable support network after the classes have finished. There is a charge for these classes. Concessions may be available for those on income support. Refresher classes (short courses for people who already have children) are available, please ask. Early booking is advised.
Virgil Clarke (NCT teacher)
☎ 727209
Louise Hunter (NCT teacher)
☎ 01235 520726
For membership information
☎ **Kirsten Burrell** 426215

The NCT also organises:
Nearly New Sales – See: *Ch. 7 Mail Order and Services*
Breast pump hire – ☎ Alison Baker 864812, Jane Higgs 375667

Having a baby in Oxford

Valley cushion hire – ☎ Nicky Scott 725661
Postnatal support groups – ☎ Joanna Steele 723266
NCT maternity sales (good quality maternity bras with personal fitting service) ☎ Mel Minns 516648.

* * *

Tip: Attend as many classes as you can – they all have something different to offer, and you will have more opportunities to meet other parents.

* * *

EXERCISE BASED CLASSES

Active birth

*Oxford Active Birth
Childbirth professionals who aim to provide a comprehensive and flexible service for prospective and new parents. This includes active birth classes, antenatal yoga classes, birth preparation for partners (group and private sessions by arrangement), baby massage. Also TENS and birthing pool hire; waterbirth workshops and birth attendance. Oxford Active Birth also arrange maternity sales, always a useful source of good, second hand clothes and equipment. Contact:
Kay Millar (active birth teacher)
☎ 554743
Kate Macfarlane (booking secretary)
☎ 760405

Yoga

*Yoga for Pregnancy (up to 32 weeks)
*Yoga for Birth (32+ weeks)
Asian Cultural Centre
Manzil Way, Cowley Road
☎ Angela 779881
Classes focus on improving flexibility during pregnancy, alleviating common ailments, relaxation and use of the breath, positions for labour and positive visualisation. To book your place please ring early in pregnancy. No previous experience required.

*Prenatal Yoga
Yoga Garden
4 South Parade, Summertown
For 12+ weeks
Wed 9.30 am
Cost: £28.00/ four 1.5 hour sessions.
☎ 311300

Aquanatal swimming

This is a very enjoyable and beneficial antenatal preparation and is available at the following pools (telephone the pools or the parent education midwives on 220458 for details of courses and booking dates).

*Ferry Pool
Marston Ferry Road
Summertown
☎ 467060
Exercise and relaxation in water. Question and answer time with refreshments afterwards. Run by a midwife and

Having a baby in Oxford

an obstetric physiotherapist.
Tues 8.00, Thurs 7.15
Cost: £33 for six weeks

*Temple Cowley Pool
Temple Road
Temple Cowley
☎ 467124
Relaxation and exercise in water.
Question and answer time.
Run by midwives.
Crèche available 11.00–3.00, free for slice card holders.
Thurs 11.15–1.15.
Cost: £33/six weeks incl. refreshments.

*The White Horse Leisure Centre
Audlett Drive
Abingdon
☎ 01235 540700
Run by midwives.
Exercise to music and relaxation in water. Question and answer time with refreshments.
Four-week courses.
Mon 12.00
Cost: £3.75/session
Crèche available at £1.30/hour.

*Antenatal Body Conditioning
Kidlington & Gosford Sports Centre
Wed: 9.00am, Fri 10.00am, Sat 9.00am
☎ Barry 873441
Exercise using resistance and aerobic equipment. Designed to meet individual requirements throughout pregnancy. Can be continued postnatally and beyond.
Good quality crèche available.

OTHER ANTENATAL HELP

*Oxfordshire Parents with Disabilities Network
☎ 01235 810949
A network supporting disabled people in pregnancy, birth and parenthood.

*The Pelvic Partnership
A support group for women with symphysis pubis dysfunction (pelvic joint pain) related to pregnancy and birth. Information booklets and regular support meetings
☎ Sarah Fishburn 01235 820921
www.pelvicpartnership.org.uk

*AIMS (Association for the improvement in maternity services)
AIMS is a campaigning organisation which seeks to improve all aspects of maternity care. If you are experiencing difficulties in accessing the care you want, they will provide emotional support and encouragement as well as information about choices and rights. They also publish a wide range of leaflets and booklets which enable parents to make informed decisions about their care.
AIMS Helpline – 0870 765 1433

IF YOU ARE HAVING TWINS, PLUS!

Having two or more babies at the same time can seem daunting at the very least, but help is at hand.
The **Women's Centre** runs special **Preparation for Parenthood** sessions

Having baby in Oxford

for multiple births four times a year (7.15pm Thurs) ☎ 220458

*Twins and Multiple Births Association (TAMBA)
National Helpline: 01732 868000
Local contact: Trudy Aries runs a twins club. Expectant parents also welcome.
☎ 772196

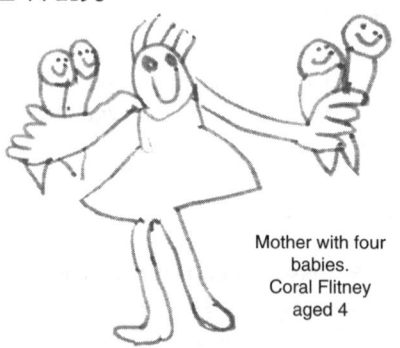

Mother with four babies.
Coral Flitney aged 4

COMPLEMENTARY MEDICINES

Complementary therapies can be very useful in pregnancy and labour, particularly massage, acupuncture, homeopathy and herbalism. Before you consider using herbal remedies, it is very important that you consult a practitioner as some preparations are not recommended during pregnancy. Look in the **Green Pages**, available from **Neal's Yard Remedies**, Golden Cross or High Street, or **The Inner Bookshop** on Magdalen Road. A practising herbalist is often available for consultation at Neal's Yard.

See: Ch. 2 - Your Child's Health for a list of practitioners of complementary therapies in the Oxford area.

THE JR WOMEN'S CENTRE

What to expect on arrival

When you think labour has started and you go to the hospital, you will be seen by a midwife in one of the admission rooms. She will examine both you and the baby to monitor progress and establish what stage of labour you are at. Depending on this, you will either be sent home to await further developments, go to the wards, or if labour is established, to a labour room.

The labour rooms

There are twelve labour rooms: one has a birthing pool and two have windows. If you would like either of these, ask! There is a bean bag, a rocking chair, a bed, a radio-cassette player, a foot stool and floor mats in each of the rooms. They can look rather bare and clinical, despite murals and wallpaper, but lighting can be dimmed which makes the atmosphere a bit more friendly and intimate. Some of the rooms have an en-suite toilet and shower.

Several pain relief options are on hand. Entonox (gas and air) is available above the bed or from a portable cylinder if you want to move about. Other forms of pain relief available include aromatherapy, TENS, meptid and epidural injection.

The 'pool' is a large, deep bath which many women find useful for pain relief. As long as everything is going OK and it

Having a baby in Oxford

is not already in use, you can opt for it. Gas and air and a baby heart monitor can be used in the pool.

If doctors need to assist with the delivery, you may be moved to a small theatre where you can also have music and dimmed lighting. Caesarean deliveries take place in an operating theatre under an epidural or general anaesthetic.

After the birth your baby will stay with you unless it needs specialist care in the **Special Care Baby Unit (SCBU)**. If you wish, you can feed your baby straight away. If you require stitches, these will normally be done in the labour room; you can also take a shower in the bathrooms adjoining the labour rooms.

Once all the medical procedures are over, you (and your birthing partner) can stay in the labour room alone with your baby. You will be offered tea and toast and many people enjoy this quiet time to relax with their new arrival.

What happens next?

For most people it's up to the wards on Level 5, 6 or 7. If there have been complications, you might have to go to the **Observation Area** first. If, on the other hand, both you and your baby are well you can, if you wish, go straight home from the Delivery Suite. Ask your midwife for advice. Otherwise, you will probably stay in hospital for two days. Your stay may be longer if you or the baby had problems during the delivery or after the birth. There are four beds in each ward and some single rooms are available. You can pay for a private room but you must book in advance. Your baby will stay with you all the time unless it is jaundiced and needs light treatment, which will be given in the nursery nearest your room. No bottle-feeds will be given to breastfed babies unless you request it.

You are expected to care for your baby yourself from the start, but you will receive help and advice from nursing and ancillary staff on feeding, bathing, dressing and general care. If you are very tired or unwell, or your baby is particularly demanding, the staff may take it off your hands for a few hours to allow you to get some sleep.

My baby brother being born.
By Ruth Hamilton aged 4

11

Having a baby in Oxford

If you are breastfeeding your baby you can seek support and advice three days/week from the excellent **Breastfeeding Clinic** on Level 5. ☎ 221695. See below.

Your baby will be checked by a paediatrician or a specialist midwife and any referrals, for instance for 'clicky hips', will be organised. A neonatal hearing test will usually be offered before you are discharged. A hospital and/or community midwife will visit you in hospital. You can always see the obstetric physiotherapist if you wish and you will be given written information about postnatal exercises. If all is well you will be discharged after two days.

Your community midwife will visit you at home for about 10 days after the birth and offer advice on feeding, general care and the overall health of you and your baby. After a couple of weeks your health visitor will take over.

Special Care Baby Unit

If your baby is in the **Special Care Baby Unit (SCBU)** you will be encouraged to spend as much time as possible with him/her and will also be given help with breastfeeding.

*SSNAP (Support for the Sick Newborn and their Parents)
Oxford SSNAP ☎ 221359.
If you need to talk to other parents who have had babies in SCBU then contact SSNAP. They can also help with transport and with accommodation if you live a long way from the hospital.

If your baby dies

The Women's Centre at the JR is recognised as dealing with stillbirth and neonatal death very sensitively. You will be able to see your baby and be given the choice of having it baptised.

If your baby has died, the following organisations can also offer support and advice. It is never too late to contact them.

*Oxford SANDS (Stillbirth and Neonatal Death Society)
National Helpline: 020 7436 5881
Local contact: ☎ Annette Grimaldi 771552

*Compassionate Friends
☎ Dinah Perkins 407496
This is a group run by bereaved parents for bereaved parents, offering friendship and support. They hold regular, informal meetings and can put you in touch with other groups and parents who have had similar experiences.

Registering your baby

By law you have to register your baby's birth within 6 weeks. The **Registrar of Births** has an office on Level 5 of the Women's Centre, which is open on weekdays between 9.00–12.00. Births can only be registered here while you are still in hospital. Otherwise you have to go to the **Registrar's Office** in Tidmarsh Lane, Oxford. ☎ 815900.

Having a baby in Oxford

Did you know?

❖ You can change or add a name within the child's first year.
❖ If you are married, your child can have either surname, both surnames or an amalgamation of the two.
❖ If you are not married, your child can have either surname but can only *automatically* have the father's if he is present at registration.
❖ You can, in fact, give your child any surname.

Getting ready for the new baby
by Coral Flitney, aged 3

NHS card

Your baby will need an NHS card so that he or she can be registered with a doctor. The registrar will give you a form which you should send to your doctor. You will then be sent an NHS card with your baby's number on it.

Naming ceremonies

Most churches are keen to welcome new members and you can contact them direct to arrange a baptism ceremony.

If you would like a non-religious naming ceremony and don't feel able to do it yourself, the **British Humanist Association** may be able to help. They have lots of ideas on how to mark the arrival of your baby.
☎ London office: 020 7430 0908
Local contact, Nigel Collins ☎ 01608 652684 can give advice or will conduct a ceremony for you.

Postnatal check-up

At six to eight weeks you will have a postnatal check-up with your GP or at the hospital. A cervical smear may be taken at the same time and family planning will be discussed.

Postnatal contraception

Breastfeeding does not stop you getting pregnant! You could be pregnant again as soon as six weeks after delivery and before periods restart, so you will need some form of family planning if you do not want another baby right away. For help, see your GP or make an appointment at the **Alec Turnbull Clinic** (See: *Contraception* above). Advice on natural family planning is also available.

Having a baby in Oxford

Birth afterthoughts

If you are frustrated, confused or uncertain about the treatment you received during labour, or if you would simply like to discuss your birth experience with access to your medical notes, contact the midwives on the **Birth Afterthoughts** confidential answerphone: 220605. There is no time limit after the birth and the venue will be one of your choice. A midwife will discuss your experience with you and offer advice, information and support.

Alternatively, if you want to make an informal (or formal) complaint about any aspect of your maternity care, you can contact the new Patient Advice and Liaison Service at the John Radcliffe Hospital ☎ 741166

YOUR POSTNATAL HEALTH

You may not feel your old self after your baby is born – or even look it! You may feel physically and emotionally tired. Getting out and about and meeting other people with babies might help (See: *Ch. 4 Meeting People*). If you have some persistent physical problems, such as piles, a bad back or unhealed stitches, see your midwife, health visitor, physiotherapist or GP. There are also other people and groups who can help you with certain problems, so please don't despair, there is help out there.

Physical problems

The obstetric physiotherapists at the Women's Centre can help you with severe backache, incontinence, pelvic pain, sexual problems and painful stitches, so don't suffer in silence – all problems are treatable. ☎ 221530 for further information.

*Perineal Clinic
This is run regularly by a consultant and a physiotherapist at the Women's Centre for follow-up checks on bad tears you may have experienced giving birth. Ask your GP to refer you.

Breastfeeding

If you want to breastfeed and are finding it difficult, embarrassing or sore, there are many people who can support and actively encourage you, and help you sort out any difficulties:

*La Leche League
National Helpline: 0845 120 2918
Local contacts:
☎ Kerry Charlton 01235 835746
☎ Jayne 768606

*NCT Breastfeeding Counsellor
National Helpline: 0870 444 8707
Local contact: Christine Hynes ☎ 862033
Breast-pump hire:☎ Alison Baker 864812

Having a baby in Oxford

*Breastfeeding Clinic
Based at the Women's Centre, John Radcliffe Hospital. Advises on a one-to-one basis. Open two-three days/week.
☎ Sally Inch 221695

Postnatal depression

Almost everyone has times when they feel low after giving birth but there are varying degrees of depression. 'Baby blues' is very common and relatively mild, usually disappearing after a short time.

If your depression lasts longer, or is very severe, then please do not suffer alone – go and see your health visitor or GP who WILL be able to help. Your health visitor should, in any case, keep a close eye on all new mothers and will ask you to fill in a questionnaire a few weeks after the birth to assess whether you may be suffering from postnatal depression. The following associations may also help:

*The Oxford Parent-Infant Project (OXPIP)
Healthy Living Centre, Cowley Road
☎ 07904 538774
Offers a confidential counselling service, for parents of babies under two. You can contact them direct or ask to be referred by your health visitor, GP or midwife. Any parent experiencing difficulties, is welcome to call. OXPIP is a charity. Trained counsellors and psychotherapists are funded by donations. You are asked to make a contribution if you can afford to.

*Association for Postnatal Illness
25 Jerdan Place
London SW6 1BE
☎ 020 7386 0868

*The Oxford Postnatal Depression Action Group (OPDAG)
OPDAG produced a useful publication called *Postnatal Depression: A Leaflet for Families*, which is available in libraries, health centres, clinics and pharmacies. Ask your GP or health visitor for a copy.

*Cry-sis
Offers 24-hour telephone counselling for parents with children who cry excessively or have sleep problems.
☎ 020 7404 5011
(See also: *Chapter 4 Meeting People* and *Chapter 3 Support for Parents*.)

*Special Experiences Register
☎ Shei Crowther 243098
If you faced particular difficulties during pregnancy, birth or parenthood and are willing to share those experiences with others, usually by phone, please contact Shei at the above number.

* * *

Tip: The New Parent Network, NCT and Oxford City Homestart can provide practical help and put you in touch with other parents who have been through similar difficulties, so do ask.

Having a baby in Oxford

Getting back into shape

If you would like advice on postnatal exercise, or a check during the first sixth months after birth, drop in at the Parent Education room on Level 1 of the JR Women's Centre on any Monday between 2.00 and 3.00. Toys available.

• • • • • • • • • • • • • • • • • • • •

Tip: After giving birth, make sure you are given a free leaflet on postnatal exercises.

• • • • • • • • • • • • • • • • • • • •

If you are feeling active and/or you are anxious to get your old shape back, then investigate these exercise classes:

*The J.R. Women's Centre

The obstetric physiotherapists run postnatal exercise classes for mothers of babies 6+ weeks old. ☎ 221530 between 9.30 and 2.30 weekdays. You are advised to book promptly after the birth of your baby for this Thursday morning 5 week course as it is run on a first come, first served basis. The classes are free.

*Postnatal mat classes
Mortimer Hal, Oxford Road Marston
☎ 248104 Georgina Evans
A postnatal class aimed at strengthening the abdominals & pelvic floor.
Fri 1.15 – Beginners
Wed 1.15 – Advanced
One-hour classes followed by refreshments. Babies welcome.
Cost: £25 for six-week course. Ring for further details.

*Postnatal yoga
☎ Kay Millar 554743
Taught by an Active Birth teacher, these postnatal classes offer 90 minutes of gentle yoga and movement for the early postnatal period. An experienced assistant is there to help with the babies.

*Exercise to music in the water
Marston Ferry Pool
☎ Ann Huggar 07740 819458
Wed 1.30–2.30
A specially designed postnatal class run by a sports therapist. An hour of exercise followed by refreshments and discussion.
Babies welcome – bring a car seat for baby to sit in by the pool.
Cost: £5.00/session

*Pilates exercise class
The Coach House
Headington Quarry
☎ Juliette Wynne 308738
Course run by a chartered physiotherapist.
Suitable for postnatal exercise.
Tues 7.30pm

Having a baby in Oxford

*Postnatal body conditioning
Gosford Sports Centre
Oxford Road
Kidlington
☎ Barry 873441
Wed: 9.00, Fri: 10.00, Sat: 9.00
An exercise class using resistance and aerobic equipment. This enjoyable personal fitness programme can continue beyond the postnatal period.

Crèche available for babies 6 weeks plus for Wednesday and Friday classes.

OTHER POSTNATAL CLASSES

*Life after birth group
Teacher's home
☎ Kay Millar 554743
Cost: £35 per five-week course
Small groups for new mothers to meet for companionship and mutual support during the first few weeks with a new baby. Flexible programming covers well-being, relationships, nutrition and exercise, among other topics.

*Infant and child resuscitation
John Radcliffe Hospital
☎ Stephanie Sparkes 308348
Cost: Single session £15.00
Four courses are organised per year through the NCT with the JR's own resuscitation trainer. It is a one-off session 8–10pm. Mums, dads, grandparents, carers and childcare workers are all welcome. The course covers all aspects of resuscitation, heart failure, breathing difficulties and choking in babies and children.

Baby massage

This special way to communicate with your baby is easy to learn and babies love it. It can help with colic, blocked noses and sleep problems. Both Kay Millar and paediatric osteopath Rosalind Jones offer courses of 4/5 sessions. Shorter courses are available from Pauline Hutton. You may find that your local Health Centre's postnatal classes include a baby massage session.

*Baby massage with Kay Millar
Teacher's or parents' home.
☎ Kay Millar 554743
Cost: £26.00 per four-week course.

*Baby massage with Rosalind Jones
Teacher's or parents' home.
☎ Rosalind Jones 778064
Cost: £30.00 per five-week course.

*Baby massage with Pauline Hutton
☎ Pauline Hutton 373919
Cost: 3 weeks/£8.00 per session.

Chapter 2 - Your Child's Health

In this section we cover common child health problems and suggest where to seek help in Oxford. We also give other pieces of local information that may help you keep your child healthy, safe and happy.

HEALTH PROFESSIONALS AND SERVICES
Health visitors

After having your baby a community midwife will care for you until around ten days after the birth. From then on your allocated health visitor will take over and will help and advise you throughout your child's life. Your health visitor will be a trained nurse who has completed postgraduate training in child health and development.

Initially your health visitor will visit you at home and will be interested in your health and recovery from childbirth. She will also weigh your baby and provide you with any support or advice you may need during the first weeks of your baby's life. You will be given a small red book in which she and other health professionals and you can keep a record of your child's health and development.

Health visitors are mainly concerned with the health and development of your child and aim to help you in whatever way is best for you and your family. They can provide you with advice and information on immunisation, contraception, breastfeeding, feeding, weaning, sleeping and common health problems. They can also refer you to more specialised services if necessary.

Health visitors run weekly child health clinics at your local surgery, at which your baby will be weighed, immunised and have developmental checks. You can discuss any health worries with your health visitor at these clinics and also see a doctor on request. A doctor usually performs a baby's first immunisations and the practice nurse may do the subsequent ones.

Your child's health

Health visitors often run postnatal classes for mothers and can give you information about local groups or services for families. They are usually available by phone early mornings and late afternoons or you can leave a message on their answer phone and they will return your call.

If you suspect your child is ill contact your surgery directly to make an appointment to see a doctor as soon as possible.

General practitioners

These are doctors who provide family health services to a local community. They are usually based in a surgery or GP practice and are often the first port of call for parents who are concerned about their child's health. GPs refer patients who need more help to specialists, such as paediatricians.

Generally a GP is available at the health visitor's weekly clinic. This doctor can be seen on request and he or she will examine your child thoroughly at 6-8 weeks of age prior to your baby's first immunisations. The GP will also be involved in other developmental and physical checks during the first few years of your child's life.

Paediatricians

Paediatricians are doctors who have specialised in the care of children. Your GP may refer your child to a paediatrician for a specialist opinion and paediatricians and paediatric nurses are responsible for the care and treatment of children in hospital.

School nurses

School nurses are responsible for groups of schools in Oxford. A head teacher will contact the nurse if he or she has concerns about a particular child's health or requires information on a health issue. When your child starts school, you may meet your school's nurse. The school can give you the name and telephone number of the nurse if you wish to seek her advice.

Pharmacists

Pharmacists can advise on prescription and non-prescription medication, as well as offering invaluable quick and free advice on minor health problems. Do get to know your local pharmacist.

Hospital Services

Within Oxford there are five hospitals with children's facilities and services:

*John Radcliffe Hospital
Headington, Oxford
☎ 741166
The hospital has several children's wards, 2 medical wards, 1 surgical ward, an adolescent unit, a paediatric intensive care unit, a special care baby unit and a day ward. A children's outpatients department is also based at the JR.

*Radcliffe Infirmary
Woodstock Road
☎ 311188
This hospital's children's services specialises in head and neck surgery and ear nose and throat, neurology and craniofacial medical and surgical care.

Your child's health

*The Horton
Banbury
☎ 01295 229415
There is one medical and surgical children's ward as well as community children's services.

*The Churchill
Headington
☎ 741155
Community Paediatrics and Ounsted clinic are based at the Churchill Hospital, where children with disabilities are assessed by a team of specialists.

*The Nuffield Orthopaedic Trust
Headington
☎ 741155
Children are referred here for specialist orthopaedic opinion, treatment and therapy.

New children's hospital

In September 2002 the Children's Hospital Campaign was launched. The aim is to build a three-storey hospital by Dec 2005 dedicated to the needs of children in the Oxfordshire area transforming the city into a centre of excellence for paediatric care.

If you want to know more about the campaign and how to support it contact
The Campaign Officer,
Osler Lodge,
Osler Road,
Headington, Oxford, OX3 9RJ
☎ 222594
email: campaign@orh.nhs.uk.
www.chox.org.uk

Hospital stays

If your child has to stay in any Oxford Hospital you will find the atmosphere on the wards very informal and friendly. You will usually be able to stay with your child sleeping overnight on a camp bed or in hospital based parent accommodation. There are no restrictive visiting hours (although there is usually an hour after lunch when visitors are discouraged).

Most of the wards have well-equipped playrooms for all ages and some will have play specialists who will organise appropriate play activities for your child. Children over five in hospital for any length of time will receive teaching from the Hospital Education service.

The Radcliffe Infirmary children's ward and the Ear, Nose and Throat Department have pre-admission visits at which all members of the family are welcome.

Health support services

Within Oxfordshire there are several health support services dedicated to sections of the community. Do contact them for advice on health and social issues.

*Home-Start Oxford
Youth and Community Centre
Blackbird Leys Road
☎ 779991
Home-Start is a charity in which volunteers offer regular support, friendship and practical help to families with at least one child under the age of five, at

Your child's health

times of stress. This support is provided in the family's own home, helping to prevent crisis and encouraging the enjoyment of family life. Your health visitor or GP can refer you to Home-start or you can refer yourself.

*Homeless families
East Oxford Health Centre
☎ Gilly O'Mara 456626
If you and your children are living in temporary accommodation, phone your health visitor for support and advice.

*Oxfordshire Health Advocacy Team
East Oxford Health Centre
Manzil Way, Cowley, Oxford OX4 1XD
Indian and Pakistani Communities
Mrs Jagjit Gurm ☎ 456622
Yaser Mir ☎ 456618
The Bangladeshi Community
Mrs Labli Bakth ☎ 456623
The Chinese Community
Jennifer Siu ☎ 456619
Kwai Coll ☎ 456619
Traveller Gypsy Communities
Jan Brown ☎ 456624
Refugees and Asylum seekers
Primary Healthcare Facilitator Mary Hardwick ☎ 456687

*Sure-Start
The Oval, Rose Hill
Family Centre: ☎ 716739
Health Team: ☎ 778765
Sure-Start offers a wide range of services for families living in the Rose Hill and Littlemore area. Contact them for more details. The geographical range of Sure-Start may increase in the future.

Finding local health services

You can phone **NHS Direct** 0845 4647 who will be able to give you the names of all doctors or dentists who are under contract to provide NHS treatment in your area. There is also a good website that provides detailed information on local health services. *www.nhs.uk* click on Local Services search on the Home page and this will take you to a page where you can find details of your local dental and GP practices, opticians, pharmacies and hospitals.

Out of hours health services

If you are concerned about your child's health out of surgery hours phone your surgery and obtain the out of hours service number, usually recorded on an answerphone message. When you phone this number you will either speak to a doctor directly or the doctor will phone you back. They may want you to come to them or when necessary they will do homevisits or advise you to call 999 or go straight to your local Accident and Emergency Department.

Or you can phone **NHS Direct** on 0845 4647 and talk to an experienced nurse or professional adviser who will be able to give you advice you on what action to take. Calls to NHS Direct are charged at the local rate and for patients' safety all calls are recorded.

Pharmacists can also provide helpful advice if your surgery is closed or you have to wait for an appointment.

Never hesitate to seek for help if you are worried about your child's health.

Your child's health

Changing your doctor/surgery
These days it is very easy to change your child's doctor/surgery. First find another doctor/surgery who agrees to take you and fill in part B of your NHS card to register. Inform your old surgery that you have changed.

*Community Health Council for Oxfordshire
Churchill House
St. Aldates
☎ 732569
Contact the council if you wish to make a complaint related to health care. The health council can also give you help or advice on finding local health services.

PROMOTING YOUR CHILD'S HEALTH

Three best tips for first-time parents are:
1. Join a postnatal group run by your health visitor or nursery nurse. These often have good educational content as well as a social function.
2. Read *Birth to Five*, which should be given to you free of charge by your health visitor. Keep it handy to refer to over the next few years.
3. Attend child health clinic at your local GP surgery whenever you have questions or doubts at all about your child's health, development or behaviour.

Breastfeeding
Breastfeeding (see Chapter 1 *Having a baby in Oxford*) is now encouraged as being the ideal way to feed a young baby. But it isn't always easy or possible. Don't feel guilty if it's not for you – modern formula milk provides all the nutrition your baby needs.

But if you do need advice, help or support regarding breastfeeding you can contact the following organisations.

*La Leche League
National Helpline: 0845 120 2918
See Chapter 1 for local contacts.

*NCT Breastfeeding Counsellor
National Helpline: 0870 444 8707
See Chapter 1 for local contacts.

*Breastfeeding Clinic
Women's Centre,
John Radcliffe Hospital.
Open two-three days/week.
☎ Sally Inch 221695

If you are breastfeeding successfully, and have a plentiful milk supply, you could consider donating some excess milk to the Human Milk Bank – you could help to save a premature baby's life! ☎ 221695 to find out what is involved.

Healthy eating and drinking
Weaning normally starts at around 4 months and you will be given advice and support from your health visitor. Detailed guidance on how to start, suitable first foods, and the way nutritional requirements change over the first years, is included in *Birth to Five* (see above). If you are concerned or need

Your child's health

more information about healthy eating you can contact Maggie Dent at:
*Health Promotion
Oxford City Council
St Aldates Chambers
St Aldates
Oxford OX1 1DF
☎ 252373
for information, talks and promotions on healthy eating.

Water and lead content
High levels of lead have been implicated in certain health problems. Water companies ensure that the water they put into supply does not contain lead. However older properties built before 1970 may still have lead pipes and sometimes water can pick up lead from these pipes. To have the lead concentration in your tap water checked (free of charge) contact 0118 9642706. Be patient - from experience it can take some time to get an appointment.

Visiting the dentist
NHS dental treatment is free for children and for mothers expecting until up to one year after giving birth.

It's important to encourage regular brushing as soon as your baby's teeth start to appear. Your health visitor can advise you on dental care. It is also wise to register your child with a dentist even before the first teeth come through.

If possible, register with your own dentist and take your baby or small child with you when you have your check ups so that they get used to the idea.

Tip: It's not always easy to find a dentist who will register you, if you are concerned to find a dentist who is good with young children try asking friends with children to recommend one.

Your dentist can advise you on how to prevent tooth decay, what type of toothpaste to use and whether your baby needs fluoride drops or tablets.

They will check your child's mouth regularly for signs of tooth decay, erosion or gum problems.

Emergency dental care
If you can't immediately find a dentist where you can register your child and they need urgent dental attention you can contact the **Community Dental Service**. This service is open for emergency appointments on Mon-Fri 9.00-17.00 and Saturday mornings. You have to phone on the day to make an appointment.

*East Oxford Health Centre
Cowley Road
☎ 456640

Immunisation
Immunisation is the safest and most effective way of protecting your child against serious infections. Vaccines are tested thoroughly to ensure that they are safe before being used. They have saved thousands of lives in the UK since their introduction. Dangerous diseases such as tetanus, diphtheria and polio

Your child's health

have practically disappeared in this country because of the national childhood immunisation programme. But these diseases could come back, which is why it's so important for everyone to keep up their immunity.

Vaccines are given to babies and young children according to a timetable and in the UK children are vaccinated (at time of printing) against polio, whooping cough, tetanus, diphtheria, meningitis C, haemophilus influenza type B (HIB), and measles, mumps and rubella (MMR). For most of these illnesses there is no cure either from the disease itself or the possible long-term side effects.

Following immunisation it is quite normal for your child to be irritable, develop a fever or feel slightly unwell for a couple of days. There may also be a reaction at the site of the vaccine. This will slowly disappear on its own.

After MMR, children may develop a mild rash with fever up to 10 days after vaccination, which disappears after about three days. Rarely a child may develop a mild form of mumps 3 weeks after being vaccinated. This is not infectious. Talk to your GP about how to keep your child comfortable. Children's paracetamol, such as Calpol, Disprol or Medinol can be given to reduce fever and relieve any pain felt at the injection sites.

If after any immunisation your child cries persistently, seems listless or unresponsive, then seek medical advice immediately.

Immunisation concerns
If you have any concerns about vaccination you can also discuss these with your GP or health visitor. They can also provide you with useful literature and other resources. The following websites are helpful sources of information:
Health Promotion England
www.immunisation.org.uk
Public Health Service Laboratory
www.phls.co.uk
This website provides a schedule for childhood immunisations.

In response to recent concerns over the MMR vaccine a dedicated website has been put together to answer any questions This is a very useful resource and well worth looking at:
www.mmrthefacts.nhs.uk. If you do not have access to the Internet your health visitor will be able to provide you with some literature from this website and either address your concerns directly or seek expert advice for you.

Accident prevention & First Aid

More accidents happen at home than anywhere else and your health visitor will discuss ways of minimising these risks with you. There are also other useful resources she may provide you with such as the Footsteps video. **Maggie Dent** the **Health Promotion Officer** at Oxford City Council is also a useful contact. She can come and give talks to small groups about accident prevention and will be able to give you practical advice, information and resources. ☎ 252373

Your child's health

Knowing what to do in an emergency can save vital minutes. Check out your local family centre (see Chapter 4 Meeting People) for free courses. Some health visitor postnatal groups also show you how to resuscitate a child.

*The British Red Cross
☎ 01235 555811/539100
1. *First Aid for Child Carers* (Parents and Child Minders)
Two-day course held on Saturdays from 9.30-15.30 (Total of 12 hours). It runs at least once a month.
Cost: £60 +VAT.
2. *Save a Life*
Two-hour course on basic adult resuscitation for groups of twelve. It is held in venues of your choice.
Cost: £220+VAT.

*St John Ambulance Brigade
☎ 378228
1. *Emergency Aid Certificate for People who Work with Young Children*
This course runs over two days 9.30-16.30 and contributes towards the NVQ in Childcare and Education.
Cost: £70+VAT.
2. *Lifesaver-Babies and Children*
This course runs over two evenings 19.30-21.30.
Cost: £30+VAT.

*National Childbirth Trust
☎ Stephanie Sparks 308348
Infant Resuscitation Training Course
This two-hour evening course covers infant to pre-school age resuscitation techniques. It is run four times a year by the John Radcliffe Resuscitation Officer.
Cost: £15 (concessions are not available). Spaces are limited so book early.

*EASOCEC (Adult and Community Learning in East and South Oxford) in association with Sure-start.
☎ 749692

*Child health and development
Sure-Start Family Centre
Rose Hill
☎ 776765
A free course with a free crèche for parents of under fours who would like to know more about children's development and behaviour, when to call a doctor, and what to do in an emergency. 10 once weekly morning sessions.

COMMON CHILDHOOD PROBLEMS

Apart from your GP and local pharmacist there are several other sources of help and advice on common childhood

My baby brother with roseola.
By Coral Flitney aged 3

Your child's health

ailments. You should be given the *Birth to Five* handbook which lists all the major childhood ailments and problems. The NHS Direct helpline 0845 4647 and their website www.nhsdirect.nhs.uk or are excellent first ports of call for health information. NHS Direct Self-Help Guide is also available free from pharmacies and branches of Safeway containing pharmacies.

Below are listed some national and local helplines and support groups that deal with the following problems.

Allergies

*Allergy UK
Deepdene House
30 Bellegrove Road
Welling, Kent DA16 3PY
Helpline: 0208 303 8583 (09:00-21:00)

*Oxford Allergy Centre
Bell Trees Clinic
Raleigh Park Road, Botley
☎ 200365

Asthma

In most doctors' surgeries there are special asthma clinics usually run by nurses. If you think your child has asthma, it is best to contact your GP as they can make the diagnosis and initiate the most appropriate treatment

*National Asthma Campaign
Helpline is manned by specialist asthma nurses Mon-Fri 09:00-17:00
☎ 0845 7010203

Bedwetting

This shouldn't really be considered a problem until your child is over five. Your health visitor or school nurse can give you helpful advice and your doctor can check whether there are any physical problems.

*South Parade Health Centre,
Summertown,
☎ 510114
Holds a special Saturday morning clinic.

Behavioural problems

*Family Nurturing Network
☎ 777756
Runs programmes for parents and children up to age 10 experiencing behavioural or emotional problems.

Breastfeeding

(See: *Ch. 1 Having a Baby in Oxford*).

Crying

*Cry-sis
☎ 020 7404 5011
24-hour telephone counselling for parents with children who cry excessively or have sleep problems. A source of information, books and practical ideas.

Dyslexia

*Dyslexia Research Trust
☎ 552303
www.dyslexic.org.uk

Your child's health

Runs clinics to research the visual causes of and develop effective treatments for dyslexia. Using simple visual treatment, they can help most children with dyslexic reading problems to double their rate of reading.

*Oxfordshire Dyslexic Association
☎ 428234
www.oxda.go.to
Organises frequent meetings and talks.

Eczema

*Eczema Group
Kaleidoscope Family Centre
Kidlington
☎ Caroline Abbot 01844 276230
First Saturday of every month 10.00–12.00. Offers support, encouragement advice and samples and gives parents a chance to compare notes on efficacy of different treatments. Specialist speakers and dermatologists sometimes attend, and a newsletter is produced. Anyone may drop in at any time during the session.

*National Eczema Society
☎ 01844 276230.

Emotional upsets

There can be times, for instance when a partnership breaks up, bereavement or the arrival of a new baby when your child is more than normally upset. One of these organisations may be able to help but don't forget that friends and relatives can also offer support.

*CRUSE
Wesley Memorial Hall
New Inn Hall Street
☎ 245398
Mon–Fri 10.00–12.00
Support group for the bereaved, including children.

*Compassionate Friends
53, North Street
Bristol
☎ 0117 966 5202
Bereaved parents' organisation offering friendship and understanding.

*Parentline Plus
Freephone: 0808 8002222
Help for all carers of children.

*Childline
Freephone: 0808 800500
NSPCC Child Protection Helpline

*Cot Death Helpline
☎ 0207 235 1721 (24-hour)

Faddy eating

There may come a day when your small child closes his or her mouth and refuses to eat anything but chocolate chip ice-cream or coco pops! Faddy eating is very common but if you are really worried, contact your health visitor who can refer you to the **community dietitian**.

Tip: Offer small portions at mealtimes, second helpings can always follow.

Your child's health

Feet

Free booklets on foot problems such as athlete's foot, fungal nail infections and verrucas are available from chemists where you can also buy treatments over the counter. If the problems persist, or if you would like a free prescription, see your GP, or try:

*Children's Podiatry Clinic
St Barnabas Health Centre
Albert Street
☎ 311312
This clinic will treat children under 8. You can get a referral from your GP or phone direct for an appointment. Clinics are held all around the county.

Tip: Buy a plastic swim sock from the swimming pool if your child has a verruca but still wants to swim.

Headlice

Very common but harmless, lice move by direct contact from head to head and prefer clean hair. They can be treated with proprietory lotions that use insecticides or by the "Bug Busting" method which aims to remove live lice by combing. You can get a "Bug Busting" kit from some pharmacies, or by mail order from: **Community Hygiene Concern** (Helpline: 020 8341 7167). A leaflet *The Prevention and Treatment of Head Lice* is available from the Department of Health, PO Box 777, London SE1 6XH email: doh@prologistics.co.uk

.Sleeping

Feel like a walking zombie during the day? Be assured there are plenty of us about! Some children do wake several times at night, or very early, or refuse to go to bed; this is perfectly normal. But if you want to try and change thins, there are several 'sleep programmes' that might be worth trying.

Gill Brown is a local sleep counsellor who helps parents of children with sleep difficulties. She will work with your family to assess your needs and design an individual sleep programme. Contact Gill for more details and cost.
☎ 01491 825664

Special needs

If you have any concerns about your child's physical, social or emotional development please do not worry in isolation. Your GP and your health visitor will be able to refer you to specialist health professionals or support services.

The **Oxfordshire Parent Partnership** has developed an information pack for parents called *Children with Special Needs in Oxfordshire-Information for Parents*. This is sometimes referred to 'The Green Pack' and copies are available from:
Parent Partnership Coordinator
Education Department
Macclesfield House
New Road, OX1 1NA
☎ 810516
(Contacts Marian Roiser, Wendy Cliffe)

Your child's health

*Oxfordshire Children's Information Service
26 Hanborough Business Park
Long Hanborough
Witney OX29 8SQ
☎ 01993 886933
Fax: 01993 886937
email: enquiries@oxoncis.org.uk
In addition the Green Pack is available on the Internet at:
http://www.oxfordshire.gov.uk/index/learning/spec_educ_needs/special_needs_green_pack_contents.htm
The pack contains information on how to navigate the system and also a directory of useful resources and contacts. It also lists specialist services and support offered by a wide range of voluntary organisations – from transport to drama groups, respite care to toy libraries.

A ten-page A5 booklet called *Local Guide for Parents of Disabled Children and Young People and those with Special Needs* is also available from Oxfordshire Children's Information Service, or contact:

*Childcare Development Officer
(Disabilities)
☎ 01235 549326

Speech

Children learn to speak at different ages but if you are worried about the speech development of your child consult your health visitor or contact:

*The Speech Therapy Department
Radcliffe Infirmary
☎ 224559
Speech therapists see children who have language or speech problems. They will see children of any age, even from birth if they have feeding problems or congenital defects such as a cleft palate. They can also advise about support groups.

Teething

There are various proprietary remedies such as *Bonjela* which can be bought over the counter.

Homeopathic treatments including *Ashton Parsons Powders* and camomile preparations are also available from chemists. Baby paracetamol, such as *Calpol* is a trusted standby.

Tip: Keep teething rings in the fridge so that they are soothing and cool on your baby's gums.

University of Oxford Development Studies

This group is researching into babies' and young children's perceptions. What do babies know about the world they live in? How do young children learn to recognise spoken words, to understand numbers, about the physical properties of objects? These are just some of the questions that they are trying to answer. If your child is between one month and 36 months old, and you would like to partici-

Your child's health

pate in the study, which involves short and simple games, contact:

*The Oxford Baby Lab
Infant Development Group
FREEPOST, Dept. of Experimental Psychology, University of Oxford, South Parks Road. Oxford OX1 3YZ.
☎ 271393/271400
You will be contacted with further information when there is a study suited to your child's age. You will receive a bib or T-shirt in lieu of your travel expenses.

COMPLEMENTARY MEDICINE

The term 'complementary medicine' is used to describe a natural approach to health and well-being, that is, one not using synthetic drugs and medicines. There is an increasing interest in complementary therapies, many of which can be used safely and effectively before, during and after pregnancy and for all the family.

Many therapies and treatments come under the Complementary and Alternative Medicine (CAM) umbrella, and include reflexology, aromatherapy, homeopathy, chiropractic, Chinese herbal medicine, acupuncture, osteopathy and Alexander technique.

Some CAM professions are very well regulated. For example, osteopaths and chiropractors are statutorily regulated under the Osteopaths Act 1993 and the Chiropractors Act 1994. Other professions have well-developed voluntary regulatory systems that require the possession of specific qualifications and adherence to a code of professional conduct. However, this does not apply across the board so some practitioners who advertise their services are not subject to any regulation at all.

If you are thinking about using a complementary therapy it is worth doing a bit of background research to find out whether a particular therapy would suit you or your child

Information is widely available - for example *www.nhsdirect.nhs.uk* is a useful start, as are the CAM regulatory and professional bodies and self-help charities. Here are some guidelines for choosing a reputable practitioner and using complementary therapies:

1. Ask your GP if he or she can recommend a practitioner. Sometimes, GP practices allow CAM practitioners to use rooms on their premises though this does not necessarily mean that they will provide treatments at NHS expense.
2. If there is a regulatory body contact it for information on standards and to obtain a list of registered practitioners in your area.
3. If you do not obtain CAM treatment on the NHS or on the recommendation of your GP, make sure your GP is aware of any therapies or products you or your child use. This is essential if you or your child are already receiving conventional medical treatment as some CAM treatments can cause conventional drugs to be less effective, or give rise to unexpected side effects.

Your child's health

Most services are offered privately and fees for consultation and treatment will vary widely.

Where to find out more
Practitioners are listed in the telephone directory and *The Green Pages-the A-Z of living well in Oxfordshire*. The latter is updated annually and available from libraries, health food shops and health clinics (or contact Living Well P.O. Box 980, Oxford OX2 02Q
☎ 0845 458 4050 for a copy). Also check the registers of national associations of practitioners in local libraries.

*The Inner Bookshop
Magdalen Road (see *Suppliers* below) Has a comprehensive range of books and other publications (including a section devoted to raising children, child development etc.) as well as notices in the window for local practitioners, classes and so on.

Local practitioners
Below you will find some practitioners listed that have been recommended by members of the New Parent Network. Only a selection of the many therapies practised are included here. The list is by no means comprehensive and should be seen as an initial starting point only. You should always be sure to check their credentials yourself and it is wise to ask your GP, health visitor or midwife for advice before you or your child commences any treatment.

It is also important to advise the practitioner of any medical treatment you are undergoing and to make it clear if you are planning a pregnancy or are already pregnant, as they will often need to take this into account in the treatment.

*The Oxford Complementary Medicine Group
☎ 200365.
Holds regular meetings which provide a good introduction to a variety of topics.

Acupuncture

A well-established Chinese therapy in which needles are inserted at specific points in the body to ease pain, tension, fatigue and symptoms of disease.

*The Bell Trees Clinic
Raleigh Road, Botley
☎ 200365

*Dr Gilbert Shia MB Bchir TCM
Dao Clinic of Traditional Chinese Medicine
30 Beaumont Street
☎ 311871

*Oxford Acupuncture Centre
41 Walton Crescent, Jericho
☎ 544631

Alexander Technique

Instruction for posture improvement. A gentle, hands-on therapy usually conducted one-to-one, although group workshops exist. Sessions (referred to as 'lessons') usually last for 30–45 minutes. The technique affects the whole

Your child's health

body and can lead to breathing improvement and a sense of well being.

*Lucia Walker
☎ 726307

*Sharyn West
☎ 726307

Aromatherapy

Involves the use of essential oils in massage, inhalations, skin creams etc, for a wide range of symptoms. It is often used for relaxation.

During pregnancy certain oils should be avoided and it is wise to contact a qualified aromatherapist before using them at home. However, used properly, aromatherapy can be beneficial during later pregnancy (third trimester) for relaxation, back pain and circulation. Oils can also help minimise stretch marks. Some midwives have basic training in the use of essential oils and will offer them to you for use during your labour and afterwards to help with the healing of stitches etc. Aromatherapy can also be beneficial for childhood illnesses.

*Marianne Thrower MISPA
☎ 456234

*Ora Sapir
☎ 373241
www.healingnature.co.uk

*Culpeper Herbalists
New Inn Hall Street
Weekly aromatherapist advice session.

Cranial osteopathy

Cranial osteopathy uses very gentle manipulative techniques and includes treatment of the head as well as the rest of the body. It is suitable for all ages, particularly children. Osteopaths believe that all babies should be routinely checked osteopathically after birth, and particularly if the birth has been difficult. Positive results with babies and children for a wide range of medical conditions, including ear infections, 'glue ear', sleep problems, colic, hyperactivity, eczema etc have been reported.

*Nina Manston DO
Horspath
Oxford
☎ 875854

*Rosalind Jones DO
Qualified paediatric/cranial osteopath Specialises in problems during and after pregnancy: sciatica, back and pelvic pain including pelvic symphysis disorder (PSD), babies and children with colic, feeding or sleeping difficulties, asthma, sinusitis, glue ear, hyperactivity and learning difficulties.

*Kelston Chorley DO MCO
Focus 4 Health
☎ 790235

*Family Osteopathic Practice
☎ 778064
Botley ☎ 200365
Headington ☎ 484157

Your child's health

*Ghislaine Gautreau DO
Summertown Clinic
362 Banbury Road
☎ 558561

*London Osteopathic Centre for Children
109 Harley Street, London
☎ 020 7486 6160
Five-day clinic (Mon-Fri) with top paediatric osteopaths and trainees that treats premature babies up to children of 16, and pregnant women. Treatment includes cranial techniques. The centre has experience of treating a range of childhood conditions including autism, cerebral palsy and coordination problems. The centre operates as a charity and a donation of £30 (at time of printing) is invited if you can afford it.

Herbalism

Herbal remedies are increasingly popular. A trained herbalist at Neal's Yard can offer advice. Otherwise try:
*The Bell Trees Clinic
Raleigh Park Road, Botley
☎ 200365

*Janet Scanlon BSc, MNIMH^
Medical Herbalist
Summertown Clinic
362 Banbury Road
☎ 513388

*Dr Gilbert Shia, Dao
Clinic of Traditional Chinese Medicine
30 Beaumont Street
☎ 311871

*Nina Manston MNIMH^
Horspath
☎ 875854
^Member of the National Institute of Medical Herbalists

Homeopathy

Homeopathy is used for a range of common children's ailments such as ear infections, general low immunity and teething, as well as emotional symptoms (e.g. separation anxiety, anger etc).

Even though homeopathic remedies for specific symptoms are widely available over-the-counter, it is well worth seeking initial advice from an experienced homeopath who will look at the person as a whole—the symptom is seen as part of an overall picture of your health. As a result, two children with earache will often be given completely different remedies. Because of this, initial consultations tend to be very thorough (typically lasting over an hour).

*Homeopathy Helpline
☎ 09065 343404

*Elisabeth Austin
☎ 794363 also at:

*Oxford Natural Health Centre
Church Cowley Road
☎ 715615

*Dr Ferguson
Beaumont Street
☎ 311811
GP and trained homeopath. Full consulta-

33

Your child's health

tions, private only, but basic homeopathic advice is offered to NHS patients.

*The Bell Trees Clinic
✺✤●✻✼✽✾ ✩✤◐☐✻ ✻☐✤✽✾ ✛☐▼●✱
☎ 200365

Nutrition and diet

The following specialise in treatment by dietary control. This includes food supplements and the detection/elimination of allergenic or irritant foods.

*Community Dietitian's Office (EOHC)
☎ 456630

*Michael Franklin MA, Dip Nutritional Studies.
Oxford Nutrition and Allergy Centre
☎ 459553
Centre specialises in finding lasting solutions for childhood eczema, recurrent ear infections, hyperactivity and ADHD. It also investigates metabolic reasons for autism.

*Foresight (Association for the Promotion of Pre-Conceptual Care)
28 The Paddock
Godalming
Surrey GU7 1XD
☎ 01483 427839
This charity promotes research and provides a hair analysis service, courses and a programme of pre-conceptual care based on good nutrition. It has a national network of GPs and nutritionists.

*Higher Nature
Burwash Common
East Sussex TN19 7LX
☎ 01435 882880
This mail order company supplies high quality food supplements (including products for children), produces an interesting newsletter and runs workshops nationally.

Basic nutritional advice is offered free to customers, and a full private nutritional consultation (over the phone) is also available.

Massage

*Rosalind Jones DO
☎ 778064
Qualified paediatric/cranial osteopath Runs classes and private sessions in Massage for Pregnancy and Birth. Also baby massage.

Osteopathy

A well-established therapy often seen as the first resort for back pain. Osteopathy is recommended for most skeletal and muscular problems (back, joints etc) and often recommended for women after childbirth to ensure correct re-alignment of the spine and pelvis. See also Cranial osteopathy practitioners listed above.

*David Ruddick DO MRO
Summertown
☎ 558561

*Kelston Chorley DO MCO
Focus 4 Health
☎ 790235

Your child's health

Reflexology

A gentle, non-invasive treatment which involves pressure and massage to specific reflex points on the feet or ankles. It is based on a similar principle to that of acupuncture. Used for relaxation, and to help with a full range of physical symptoms. Suitable for babies and children. Reflexology is sometimes used with premature babies with a view to stimulating parental bonding and physical development.

*Marianne Thrower MAR
☎ 456234

Suppliers

Most chemists and health food shops stock essential oils and food supplements of variable quality. Many clinics in Oxford also stock them, and sell treatment vouchers. In addition, there are several suppliers of oils, herbal remedies and books on complementary medicine in Oxford. Here is a selection.

*Culpeper Herbalists
7 New Inn Hall Street
☎ 249754
Herbs, essential oils, books.

*Inner Bookshop
111 Magdalen Road
☎ 245301

*Neal's Yard Remedies
5 Golden Cross
Cornmarket Street
☎ 245436
Medicinal herbs, herbal tinctures, supplements, books homeopathic remedies, essential oils etc. The shop is manned on different days by a herbalist, homeopath, aromatherapist and naturopath, all of whom can give basic advice.

*TCM (Traditional Chinese Medicine)
Cowley Road

*Holland and Barratt
6 Golden Cross
☎ 792102
London Road, Headington
☎ 764578
263 Banbury Road
☎ 552523

NAPPY CHOICES

Babies need nappies but what type should you choose? Most people use disposables and there is no doubt these are very convenient. However, there is a growing awareness of their adverse environmental implications.

Tip: You can cut down on the number of disposables you get through by using flushable liners to dispose of solids

In Oxfordshire alone, over 100,000 disposables are thrown away every day, and it's estimated this waste will still be with us in 200 years' time. You may wish to consider other options.

Your child's health

Real nappies

Apart from the environmental benefits, there are very real financial benefits to using washable nappies. Estimates vary but you could be looking at anything up to £1000. How much you save depends on many factors, nappy system used, whether you reuse nappies with younger siblings, washing and drying costs, and so forth. Oxfordshire County Council will give you £30.00 towards the cost of using washable nappies. To receive this you need to register with Nappy Tales, ☎ 01235 812747, whether you are using their laundry service or washing your own. If you are buying your own nappies, keep the receipts for all the wraps, as you will need these, plus a copy of the baby's birth certificate, to receive the payment.

The variety of real nappies available today is greater than ever before. In addition to traditional terry and muslin squares, there are all-in-ones (fitted cloth nappies with Velcro closings and attached waterproof shell), quick-release nappies (fitted cloth nappies with Velcro closings for use with an over-pant), two-piece systems (cloth nappies designed to fit special water-proof pants with Velcro closings), and wrap-around (cloth nappies with ties). Overpants have changed too and are now available in breathable waterproof fabrics or wool.

Terries

These are still the cheapest and quickest drying option. They can be fastened with a plastic gripper or pins and will need a wrap over the top.

There is a growing army of work-at-home mums making nappies in different patterns to their own designs, and even terries now come in a range of pastel and bright colours. Wraps can be obtained in gingham, leopard print, or traditional white.

Shaped nappies

These are usually fastened with Velcro or poppers and are the simplest and most popular choice to use. They are available in different sizes (from new born to toddler) or a one-size-fits-all option (more economical). These also require a wrap.

All-in-ones

These are the most expensive option but the easiest to use. New all-in-ones have an inner absorbent section removed for washing, ensuring that they are quick drying.

Tip: The best way to dry real nappies is outside as the sun naturally bleaches the cotton.

Washing

Some people wash every day, others every two or three days. You can use a biodegradable liner to contain any solids which can be flushed down the loo. Alternatively, many people use fleece liners—the solids are tipped into the loo and the liner washed with the nappy. Soaking can extend the life of a nappy, but it is not essential.

36

Your child's health

Tip: adding vinegar to the final rinsing can help prevent nappy rash

If washing still seems too much, a laundry service can deliver clean nappies to you each week (see *Suppliers*) or you can use compostable nappies.

Nappy rash

Some babies are sensitive to wipes and creams—try using water and cotton wool. The plastic component in disposable nappies and the plastic pants over terries can cause nappy rash so it may help to try a different sort or brand. You could try a woollen nappy cover (for non-disposables) as they allow more air to reach the baby's skin.

See your health visitor or doctor if the rash is very bad.

Tip: Letting babies go bare whenever possible will help bottoms stay healthy and rashes heal more easily.

Suppliers and information

*Oxfordshire Real Nappy Network
☎ Jenny 880592
Non commercial advice service.

*The Real Nappy Association
PO Box 3704
London SE26 4RX
☎ 020 8299 4519
www.realnappy.com

*Women's Environmental Network
☎ 01983 401959
www.wen.org.uk

*Babies R Us
Botley Road
Limited stock of washable nappies and training pants.

*Boots Nappy Home Delivery Service
Nottingham
☎ 0800 622 525
Free delivery of a range of brands. Order by phone or from local stores.

*Cotton-tails
For local information, demonstration and advice on choosing and using comfortable and convenient cloth nappies to suit your baby. Stockists of fitted washable nappies and other products, including eco-friendlier disposables.
☎ Stephanie 744977
www.cotton-tails.co.uk

*Enviro (UK) Ltd
☎ 01582 484899
Makers of 'Weenies', disposable pads and nappies that decompose naturally.

*First Born
32 Bloomfield Avenue
Bear Flat, Bath BA2 3AB
☎ 01225 422586

*Jenners Pharmacy
Cowley Road, opp Manzil Way
Biodegradable, compostable and flushable brands including Weenies, Kooshies.

Your child's health

*Lollipop
☎ Hazel 01869 249091
Wide range of washable nappies.

*Mothercare
Oxford Retail Park, Cowley
Limited stock of washable nappies and training pants.

*Nappy Tales
☎ 01235 812747 (8.00–6.30) + answerphone.
Delivers weekly clean cotton re-usables and takes away soiled ones in the bin provided. Registration fee and standard service charge regardless of number of nappies required each week.

*Twinkle Twinkle
☎ Caroline 841359
Washable nappies and accessories.

*Sainsbury's
'Nature' brand. Claims to be an environmentally friendlier disposable nappy.

*Uhuru Wholefoods
Cowley Road
Environmentally friendlier disposables Tushies (gel-free, dioxin-free, made of cotton and wood pulp).

Weblinks
Web-based nappy businesses, the majority are mums working from home.

www.twinkleontheweb.co.uk
Probably the largest range of cloth nappies in the UK. Also includes nappy auction and 'nappy natter'.

www.plushpants.co.uk
Sells nappies and has a hire scheme to try before committing.

www.thenappylady.co.uk
Useful hints and tips section.

www.ellashouse.com
Hemp nappies in lovely prints.

www.nappysaurus.com
Colourful fleece wraps and 'make your own' kits.

www.ukparents.co.uk
Check out for its active nappy forum.

www.snazzypants.co.uk
All-in-one nappies and wraps you won't want to cover up.

Chapter 3 – Support for Parents

From reading this guide, you will see that there is a wealth of opportunity for you and your under-8s in Oxford and a huge number of groups and individuals working with babies and young children. We have attempted to organise the guide under specific headings such as shopping, activities and so on, but there are some schemes and organisations which cover a range of issues of interest to parents of young children. These include funding, welfare, counselling and support groups. In this chapter we have tried to pull these together under the broad heading of support for parents.

UNDER 8S IN OXFORD

You may feel that you would like more of a say in the kind of facilities provided for you and your children. If you do, contact Oxfordshire's **Early Years Development and Childcare Partnership** (EYDCP) which works with the County Council to plan, develop and coordinate early years education (aged 3-5), childcare (aged 0-16) and learning and support opportunities for families across Oxfordshire. Contact details: **Early Years Information Line** ☎ 815630, Katie Bailey, Clerk to the EYDCP ☎ 815174 www.oxfordshire.gov.uk/index/learning/early_years. Email: earlyyears.education@oxfordshire.gov.uk

The EYDCP has members representing groups with an interest in early education and childcare: parents, playgroups, day nurseries, schools, ethnic minorities,

Support for parents

District Councils, Oxfordshire County Council, after-school clubs, holiday play schemes, health visitors, employers and colleges of further education. It holds full meetings every two months open to the general public. For more information ☎ Early Years Information Line 815630.

The EYDCP also advises the County Council on the spending of the **Early Years Grant** (funded education for 3 and 4 year olds) and the **Childcare Grant** (support for the development of childcare). It issues small grants of up to £500 through its five **Divisional Liaison Panels** (DLPs) to fund projects supporting local services for children. To find out details about your local DLP and/or if you would like to put forward a bid for funding a project, call 815346.

There is one local Early Years development and Childcare Partnership group:

*Cutteslowe for Under-8s,
David Trebilcock or Sue Weinstock
☎ 311172

WELFARE RIGHTS AND ADVICE

Benefits and NHS treatment

Leaflets about the benefits and free NHS treatment you may be eligible for once you are pregnant or have children are available from your local Social Security Office, Post Office, maternity or child health clinic or dentist. See box on page 41 for details of benefits available.

Advice Centres

If you are finding it difficult to get the help and advice you need from your Social Security Office or the Oxford City Council Housing Department, try one of the following centres:

*Citizens' Advice Bureau
95-6 St Aldates
☎ 0870 264114 (opening hours can be obtained on this number)
www.adviceguide.org.uk
Information and advice including legal advice.

*Barton Information Centre
Barton Neighbourhood Centre
Underhill Circus
☎ 744152
Mon & Thurs 10.00-1.00 drop in
Other times by appointment.
Comprehensive welfare rights and information service.

*Agnes Smith Advice Centre
96 Blackbird Leys Rd
☎ 770206
Mon & Fri 10-12.30 drop in
Tues-Thurs 10-5.00 by appointment
General information and advice on welfare benefit take-up and representation, money advice and representation at County and Magistrates' Courts.

A solicitor is available by appointment on Thurs afternoons, 2.30-4.00 pm, offering free legal advice, and there are outreach advice sessions at the following centres:

Support for parents

The Clockhouse
Long Ground
Mon & Tues 10.00-12.00 Drop-in

The Farmhouse
Nightingale Avenue
Tues & Thurs 10.30-12.30 Drop-in

*Oxfordshire Chinese Community and Advice Centre
44B Princes Street
☎ 204188
Mon & Thurs 10.00-4.00
Benefits, housing, legal and immigration advice, translating/interpreting service.

*Oxford Housing Rights Centre
11 New Road
☎ 247853
ohre@btinternet.com
Mon, Wed, Fri 10.00-5.00
Tues, Thurs 10.00-1.00
Housing advice and a weekly list of rental property.

*Rose Hill and Donnington Advice Centre
The Cabin
The Oval
☎ 438634
Mon-Thurs 10.30-12.30 Fri 11.30-12.30

Non means-tested benefits relevant to young families
- Statutory Maternity Pay
- Maternity Allowance
- Child Benefit
- One Parent Benefit
- Free prescriptions and dental treatment if you are pregnant (and for one year after your baby is born)
- Free NHS prescriptions, dental treatment and vouchers for glasses for children.

Means-tested benefits include:
- Income Support
- Child Tax Credit - *provides a seamless system of income related support for families with children, paid directly to the main carer in the family. May include help with childcare costs. (See: Chapter 16 - Childcare)*
- Working tax credit - *paid to low-income working people. It also provides extra support for disabled people in work.*
- Child Maintenance and Child Maintenance Bonus
- Housing and Council Tax Benefit
- Free milk, vitamins and school dinners
- Budgeting and crisis loans

Support for parents

Benefits and money debt advice and representation at County and Magistrates' Court. Home visits are offered to anyone unable to get to these sessions.

Outreach sessions available at:

Parents Open Door (POD) Centre
Sure-Start
Littlemore
Mons 10.00-11.00 Drop-in

St Luke's
Canning Crescent
Weds 11.00-12.00. Drop-in

Sure-Start Family Centre
Rose Hill
Thurs 10.00-11.00. Drop-in

Informal support is also available at Donnington Doorstep in Townsend Square.

Help for lone parents

For advice on a range of issues including in-work benefit calculations, training and childcare advice try:

*Gingerbread
Advice Line: 0800 018 4318.
Mon-Fri 9.00-5.00
www.gingerbread.org.uk
National organisation offering practical and emotional support to lone parent families and their children.

*National Council for One-Parent Families
Freephone 0800 018 5026
Mon-Fri 9.00-5.00
www.oneparentfamilies.org.uk
info@oneparentfamilies.org.uk
Promotes the welfare of lone parents and their children. It offers parents the means to help themselves and their families by providing information and advice and working with communities.

Useful Helplines:

- **Child Credit** and **Working Tax Credit** 0845 300 3900 (8.00a.m.-8.00p.m.)

- **Child Support Agency** National Enquiry Line (Mon-Sat) 0345 7133133

- **DSS and Inland Revenue** for general enquiries 788400 (Mon-Thur 8.30-5.00, Fri 8.30-4.30) www.inlandrevenue.gov.uk

- **Social Security Office** 443333 (Mon-Thur 8.30-4.00, Fri 9.00-3.00)

Support for parents

*New Deal for Lone Parents
This is a service to help lone parents on income support to find work. A personal adviser will help you through the process of getting a job (preparation of a CV, dealing with interviews etc) and arranging childcare.
    Call the helpline or your local Jobcentre or Social Security Office
☎ 0800 868 868
www.newdeal.gov.uk

BRINGING UP KIDS—HELP & SUPPORT

Bringing up children can be hard. In this section we list some self-help groups and organisations which offer parents practical help, emotional support, counselling, parenting courses and helplines. Don't forget your doctor can help too. Some GP surgeries have counsellors attached to the practice or are able to refer you to an NHS or independent counselling service. See also *Ch 4 – Meeting People*, for other support groups
    These organisations all offer a sympathetic ear. Some of the services listed are free, others you have to pay for. Try the following:

*Black Child Mixed Parentage Group
☎ Sue 776691
Sue.funge@btopenworld.com
If you are a parent of a black, mixed parentage child, why not join this group? Parents and children concerned about the effects of racism on their families give each other support and arrange occasional family events.

*Cutteslowe for Under-8s
David Trebilcock or Sue Weinstock
☎ 311172

*Deaf and Hard of Hearing Centre
St Ebbes
☎ 243447 (9.00-5.00 weekdays)
Fax: 249823   Minicom: 722247
Support group for deaf children and their families. Contact centre for further information.

*Disabled Parents' Network (DPN)
☎ 0870 241 0450
National Centre for Disabled Parents
Unit F9, 89-93 Fonthill Road
London N4 3JN
enquiries@disabledparentnetwork.org.uk
A national organisation for people with a vested interest in disabled parenthood. Register with the DPN to obtain details of other disabled parents with whom to share experiences.

*Home-Start UK
☎ 0116 233 9955
Freephone national information line: 0800 686368
info@home-start.org.uk
www.home-start.org.uk
Family support organisation which provides regular support, friendship and practical help for families with at least one child under five, in their own homes. The service is free and confidential.

*Home-Start Oxford
Blackbird Leys Community Centre
☎ 779991

Support for parents

Regular visits by volunteers for those with at least one child under 5, facing difficulties or needing advice.

*Isis Centre
Darlington House
Little Clarendon Street
☎ 556648 (Mon-Fri 9.00-5.00 pm)
Free counselling and group therapy for anyone suffering from personal or emotional difficulties. Available to parents aged 18+ located in Oxford or registered with a GP in Oxford. Waiting list.

*National Childbirth Trust
☎ 717182
Can offer practical help with problems. Runs local postnatal support groups in all areas of Oxford.

*New Parent Network
☎ 775832/249466
Can put you in touch with other parents with similar experiences or problems.

*Oxfordshire Children's Information Service
26 Hanborough Business Park
Long Hanborough
Witney, Oxon
☎ 01993 886933
enquiries@oxoncis.org.uk
www.oxoncis.org.uk
A free service for parents which provides impartial, confidential information about childcare provision, play facilities and other child-related services for children aged 0-16 years within Oxfordshire.

*Oxford Parent Infant Project (OXPIP)
Appointments 07904 538774
Healthy Living Centre
Temple Cowley
oxpip@gn.apc.org
OXPIP provides emotional support to parents finding it difficult to cope with bringing up their babies. It offers a confidential counselling service for parents and their babies under two, and also for parents-to-be. OXPIP's trained counsellors and psychotherapists help parents to understand their relationship with their baby and to develop new ways of behaving. The service has no charge but parents are asked to make a contribution.

*Oxfordshire Family Mediation Service
125 London Road
Headington
☎ 741781 Mon-Fri 9.00-5.00 pm
24-hour answerphone
mediate@ofms.fsnet.co.uk
If you are at any stage of separation or divorce the service can help you both discuss your children's needs and make joint decisions about the best arrangements for them. They cannot offer legal advice but can help you find a local solicitor who specialises in family law. Free if legally aided; otherwise a sliding scale, depending on income. You can arrange an appointment yourselves or through a solicitor or social worker. Offer a separate Children's Support and Information Service to children

Support for parents

aged six and over, which gives children the opportunity to talk about the changes in their families in a relaxed and confidential setting.

*Parentline Plus
☎ 0808 8002222 24 hour
www.parentlineplus.org.uk
If you are feeling under stress or are worried about a child and would like to talk about it in confidence, please call.

*Springboard Family Project
Unit 5 Ramillies House
Alvescot Road
Carterton
☎ 01993 841740
Crisis line 07770 713248
A centre managed by Oxfordshire MIND for parents and children which provides support in relation to mental health issues (e.g. anxiety, self-confidence, postnatal depression). It includes groups for children to develop their self esteem through structured play. Crèche facilities available. Home visits can also be arranged.

Tues 10.00-3.00. Drop-in
(Specific groups are also run)

Wed 9.00-2.00. Drop-in
(soft play room open 9.00-1.00)

Thurs 1.15-2.45
Parent group with separate crèche
3.30-5.00
Children's groups - 4-6 and 7-9 years old, plus crèche

*Sure-Start - Rose Hill/Littlemore
The Oval
Rose Hill/Littlemore
☎ Tan Lea, Director 716739 (Mon-Fri 9.00-5.00)
tan.lea@sure-start.org.uk
www.surestart.gov.uk
One of the government's sure start programmes which supports children, parents and communities from disadvantaged areas through the integration of early education, childcare and health and family support services. The programme supports children and families living in the Rose Hill/Littlemore area. Among it's many services it offers a drop-in centre, counselling services, home visits, free transport and child care to families in need, a lending and recycling service of children's equipment, translation and interpretation (for Asian families), and training for parents and workers. Littlemore Community Centre has been extended to offer drop-in and training for families in the area. The Rose Hill Family Centre has also recently opened a new playroom, community café and crèche. The playroom is open:
Mon-Wed & Fri 9.00-12.00 & 12.30-3.00
Thurs 9.00-12.00

*Young Dads
Sure-Start Family Centre
The Oval, Rose Hill
☎ Rob 716739
www.oxdads.org.uk
Free drop-in group for young dads (up to 25 years) with their kids. Toys, play

Support for parents

area, activities, information, advice, free trips. Meets second Saturday of each month in the Sure Start playroom.

Other Support Groups

Other self-help groups and organisations which are not just for parents but also offer emotional and practical support that may be useful to you are:

*Asian Women's Helpline
☎ 0800 052 6077
Mon–Fri 9.30–4.00
Free, confidential phone advice on anything.

*Asylum Welcome
Diana Tickell/Mercedes Cumberbatch
276a Cowley Road
Oxford
☎ 722082
asylum-welcome@supanet.com
Mon–Wed & Fri 10.00–3.00
Thurs 11.00–1.00 women and children only.
Support agency for refugees and asylum seekers that provides practical help and advice on such matters as health care, children's education and employment. Children are welcome – mother and toddler group on Thursdays.

*CRUSE Bereavement Care
Day by day Helpline 0870 167 1677
helpline@crusebereavementcare.org.uk
www.crusebereavementcare.org.uk
A national organisation offering free information and advice to anyone who has been affected by death. It also provides support and counselling one to one and in groups.

*Marriage Care
☎ 749806
Crisis Helpline: 0845 7573921
Mon – Fri 10.00–4.00
Trained counsellors offer individuals or couples confidential one-hour counselling sessions, normally weekly, for an agreed number of visits (typically six). Initial meeting and counselling sessions are by appointment at accessible premises to central Oxford. No fee is charged, but those who are able are invited to make a donation.

*Oxfordshire MIND
125 Walton Street, Oxford
☎ 511702
office@oxmind.freeserve.co.uk
Provides information and advice on all issues relating to mental health.

Oasis
125 Walton Street
Mon 5.00–9.00pm, Fri 11.00–3.00
☎ 511702
An all women drop-in centre for women in distress needing emotional support. It is especially suitable for new mums suffering from bad postnatal depression. Meals and refreshments are provided. It also offers financial support for childcare costs.

Crisis Line
Mon-Thurs 7.00–1.00 am
Weekends 24 hours (Fri 7.00pm – Mon 7.00 am)

Support for parents

☎ 251152
Confidential Helpline for people in distress relating to mental illness.

*Oxfordshire Mental Health Resource Centre
19 Paradise Street
☎ 728981
mhrc@oxford-mentalhealth.org
www.comcom.org/oxmhrc
Free, confidential information and advice on mental health issues (including anxiety, depression, stress) in a friendly, supportive environment.

*Oxfordshire Women's Aid
PO Box 255, Oxford
☎ 791416 (office hours), Duty Social Worker 0800 833408 out of hours
owa@line1.net
Phone or write if you are threatened by physical, emotional or sexual violence and would like someone to talk to for advice and support. Also provide emergency accommodation for women fleeing from violence.

*Oxford Women's Counselling Centre
☎ 725617
Professionally trained female counsellors who offer low-cost counselling for women unable to afford private counselling fees.

*Relate
33 Iffley Road
☎ 242960
relate_oxon@hotmail.com
www.relate.org.uk

Counselling services for people experiencing difficulties in their relationships. You are generally asked to pay but will be seen if this is not financially possible.

*Samaritans
☎ 722122
Offers confidential, emotional support to anyone in crisis.
Lines open 24 hours a day.
Drop in at 123 Iffley Road 08.00–22.00

*Women of Colour
Mill Day Centre
46 Cowley Road
☎ Farah Zeb or Beth Brown Reid 716633
Mobile: 07765 253065
Fri 10.00–2.00
A welcoming and culturally aware environment where women suffering mental illness or distress can get support and information. No referral required, just pop in. Support with childcare costs available. Low cost refreshments.

*Worktrain
www.worktrain.gov.uk
Worktrain is an online jobs and learning site provided by the Department of Works and Pensions. It puts the most popular services for jobseekers online, including information on childcare.

Parenting education

As well as the organisations listed below, family centres, health visitors, community education centres (see

Support for parents

Chapter 9) and churches often run free courses on parenting. Look on notice boards at health and family centres, churches, community halls and libraries for more information. It's worth asking at your child's school as many courses are run in partnership with schools.

Don't forget that groups such as **New Parent Network** and **National Childbirth Trust** (See *Ch 4 – Meeting People*) also organise meetings on topics of interest to parents.

*Courses for Parents
Abingdon College
Northcourt Road
Abingdon OX14 1NN
☎ Christine Long 01235 216269
Free day and evening courses on how to encourage literacy and numeracy skills with very young children and how to build on the work your child does at school. The courses also provide the opportunity for you to develop your own skills and confidence.

*Family Nurturing Network (FNN)
Ground Floor, Temple Court
109 Oxford Road
Cowley
☎ 777756
info@fnn.org.uk
Provides parenting support and education to families with children aged 2-12 within Oxfordshire. It offers programmes which are aimed at improving relationships within the family and to help children succeed at home, with friends and at school.

1. Family Connections
Run at various venues throughout Oxfordshire.
The FNN and the Pre-School Teacher Counselling Service in Oxfordshire have joined to offer this free programme specifically designed for families with pre-school children (2-8 year olds). You are welcome to refer yourself or ask your health visitor or any other family educational service to recommend you.

2. The Dinosaur School
The Dinosaur School is run by the FNN for children (aged 5-10) whose parents are participating in one of their parenting courses. The aim of the school is to promote children's self esteem, social competence and acceptance by peers.

*'Man Enough' courses
☎ Albert Ford 863539
Parenting programme for dads who want to be more effective and understand how important dads are to their children. Has created a thriving group of dads who, after completing the course, continue to meet and plan joint activities for ongoing mutual support, from dads-only minibus trips to dads-and-kids camping weekends.

*Oxfordshire Parenting Forum (OPF)
☎ Julie Smith, coordinator 247190
c/o West Oxford Primary School
Ferry Hinksey Road, OX2 0BY
oxonparentforum@aol.com
The OPF brings together people concerned with the preparation, education and support of parents. It runs a series

Support for parents

of seminars for parents and people working with parents on a wide range of parenting issues.

There is a charge but concessionary rates are available. It also offers small grants towards the set-up and running costs of new parent group projects.

***Parent Education Development Team**
☎ Kathy Peto or Gill Warland 428078
Works with Oxford primary schools and the Oxford Parenting Forum to develop and run parenting courses for parents of children attending local schools. Contact Kathy or Gill or ask at your child's school for details.

My Family
by Catherine Godfrey
aged 3

Chapter 4 – Meeting People

Staying at home to look after babies and young children can make you feel isolated, especially if you are new to the area. Don't despair! You happen to be living in a city with all sorts of child-friendly activities on offer. See also: *Chapter 15 Activities for Kids.*

There are plenty of places in Oxford to meet other people with children and you may be surprised how quickly you can widen your circle of friends. Indeed some of the people you meet may well become close friends as your children grow up together. If you are missing work, why not get involved in running some of these groups and organisations? It can be interesting, rewarding and an excellent way for both you and your children to make new friends.

Tip: if you are nervous about going to a group for the first time, either take a friend or phone Donnington Doorstep on 727721. Their outreach workers will go to any group with you and stay until you feel settled.

POSTNATAL GROUPS AND CONTACTS

If you have just had a baby you may find it helpful to meet regularly with others in the same situation. Postnatal groups are generally very relaxed and baby-friendly. Some are run by health visitors in your local surgery or family centre, others are run by organisations such as the New Parent Network (NPN) or the National Childbirth Trust (NCT) and take place in people's homes.

If you would rather not go to a group, but would like to meet people in your area, contact either the NPN or the NCT who may be able to put you in touch with other parents (see: "Other support groups" in this chapter for contact numbers).

Meeting people

Health visitor groups

These are usually run on a weekly basis, sometimes involving discussions on topics relevant to the group. Most are open to all, although some require you to be registered with a particular practice or surgery. Most surgeries and some family centres run regular baby clinics on a drop-in basis. Ask your health visitor for details of current groups in your area as new ones may be available. Phone to check that times and venues are correct as this information may have changed since publication.

*Parent and Baby Group
St Clements Family Centre
Cross Street
☎ health visitors 793665
Fri 10.30-11.30
For parents living locally with babies up to a year old. Led by health visitor or parents. Health bias but agenda set by group.

*Parent and Baby Group
Bury Knowle Health Centre
London Road
Headington
☎ health visitors 762326
Fri 2.00-3.00
Topic discussion for first half hour. Informal and friendly.

*Temple Cowley Health Centre
Temple Road
☎ 772505
Occasionally runs a postnatal group. Call for up-to-date details.

*Parent and Baby Group
Jericho Health Centre
Walton Street
☎ Fiona Newton 513231
Tues 2.00-3.30

*Summertown Health Centre
Banbury Road
☎ health visitors 311898
Various sessions led by health visitor on different topics for parents and babies/toddlers, depending on demand. Contact for details.

*Postnatal Group
Florence Park Family Centre
Rymers Lane
☎ 777286
Group led by health visitor and family centre staff. Contact for details.

*Littlemore Community Centre
Giles Road
Littlemore
☎ 771764
At time of publication there are plans for a baby health clinic at the new **Sure Start** centre here. This may be on a drop-in basis, rather than a group. Contact for more details.

*Kaleidoscope Centre for Families
Oxford Road
Kidlington
☎ 372591
Postnatal group with crèche on Thurs. Contact for more details.

Meeting people

Other support groups

See also: *Chapter 3 Support for Parents* for various other special interest groups.

*New Parent Network
☎ Heather Dalitz 249466
☎ Nichola May 775832
website: *www.new-parent-network.org*
The NPN is an Oxford-based association run by parent volunteers. It aims to provide information and support for carers of children up to 8 years of age who live in Oxford and surrounding areas. Members receive a regular 40-page magazine, which include articles on parenting issues, a dads' section, and information on local groups, activities and events. The NPN organises informal coffee/social groups, monthly pub evenings led by speakers on parenting issues, a Dad's Group, PEEP groups, an annual Baby Day, parties and other activities. Dads are always welcome at events. Members can exchange parenting news and views via the NPN email group. The NPN also publishes this book, *Oxford for the Under Eights*. Annual membership is £6, which includes three magazines. To join, please use form at the back of this book.

*National Childbirth Trust
☎ Julia Horsnell (Chair) 717182
☎ Joanna Steele (postnatal support) 723266
☎ Virgil Clarke (antenatal classes) 727209

The NCT is a national organisation aiming to help families achieve greater enjoyment of childbirth and parenthood. They organise antenatal classes and postnatal support groups, child resuscitation classes, social events and regular 'nearly new' sales as well as providing information about other local groups and NCT services. A local agent provides a maternity bra fitting service. The NCT produces a regular newsletter also available to non-members. There are several postnatal supporters each covering a different area of Oxford.

*Oxford Twins Club
☎ Trudy Aries 772196
☎ Susan Fyvie 769275
☎ Sue Floyd (Kidlington) 460963
Meets as a parent and baby/toddler group on Wednesdays in Headington and Kidlington. Also arranges social evenings. £5 per year membership (2003). Entry fee for toddler group session.

*Wallingford/Benson Twins Club
At time of publication a twins group is planned for this area.
☎ Kate Bennington 01235 528381

*Abingdon Twins Club
☎ Kate Bennington 01235 528381
Meets regularly as a parent and toddler group and holds evening social meetings. Do get in touch if you have, or are expecting, twins or more! £6.50 per year membership (2003). Entry fee for toddler group.

Meeting people

See also: *Ch 1 Having a Baby in Oxford* for parentcraft classes at the JR Women's Centre for those expecting more than one child.

*Saturdads
☎ Rob 716739
Sure Start Centre
The Oval, Rose Hill
Second Saturday of each month. 10.00-1.00. Occasional outings.

*Young Dads
☎ Rob 716739
www.oxdads.org.uk
As above, Sure Start Centre, 2.00-4.00
Free, drop-in group. Toys, play area, information, advice, free trips.

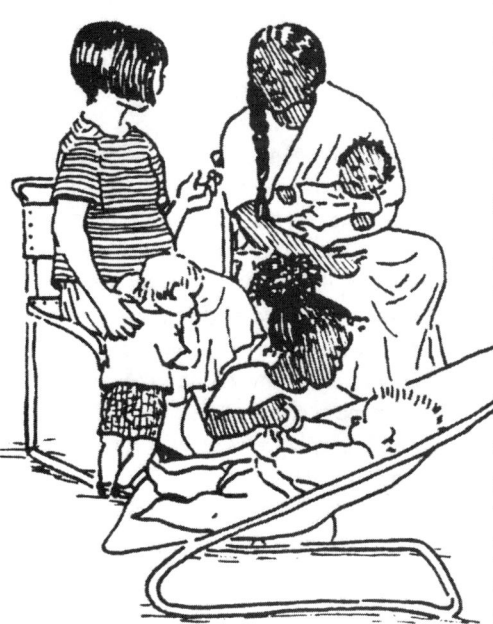

*Dads and Kids
☎ 775832/249466

*Parenting morning/study circle
8 St Omer Road, Cowley
☎ Maryam Ramzy 714398
Fri 11.30-2.30
For Muslim mothers of all nationalities. Contact for more details.

*Muslim Saturday Group
☎ Rayhana Khan 240808
Sat 10.30-1.00. Information on child development, health and diet. Social group. This is followed by Arabic classes for children up to age 8 and their parents (1.30-3.30).

*Asian Cultural Centre
Manzil Way
Cowley Road
☎ 425000
Provides a wide range of activities for all the community. Offers various groups including:
lunch club for women to meet and socialise on Mondays 12.00-1.30 (children welcome); Urdu class with crèche; sewing class with crèche. Support groups and advice available. Phone or call in for more details.

*The Café Club
Rose Hill Community Centre
Tues 12.30-2.30
For young parents/parents-to-be. Meet others in a relaxed and friendly environment. Partners and friends welcome.

Meeting people

*African Caribbean Women's Support Group
Unity Office
East Oxford Education Complex
51 Union Street
☎ 722999
email: unity@owts.org.uk
Last Thursday of the month 7.00-8.00pm

*Black Child Mixed Parentage Group
Barton Neighbourhood Centre
☎ Sue 776691
email: sue.funge@btopenworld.com
Contact for more details.

*Oxfordshire Chinese Community Centre
44B Princes Street
☎ 202266
Occasionally runs social groups for Chinese families. Contact for more details.

*MAMA: Mothers and Children at Asylum Welcome
Asylum Welcome,
276A Cowley Road
Oxford.
☎ 722082
Thurs 11.00–1.00 women only. For asylum seekers/refugees. Social, meet other women, talk, eat, drink. Children can play together – toys and clothes.
Note: Asylum Welcome is a charity providing advice and assistance to asylum seekers and refugees on all matters ranging from housing, immigration to welfare benefits.

Open 10.00-3.00 every day, except Thurs. See signposts at start of book for more details of services for asylum seekers and refugees.

Family centres

These are great, informal places to meet friends with young children. Generally they are free. The centres are run on a 'drop-in' basis and you can stay for as long/short a time as you like. They welcome carers and children up to the age of eight and try to provide for all their needs with fun activities indoors and out, food and drink at reasonable prices (or most will let you bring your own food) and nappy changing facilities. Some also organise specific activities for the over-fives during school holidays. It is fine to breastfeed at these centres and most have facilities to warm bottles.

Staff are available to give support and information where needed, which may be one-to-one or group sessions covering particular topics. These sessions may also have a crèche facility. Each family centre is different so it is worth trying more than one.

If you are nervous about visiting a new centre, contact the staff first as they will usually be pleased to meet you and to show you around.

*BOD (Barton's Open Door)
Waynflete Road
Headington
☎ 764952

Meeting people

Mon, Wed, Thurs 10.00–2.00 drop-in sessions
Tuesday Toddler Group, 12.45–2.45. Lots of play activities for children and group activities for carers e.g. health, adult literacy groups. Bring and share lunch every Monday. Inexpensive refreshments all day. Workers can offer help and support if you want it; just pop in any time up to 4.00.
Contact space for parents separated from their children. Please call for current news and groups.

*Cuddesdon Corner
61-3 Cuddesdon Way
Blackbird Leys
☎ 773263
Fax 747415
Email: pc@cuddcorn.freeserve.co.uk
Drop in & play Mon, Thurs & Fri 10.30-2.30. **'Creative kids' activity group** Tue 10.30-11.30. **Creative group for adults**, with crèche, Tues 1.15-2.45.
UK Online Centre - IT and Internet access every day 10.30-2.30.

Other groups and short courses at other times - check with the Centre for details. Other family support, either Centre-based or in your home on request. Free independent **counselling** service - TLC - Mon 3.30-5.30, Tues-Thurs 3.30-8.30, ☎ 374370 for more information.

*Donnington Doorstep
Townsend Square
(off Donnington Bridge Road)
☎ 727721

Mon–Fri 10–4.00 Drop-in.
Independent, grant-aided family centre. Indoor play area with plenty of toys for babies and older children and lots of messy activities. Outdoors has activity toys, slide, sand etc. Everything is packed into one room, so easy to keep an eye on the kids, indoors or out. Books for adults to browse while children play. Cheap refreshments throughout the day and excellent home-cooked lunch from 12.00, usually with vegetarian option. Craft materials, stationery, some toys and second-hand clothes for sale at competitive prices. Children's book library and toy library Friday 10.30-11.30. Training courses open to all in play-leading and catering. Crèche Mon 9.45-11.45. Very friendly and welcoming. Free entry, but contributions always welcome.

*Florence Park Family Centre
Rymers Lane
☎ 777286
Open access drop-in Mon, Thurs and Fri 10.00-3.00. Tues and Wed groups. County Council resource run in partnership with education and voluntary agencies. £1.00 per adult, children free (includes refreshments). Cheap lunches available, or bring your own. Indoor craft activities, messy play, books, home corner, lots of toys, puzzles etc. Outdoor play with climbing bridge, trikes, cars. Groups running or planned at time of press: music, postnatal, women's, Early Start and PEEP; crèche available for some adult groups.

Meeting people

Support and information available. Speak to staff on your first visit and they will show you around. The centre is situated in Florence Park – a spacious park with children's playground, crazy golf, bowling green and tennis courts (see Ch. 11 – Out and About in Oxford for more details).

*Kaleidoscope Centre for Families
Oxford Road
Kidlington
☎ 372591
Drop-in centre on Tues 9.00–12.30, Weds 12.30–3.30, Thurs 9.00–1.00, Fri 9.00–12.30. Small entry charge. Toy library, crèche, postnatal group (with crèche) on Thursdays, eczema group etc. Phone for further details and times.

*Littlemore Community Centre
Giles Road
Littlemore
☎ 771764
Holds drop-in 'snack and play' sessions. Toy library Weds afternoons. Also, at time of publication a new Sure Start Centre has just opened. There will be groups for under 4s, parents with young babies, PEEP sessions, as well as a crèche, a health clinic and drop-in play sessions. Please contact the Community Centre or Sure Start ☎ 716739 for more details.

*Rainbow House
Wesley Memorial Hall
New Inn Hall Street

Wed–Fri 10.30–2.00 (term-time only) Drop-in centre for parents and carers with pre-school children in the centre of Oxford. Good cheap lunches, high-chairs and plenty of toys and space for children to play.

Parents are *discouraged* from bringing own food as refreshment sales provide much of the centre's income. See: Ch. 10 - Eating Out.

*Sure-Start Family Centre
The Oval
Rose Hill
☎ 716739
Mon–Fri 10.30–3.00. Open daily for drop-in play at the playroom 9.00-12.00 & 12.30-3.00 (toys are available in the café area during lunch period). Closed Thurs pm.

Great provision for babies as well as older children. Cheap refreshments and lunch, with vegetarian option. Messy play, baby play, song & dance, baby clinic, etc. Cheap laundry. Lunchtime/shoppers' crèche Wed & Fri (only £2). Toy library Mon 10.00-12.00 and Fri afternoons.

Regular courses for adults living locally e.g. basic skills, English for speakers of dual languages, computers, women's sewing, parenting, childcare, first aid etc. Also benefits/debt advice, relationship counselling. Regular trips, fun days etc.

After school club, holiday playschemes during Summer and Easter.

Ring for more information.

Meeting people

Baby and toddler groups

These are very good places to meet other families with young children in your area—and for your child to burn off some energy and learn to relate to other children. It's a good introduction to the art of 'sharing'! These groups are informal—you can drop in at any time during the session. They are often run by other parents or childminders and usually involve a hall full of toys with activities and refreshments for carers and children. Some have organised singing/music/special activities and most charge up to £1 per session to cover costs. It is worth trying a few. You may find yourself travelling to another part of the city for a particularly good group. Some are suitable for 0-4 year olds, so not strictly toddlers. If you are unsure, enquire about the age range of children that attend. For nursery and pre-school playgroups see: Ch. 16 - Childcare and Ch. 17 - Playgroups and Nurseries. For other groups, such as music or gym, see Ch. 15 - Activities for Kids.

Where to find toddler group information

It is almost impossible to keep up with current toddler group listings as the details change rapidly. This list is, to the best of our knowledge, correct at the time of publication.

If a contact number has changed, check the noticeboard of the listed venue. Try local community places such as your church hall, primary school, library or family centre. Ask at other groups and drop-in centres—sometimes word of mouth is the best way to find a suitable group. Look out for parish magazines and local newsletters (especially New Parent Network and NCT). You could also try contacting Oxfordshire's **Children's Information Service** 01993 886933 www.oxoncis.org.uk. The following is a fairly comprehensive list of what is available, but if you find anything new, please let us know on 775832, or oxfordforunder8s@oxoncis.org.uk.

Central/Jericho

*St Ebbe's Toddler Group
St Ebbe's Church
☎ Annabel Heywood 240438
Wed 11.00-2.45 term-time. Lunch provided for small charge. Singing, stories, crafts. For preschool children & carers.

*St Barnabus Mums and Prams
St Barnabus Community Centre
33A Canal Street
☎ Trudy Foulks 511561
Tues 9.30-11.15. For 0-4 year olds. Free, donations welcome.

*Toddle in
St Aldates Parish Church
Pembroke Street
☎ Vanessa Watts 436537
Mon 10.00-11.30
Singing, storytime and toys for babies and toddlers. Refreshments.

Meeting people

South Oxford

*Sth Oxford Parent & Toddler Group
South Oxford Baptist Church
Wytham Street
☎ Church office 201744.
Thurs 9.30-11.30. 0-2 year olds. Toys, refreshments. Small entry fee. Please contact the Church to confirm details.

*Parents with Disabilities Toddler Group
South Oxford Baptist Church
☎ Church office 201744
Wed 9.30-11.00. At time of publication we have been unable to confirm if this group is still running, please contact the Church to confirm details.

*Messy Play
St Matthew's Church Hall
Marlborough Road
☎ Church Office 798587
Tues 9.30-11.30. Lots of messy fun for the under threes.

East Oxford/St Clements

*Bartlemas Toddler Group
Community Room
Bartlemas Nursery School
269 Cowley Road
☎ School Office 245768
Tues 9.30-11.30 term-time.

*Bartlemas Messy Play
Bartlemas Nursery School (see above).
Thurs 9.30-11.00 for the over twos.
Toy library after messy play session.

*Bartlemas French Group
Bartlemas Nursery School (see above) Toddler group for French-speaking families, Fri mornings.

*St Clements Toddler Group
St Clements Family Centre
Cross Street
☎ Helen Garfitt 246674
Thurs 10-11.30 term-time. 0-3 years. Very friendly, large warm hall, fun & educational toys, crafts, action songs. Entry fee, refreshments included.

*St Clements Tiddlers Praise Group
St Clements Church
Marston Road
☎ Helen Gillingham 248735
Mon 10-11 term-time. For 0-3 years. Action songs, story box with 'Barnabus bear', many children's books. Entry and refreshments free.

*Jeune Street Parent and Toddler Group
Cowley Road Methodist Church
Main Entrance (corner of Jeune St)
☎ 735569
Mon 10-11.30. Toys, books, dough, sand etc. For babies and preschool children. Entry fee, includes refreshments.

Cowley/Temple Cowley

*Church Cowley 0-4s
Church Cowley St James School
Bartholomew Road
☎ School Office 778484
Tues 1.35-3.00. Toys and refreshments.

Meeting people

*Our Lady's Toddler Group
At the Mornese Centre (at end of Convent Grounds)
Oxford Road, Cowley
Contact number not known, but try Our Lady's School ☎ 779176
Weds 9.00–11.30.
Entry fee.

*Temple Cowley Toddler Group
(previously St Dominic's Toddler Group.)
Silver Band Hall (next to car park of Temple Cowley Swimming Pool)
Temple Road
☎ Hilary Webster
Mon, Wed, Thurs, Fri 10.00–12noon. Tricycles, push along toys, space to run around. Entry fee includes refreshments.

*Toddler Group
St Francis Church (CE)
Hollow Way
☎ Helen Doling 779626
Wed 10.10–11.30
Run by vicar. Christian emphasis. Action songs, story, music followed by coffee and toys.
Entry fee.

Iffley, Rose Hill and Littlemore

*Parent and Toddler Group
St Luke's Church
Canning Crescent (off Donnington Bridge Road)
☎ 251616
Fri 10.00–12.00 (during term-time and school holidays). Toys, friendly welcome and comfy sofas. Access to garden in Summer. Small entry fee.

*Toddler Group
Rose Hill Primary School
The Oval
☎ 777937
Wed 9.00–11.00 (ring to confirm times). Toys, informal music session. PEEP groups also held here for parents living in the Rose Hill area.

*Saturdads and
*Young Dads
Sure-Start Centre
Rose Hill
See p 53
Phone to confirm times.

Blackbird Leys

*The Dovecote Carer and Toddler Group
The Dovecote Centre
Nightingale Avenue
☎ Carol Richards 712299
Thurs 10.00–11.30 term-time. Outside play, toys. Entry fee. All welcome.

*The Dovecote Centre New Parents Group
The Dovecote Centre
Nightingale Avenue
☎ Trudy 772196, Vicki 721185, Lynn or Sue (Home Start) 779991 or The Dovecote Centre 712299.
Fri 10.30–12.00 term-time. A group for new parents. Easy parking and access.

Meeting people

Refreshments for parents, toys for the babies. Older children up to the age of 3 years welcome. Please phone to confirm details.

Headington/Barton/Northway/Marston

*Little Sharks
All Saints Church Hall (opposite church)
New High Street
☎ Anna Cahill 432740 or J. Chester (Church Hall bookings) 750531
Mon 9.30-11.30 term-time.
Informal, plenty of space and toys, singing. Friendly group for preschool children and babies. Come and socialise with other carers.

*BOD (Barton's Open Door) Toddler Group
Waynflete Road
☎ 764952
Tues 12.45-2.45. See Family Centre section for more info on other activities held at BOD.

*Coach House Toddler Group
The Coach House
Quarry Road
☎ Anne Wood 767827, Becky Paton 768731
Wed 2.00-4.00. Toys, informal music session.

*Headington Baptist Church Toddlers
78 Old High Street
Old Headington
☎ Church Office 761444 or Marion Bloyce-Smith 432436
Tue 9.30-11.30 term-time. Toys, refreshments and singing

*Headington Quarry Toddler Group
Methodist Church Hall
Quarry High Street
☎ Louise Noonan 744693
Thurs 10.00-11.30. Toys, crafts, 0-5s. Small friendly group, all welcome. Entry fee.

*Parent and Toddler Group
Tower Playbase (at the base of Ploughman Tower flats)
Maltfield Road, Northway
☎ Teresa Evans 767298
Fri 9.30-11.30 term-time. Toys, craft activities. Friendly group. Entry fee includes refreshments.

*Scallywags Mums & Toddlers
Northway Evangelical Church
Sutton Road, Headington
☎ Rachael Bell 766284
Mon 9.45-11.00 term-time.

*St Nicholas Babies and Toddlers
St Nicholas Church Hall
Old Marston
☎ Sue James 722211
Wed 10.00-11.00 Entry £1.00 inc. refreshments. Arts and crafts, themed activities, singing.

Wood Farm/Risinghurst

*Mother & Toddler Early Years Group
Wood Farm Primary School
Titup Hall Drive
☎ Margaret Warner 453968

Meeting people

Mon, Wed, Thurs, Fri 9.00-12.00 (an organiser is present from 9.30 onwards) Term-time and summer holiday (closed Easter and Christmas).
Drop-in for pre-school children. Toys, paint, dough, sand. Refreshments. Everyone welcome. Useful for parents with older children attending the Primary School or the Slade Nursery nearby. Entry fee, 50p per adult.

***Risinghurst Toddler Group**
Risinghurst Community Centre
Kiln Lane
☎ Jo Armitage 744707
Fri 9.30-11.30. Entry fee. All welcome.

***Bullingdon Parent and Toddlers**
Bullingdon Community Centre
Peat Moors (off The Slade)
☎ Kathy Partlette 450994
Mon, Tues and Thurs 10-11.30. Toys and refreshments. Phone to confirm details.

North Oxford

***Flying Start**
Cutteslowe Community Centre
Wren Road
☎ Sue Weinstock 311172
Wed 10.00-11.30 term-time.
Parents/carers and babies 2-12 months. Share songs, rhymes, books and stories.

***Parent and Toddler Group**
Cutteslowe Community Centre
Wren Road
☎ Sue Weinstock 311172
Tue, Wed, Thur 9.00-11.30 term-time.

***St Andrew's Parent and Babies Group**
St Andrew's Church
Linton Road
☎ 311212
Two groups: 0-13 months, Tues 11.00-12.30 (term-time and summer holidays); 14-24 months, Tues 9.30-11.00 (term-time only). Small informal groups for carers to chat and socialise. Entry fee.

***St Andrew's Toddler group**
St Andrew's Church
(see entry above)
Wed 10.15-12.00 and Wed 1.45-3.30 term-time only.
Play, music and crafts for 'under fives' and carers. Entry fee. Call for details.

***St Margaret's Toddler Group**
St Margaret's Church
St Margaret's Road
☎ Frances 310886, Emma 512105 or Jo 316990
Fri 2.45-4.30.

***St Peter's Under 5s Group**
First Turn, Wolvercote
☎ June Williams 511770 as there is often a waiting list.
Fri 10.00-11.45. Toys, action songs, activities. Entry fee.

***Stepplng Stones**
Baptist Church Hall
198 Woodstock Road
☎ Margaret Evans 873592
Thurs 10.00-12.00 term-time.
For preschool children and carers.

Meeting people

*Summertown Baby and Toddler Group
St Michael & All Angels Church
Lonsdale Road
☎ Sally Vine 514816 or Jan Rushton 556079
Tues 10.30-12.00.
Children's games, music, craft and messy play. Small entry fee (includes refreshments).

West Oxford

*Messy Play
West Oxford Community Centre
Botley Road
☎ 245761
Mon 10.00-12.00 term-time. For pre-school children. Paints, sticking, dough, clay. Refreshments provided. No need to book. £2 first child, £1 each additional child. Phone to confirm details.

*Mother and Baby Group
West Oxford Community Centre
☎ 245761
Mon 10.00-12.00, Wed 3.00-4.30. Phone for more details.

*Parent and Toddler Group
West Oxford Community Centre
☎ 245761
Fri 9.00-11.30.
Phone for more details.

Villages outside Oxford

Kidlington

*St Mary's Baby and Toddler Group
St Mary's Church
Church Street
☎ Church Office 841248 (on Tues or Thurs morning) or Lesley 370517
Tues and Thurs 10.00-11.30 (term-time & usually during holidays). Activities, toys, refreshments. For 0-4 year olds and carers. Entry fee.

*Parent and Toddler Group
Kidlington Methodist Church
☎ Church Office 374623
Fri 9.00-11.30 (term-time). Entry fee.

*Toddler Group
Kidlington Methodist Church
☎ Sue Warmington 371874
Wed 10.00-11.30 (term-time and school holidays). All carers and 0-4s welcome. Toys, sit 'n' ride vehicles, puzzles, outdoor activities organised in Summer. Entry fee includes refreshments. Occasionally a waiting list, but come along and try first.

*Skips Mother & Toddler Group
St Johns Church
Kidlington
Wed 1.15-2.45
For 0-5 years.
Contact number not known, but try the Church Office
☎ 372230.

Meeting people

*Bumps & Beyond
Adult Learning Centre
Gosford Hill School
Mon 10.30-12.30
☎ Sarah 370531
For pregnant mums and babies up to 1 year.

*Tots R Us
Adult Learning Centre
Gosford Hill School
☎ Helen 01869 343850 or Rachel 460796
Mon 2.00-4.00. For children 1 year +.

*Robin Toddlers
Adult Training Centre
Blenheim Road
Mon 1.15-2.45
☎ 372494
For 0-5 years. Phone for more details.

Other villages

*Cumnor Babies and Toddlers Group
United Reform Church Hall
Leys Road
Cumnor
☎ Joy Green 246873
Fri 2.00-4.00 term-time. Ring to check details for holiday periods. For 0-3 years.

*Kennington Parents and Toddlers
Kennington Village Hall
Tues and Thurs 9.30-11.30
Details not confirmed at time of publication.

*Sandford-on-Thames Village Toddler Group
Sandford-on-Thames Village Hall
Henley Road
☎ Hannah Wright 776357
Mon 10.00-12.00 term-time. Good selection of toys and activities, books, songs, games, refreshments. Informal, welcoming and friendly. Entry fee (first visit free).

*Standlake Mother and Toddler Group
Standlake Village Hall
☎ Meg 300773 or Rachael 300607
Toys, craft activities, refreshments. From newborn to preschool. Small, friendly group. Parents from outside the area welcome. Entry charge.

*Stanton St John Toddler Group
The Holford Centre
Stanton St John
☎ Pip 874566
Thurs 10.00-12.00. Toys, refreshments. Small entry fee. Details not confirmed, please phone for more info.

*Yarnton Toddler Group
☎ Karen Smith 371046
No other details at time of publication.

Do you know of any other Oxford-based toddler groups that can be included here? Please let the NPN know on 775832 or email: oxfordforunder8s@oxoncis.org.uk

Meeting people

CHURCHES & PLACES OF WORSHIP

Would you like to take your children with you to worship but are worried they will make too much noise? Don't be. Oxford has a huge range of churches and places of worship that cater for a variety of cultural groups, and most are welcoming to families and children. Here are some that are particularly 'child-friendly'. These places of worship have been recommended by other parents—please let us know if you have found any others.

Most Sunday children's groups are run by other parents and teachers from the church—you are welcome to stay with your child until they feel comfortable and settled. Otherwise most churches don't mind babies/children in the service—some have crèches—but make sure you have access to a quick exit should you need to escape!

Central Oxford

*St Aldate's (CE)
St Aldates
opposite Christ Church
☎ 244713
10.30 Family service. Crèche 0-2.
Good, organised Sunday groups for 3 years upwards. Mums' bible study with crèche Fridays 10.00am. Phone for details. Mothers and Young Children (MaYC) holds weekly meetings in Oxford City Wed 10.00, Marston and Wheatley Thurs 10.00.
☎ 874285.

*Blackfriars (RC)
St Giles
☎ 278400
9.30 Family Mass.
Organised groups, music and stories for children during the service.

*Cherwell Vineyard
☎ 433030
10.30 Service with separate activities for children.

*St Ebbe's (CE)
City centre
☎ 240438
10.00 Family service. Crèche 0-3.
Good, organised Sunday groups in different rooms for aged 3 upwards.
Phone for other activities organised at the church.

*New Road Baptist
Bonn Square
☎ 556210
10.30 each Sunday.
Crèche facility.
Sunday school groups for 3 years upwards.
Pushchair-friendly lift to upper floors. Phone for holiday club details and day events.

*Oxford Community Church
The Kings Centre
Osney Mead
☎ 297420
Sunday services with crèche. Organised children's activities for 0-14 years.

Meeting people

*Wesley Memorial Methodist Church
New Inn Hall Street
☎ 243216
10.30 Sunday Family service, children welcome, crèche also available, Sunday School. also runs Rainbow House Weds-Fri term-time (See Chs. 4, 6, 10.)

South Oxford

*St Matthew's (CE)
Marlborough Road
☎ 798587
10.30 Family service. Very good crèche and children's group provision.
A popular family church. Mums' Bible study with crèche facility every other Thursday morning. Phone church office for details.

*South Oxford Baptist Church
Wytham Street
10.00 Sunday service, children welcome. Crèche and Junior Church activities available.
(Asian Baptist Fellowship based here, see end of chapter).

East Oxford

*St Clements (CE)
Marston Road
☎ 246674
10.30 Family service. Crèche for 0-3. Baby-friendly. Good, organised Junior Church every fortnight in St Clements family centre. Phone for details of other activities.

*Cowley Road Methodist
Jeune Street
☎ 770703
10.30 service. Crèche available.

*St Francis (CE)
Hollow Way
Cowley
☎ 01494 462911
10.30 service with crèche and Sunday School for 5s upwards. Recommended informal, friendly family service on the second Sunday every month.

*Greyfriars (RC)
Iffley Road
Has a family service.

*St James' Cowley
Beauchamp Lane
☎ 747680
10.00am family service on second Sunday of the month.

*Leys Community Church
Blackbird and Greater Leys
☎ 714153
3.30pm service. The church especially welcomes families with young children. Crèche and also children's activities designed to be creative, fun and educational.

*St Mary and St John
Cowley Road
11.00 Wednesday, 'Noah's Ark' service for carers and under 5s with songs and lunch.

Meeting people

*St Mary's (CE)
Iffley village
☎ 773516
10.00 Sunday service. Crèche 0-4. Groups for 4 years upwards. Monthly family service in Rose Hill First School.

*Rose Hill Methodist
☎ 770703
11.00 Junior Church and crèche. All ages worship together once a month.

Headington

*All Saints (CE)
Lime Walk
☎ 762536
9.30 Sung communion with facilities for children. More informal family service once a month at 11.00.

*St Andrew's (CE)
Old Headington
☎ 767041
10.00 service with crèche and Sunday School for 4s upwards.
Changing and other baby-friendly facilities available.

*St Antony of Padua (RC)
Headley Way
☎ 762964
10.00 Family Mass. Children's liturgy. Child/baby friendly.

*Corpus Christi (RC)
Margaret Road
Sunday services at 9.00, 11.00, 12.00. Crèche facilities. Plenty of ramps for pushchairs. Large hall for 0-7 years.

*Headington Baptist Church
Old High Street
☎ 432436
10.30 service with crèche and full range of Sunday School activities.

*Headington United Reform Church
Collingwood Road
☎ 761648
9.30 service with play table in church for children. Also coffee lounge with books and toys.

*Holy Trinity (CE)
Quarry Road
Headington Quarry
☎ 762931
10.00 Family service, crèche in vestry. Thriving Sunday School for 3s upwards in nearby Coach House (Church Hall).
Pram service with communion taken by the vicar or curate every Tuesday at 10.00 for parents and carers with children up to school age. Refreshments afterwards in Coach House; toys.

Marston

*Marston U.R.C
☎ 761648
11.15 service with play table and crèche.

*St Michael and All Angels (CE)
Marston Road
Well-equipped play space.

Meeting people

*St Nicholas (CE)
Old Marston
☎ 247034
10.00 service with crèche usually. Room for parents to withdraw with crying babies. Junior Church for 4 years up. Once a month Family service.

North Oxford

*St Aloysius (RC)
Woodstock Road
Baby changing and feeding facilities. Sunday 9.30 Family Mass.

*St Andrew's (CE)
Linton Road
☎ 311212
9.30 service in large, lively and popular family-friendly church. Crèche with facility to listen to the service while looking after your baby. Excellent organised children's groups in a multitude of rooms. Short family service held on the first Sunday of the month at 9.30. Mothers' bible study group Mon 9.45-11.15 with crèche.

*St Gregory's
Woodstock Road
Family service

*Woodstock Road Baptist Church
Woodstock Road
☎ 515569
10.30 service, crèche and Sunday School for 3s upwards. Family service usually held on last Sunday of the month.

Outside Oxford city

*St Andrews (CE)
Sandford-upon-Thames
☎ 748848
10.00 every Sunday, Sunday club for school age children. Special half hour family/children's service is held on the last Sunday of each month at 11.15.

*Kennington Methodist
☎ 770703
10.30 service. Junior Church and crèche.

*Kidlington Baptist Church
High Street
Kidlington
☎ 373426
www.kidlington-baptist.org.uk
10.30 service with Junior Church and crèche. Family Service on third Sunday in month. Clubs for children on Thursday and Friday evenings. Open House fellowship group for mums, Men's Breakfasts.

*Kidlington Methodist Church
☎ 373958
10.00 Family service plus regular children's services. Crèche and Junior Church. Other children's groups run during the week. Call for details.

*St Mary's (CE)
Church Street
Kidlington
☎ 375611
10.00 service, families welcome. Crèche and Sunday School groups.

Meeting people

Other places of worship
Groups and contacts

Despite our best efforts, we have only been able to find limited information on other places of worship. If you have details of other centres that should be included, please let the NPN know for future publication. Contact 775832 or email us on oxfordforunder8s@oxoncis.org.uk

Jewish

*Oxford Jewish Centre
☎ 553042
For under-fives. For information contact Lizzie ☎ 558105

Christian

*Asian Baptist Fellowship
South Oxford Baptist Church
Wytham Street
Sunday 3.00pm
Punjabi speaking. Activities for children available.
☎ Mohan Masih 203699

*First Church of Christ, Scientist
36 St Giles
☎ Sally Lessiter 875529
Sunday School welcomes all ages.
11.00 Sunday service.
12.00 Children's service.
Reading room open to all; special corner for youngsters.
Opening times: Mon-Fri 12.00-3.00
Closed Weds.

*Greek and Russian Orthodox
1 Canterbury Road
☎ 552597
Phone for information about times and languages used in services.

*Oxford Chinese Christian Church
Headington Baptist Church
Old High Street
☎ the Pastor, Mr Lee on 765756
The only Chinese Christian church in Oxfordshire. Families welcome, crèche available. Sunday School classes in English, Mandarin and Cantonese every Sunday, 1.30-4.00. Bible Teaching and Chinese classes in both Mandarin and Cantonese.

*Jehovah's Witnesses
Kingdom Hall
Temple Street
☎ 372736
Two congregations share the hall and each have two family-friendly meetings every week, to which anyone is welcome. Also smaller study meetings in each others' homes.

*Religious Society of Friends (Quakers)
Oxford Meeting House
43 St Giles
☎ the Warden 557373
Quaker meeting every Sunday 11.00-12.00.

Meeting people

Sunday school classes for 0-5 year olds and older children.

Buddhist

*Thrangu House Buddhist Centre
42 Magdalen Road
☎ 241555

Muslim

*Medina Mosque
2 Stanley Road
☎ 243142
Quranic lessons held daily for 6-year olds upwards. Islamic study classes, Urdu classes for children. Once a month youth gathering. All welcome.

*Oxford Islamic School
Union Street Education complex
☎ Maryam Ramzy 714398
Mon 6.00-7.30 term-time.
Voluntarily run school providing free classes for Muslims of all nationalities from age 5. An opportunity for Muslim children to learn about their religion.

*The Mosque
Bangladeshi Islamic Education Centre
57 Cowley Road
☎ 793118
Quranic classes for age 6 upwards. Regular Islamic programmes.
All nationalities and backgrounds very welcome.

Chapter 5 - Getting About

Getting around, whether by foot, bike, bus or car, is obviously more difficult with young children in tow. In this section we've collected together ideas and information to try and make getting about in Oxford a bit easier.

By foot

Slings and backpacks

Many parents like to carry very small babies on their fronts in purpose-made carriers. This leaves your hands free and most babies like to be snuggled close to mum or dad in this way. You may even find it calming for the baby to pop him or her in a sling while you are pottering around the house. It's a great way to get a few jobs done!

There are several types of carrier available most of which adapt from inward facing to outward facing as the baby grows. The Baby Bjorn is one of the best quality, and easiest to put on and adjust quickly. Getting into the Wilkinet may look daunting, but many people find them comfortable and adaptable *Try before you buy!*

Depending on the size of your baby, and the strength of your back, you may at some stage find it more comfortable to use a backpack carrier. Babies and toddlers love these as they get a more interesting view of the world. They also allow you more freedom and are great for country walks. Back packs are quite expensive, but you can carry your baby up to the age of three or even older. The Tomy Dreamer is a popular lightweight backpack costing around £50 new or £15-20 secondhand. All-in-ones are now available with their own stands, handles and wheels so they can convert into chairs and pushchairs. But be warned, these are pretty heavy!

Getting about

Suppliers
For main suppliers of baby and toddler equipment see "Suppliers", below and Chapters 6 and 7. But in addition to standard brands available from shops and by mail order, less conventional styles of slings are sold locally by:

*Kay Millar
☎ 554743 Wilkinet slings

See also www.slingeasy.co.uk

Prams, pushchairs & buggies

There is a mind-boggling range of child transport out there. It's a good idea to examine your lifestyle before you buy and decide what will best suit your needs – mistakes can be expensive! If you do a lot of car journeys then maybe a travel system is best for you. If you only take one cross-country walk a year, then a three-wheeled off roader is probably not a practical, or cheap, option.

• • • • • • • • • • • • • • • • • • •

Tip: To prevent back problems, check that the handle height suits everyone who will be pushing the buggy regularly.

• • • • • • • • • • • • • • • • • • •

Travel systems: These integrate car seat, pram and pushchair – and more traditional **prams** and **pushchairs** are often bulky and do not collapse easily, or at all, which can make it more difficult to cope on buses. But if you shop around you can find newer models that collapse with the press of a button. Some more traditional prams allow you to use the chassis for the car seat. This is useful as sleeping children can be transferred to and from cars without waking them. The advantage of prams and pushchairs is that you can see and make eye contact with your baby while you walk and talk.

Buggies: Once your child is beginning to sit up, you can move on to buggies which are very easy to deal with. The 'umbrella' fold-up style buggy is a real bonus for urban life. These are manoeuvrable, relatively light, can be wheeled on to buses and easily folded up, thrown in the car etc.

• • • • • • • • • • • • • • • • • • •

Tip: Weights on the front wheels will stop a buggy tipping over backwards when loaded with shopping and equipment – available from the Great Little Trading Company.
☎ *08708506000*

• • • • • • • • • • • • • • • • • • •

'Off-roaders': If you are keen on cross-country walking then the small wheels on buggies can make it hard-going so you may wish to invest in a three-wheeled, purpose-built 'off-roader'. But be aware that although three wheelers are easy to push, some are too large to travel on buses or to fit into smaller lifts (such as those in Boswells or the Central Library). They also may

Getting about

not fit in the boot of small cars. They will not normally fold up as compactly as a buggy.

Two children

If you need to push two around you have three choices of **double buggy**. Children can sit side-by-side, in tandem or as a double decker! All of these are a bit of a handful and when making your choice, do consider the width of doors you are likely to have to get through, and the size of your car boot/roof box.

The best alternative (apart from sling-plus-buggy, if there is a suitable age gap) is a **buggy board**. This is like a skateboard (your kids will love it) hooked behind your pram or buggy which the older child stands on.

Suppliers

Slings, buggies, prams and off-roaders can be bought at:

*Mothercare World
Oxford Retail Park, Cowley
☎ 712309

*Oxford Pram Centre
Between Towns Road
Cowley
☎ 778898
They have great after-sales care and provide a more personal service.

*Babies R Us
at Toys R Us

Botley Retail Park
Botley Road

For more information on **buggy boards**, and free delivery in Oxford
☎ Marianne 456234.

• • • • • • • • • • • • • • • • • • • •

Tip: Buggy boards are great for short trips, but if your child tires or gets bored quickly, you may end up carrying a toddler AND pushing a buggy!

• • • • • • • • • • • • • • • • • • • •

You can purchase extra fittings for boards from **Cheeky Rascals** by mail order ☎ 01428 682488 if your buggy is not standard.

Second hand and hire

See: *Chapter 6 - Going Shopping* for second hand buggies and backpacks.
Also check out the small ads in local papers and on supermarket notice boards. NCT second-hand sales are held in March and September from which all purchases should conform to the British Standard 7409.

*Baby Borrows
88 Honey Bottom Lane
Dry Sandford
☎ Abingdon 735695
Hires baby equipment including buggies, back backs, slings, buggy boards and car seats. Special needs buggies can also be hired (these can also be useful for children with broken legs, etc).

Getting about

Tip: Baby Equipment can be loaned/hired from the Sure-Start POD Centre in Littlemore.

Websites

www.tesco.com/babystore/
A range of buggies, prams, pushchairs and accessories.

www.marksandspencer.com/
Baby travel section has a range, including reversible (forward or back facing) three-wheelers.

www.babiesrus.co.uk
Buggies, backpacks, slings, bike seat and accessories.

www.boots.com
'Out and About' and 'Mother and Baby' sections with buggies, buggy boards, carriers and accessories.

www.argos.co.uk
Pushchairs, buggies and carriers.

Many catalogue baby suppliers also have websites that are worth checking out e.g.

www.gltc.co.uk
www.earthlets.co.uk
www.bloomingmarvellous.co.uk
www.babyjunction.co.uk/babyshop

Getting about

Repairs

Baby Borrows and **Oxford Pram Centre** (see above) will repair buggies and get spare parts, where possible.
For other buggy and pram repairers, See: Ch. 7 Mail Order and Services.

BY BIKE

Oxford City Council encourages the use of bikes. Phone the Cycling Officer for details of cycling tracks ☎ 249811.

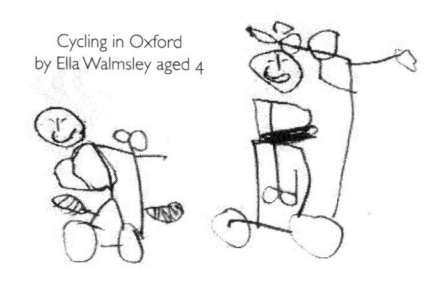

Cycling in Oxford
by Ella Walmsley aged 4

*Sustrans National Cycle Network
www.sustrans.org.uk
Sustrans has 100 miles of routes in Oxfordshire the majority of which are either on traffic-free routes, quiet country lanes or traffic-calmed urban roads. The Sustrans website has a very good detailed mapping service. A particular highlight is the path alongside the River Thames out of Oxford through the Kennington Meadow, south of the Ring road. There are also some excellent traffic free routes leading into Abingdon and north of Woodstock (along Green Lane and Dornford Lane).

Getting about

Cycling options for kids

There are many ways of travelling by bicycle with children. The options vary depending on the age and number of children and, of course, the price of the equipment. They include childseats, trailers and trailer bikes or trikes. Generally, apart from a child seat for an adult bike, prices are high, but you may feel it's worth it for the freedom gained. Always ensure your child wears a properly fitted crash helmet.

Child Seat
Age range: 9 months–5 years
Cost: £35–£150
Number of children: 1
Available from select bicycle shops. Cheapest option. Beware of bike instability when dismounting.

Trailer
Age range: birth–5 years
Cost: £150–£250
Number of children: 2
Available from: Cycle King and Reg Taylor
All weather (has cover) and safe from falls. Trailers can be combined with a child seat to take more children. They can be heavy to tow and you need to be aware of the size when manoeuvring. Also allow space for books, toys, extra equipment or picnic.

Trailer bike
Age range: 3–9 years
Cost: £80+
Number of children: 1 or 2
Available from: Cycle King, Reg Taylor, Pashleigh
The safest way to get young cyclists out and about.

Trike with seats
Age range: 9 months–5 years
Cost: £650
Number of children: 2
Available from: Cycle King and Pashleigh
Heavy and bulky but easy to park and ride.

Suppliers

Specialist suppliers include Braggs and Reg Taylor, others, such as Halfords, have bikes and cycling equipment as only part of their range. The following is a good selection. Also try Yellow Pages.

*Braggs
Abingdon
☎ 01235 520034

*Reg Taylor
Iffley Road
☎ 247040
Unbeatable after-sales service and cheap repairs.

*The Camel Trail
☎ 01208 815715
Specialists in bike trailers.

*Cycle King
Walton Street
☎ 516122
Cowley Road
☎ 728262
Widest range, frequent sales and special offers. Also children's play equipment and all-terrain, three wheel buggies.

Getting about

*Pashleigh
☎ 01739 292263
Manufacturers of cycling accessories.

*Halfords
110 Botley Road
☎ 241093
and at:
John Allen Centre
Between Towns Road
Cowley
☎ 749494

BY BUS

Children love travelling by public transport – there is always so much to look at. Two bus companies operate in Oxford city: **Oxford Stagecoach** ☎ 772250 and the **Oxford Bus Company** ☎ 785400. They often run the same routes but unfortunately ordinary tickets are not transferable, although you can now buy multi ride tickets valid for both companies. Buses are plentiful and children under five travel free. Five to 15 year olds pay half fare. Both companies have introduced new lo-liner, lowerable floor buses onto many of their routes. These are specially designed so that you can wheel on a pushchair (or wheelchair) and leave the child sitting in it. There are dedicated priority places in the bus for pushchairs - Stagecoach buses can usually fit in at least three at a time. This is a tremendous improvement, saving parents from those panic-stricken moments involving fights with the buggy, a screaming child and furious stares from the other passengers! Both companies are slowly replacing their old stock with these new buses. However, at the time of going to press, many routes still use the old type and you will need to get your child out, fold up the buggy and put it in the luggage rack - Good Luck!

Longer bus journeys

Both bus companies run coach services to London. These are both amazingly frequent (every 10 to 20 minutes for most of the day) and cheap. The journey takes about two hours but can be just 90 minutes at quieter times of day. The Oxford Tube has a loo on board and ample space for buggies and bikes.

You can also get buses into the countryside, for instance to Woodstock (Blenheim Palace).

Going by bus
by Coral Flitney aged 4

Getting about

Contact Details

Oxford Bus Company
☎ 785400
www.oxfordbus.co.uk

Stagecoach
☎ 772250
www.stagecoach-oxford.co.uk

By car

Parking in Oxford is very expensive and the City Council encourages visitors to use the Park and Ride system. Large car parks and regular buses into town can be found at Sandhills, Water Eaton, Pear Tree, Redbridge and Seacourt.

If you do travel by car with your child then it is vital that you have a safely fitted car seat. See the DETR website: www.roads.detr.gov.uk/roadsafety/seatbelt/index.htm

This recommends that children and babies are kept in the back of the car in an appropriate seat (back-facing for babies), not in a carrycot. It is against the law for anyone to sit in the front seat without a suitable restraint which must be used if fitted. *Never* use a child seat or carrier in a seat fitted with an air-bag; if they inflate on impact they can suffocate the child.

If you need more storage space consider hiring a roof box for £2-2.50/day from Wantage Motorist Centre 01235 765993, who provide free fitting. Hiring is a useful option as permanent roof-boxes can affect car fuel economy, create annoying whistling/roaring sounds and be awkward to store – again, try before you buy!

Car seat fitting

See details of expert car seat fitters in *Ch. 7 - Mail Order and Services*.

Road safety

When children are walking competently and independently the biggest worry is road safety. It is the parents' responsibility to teach the child how to cross a road safely. For advice contact the **Road Safety Group** ☎ 815717. This organisation has produced a video and booklet showing you how to teach road safety. You should be given the booklet by your health visitor at the two-year health check. If not, or if your child is over two already, then phone the group to get a copy. There are also training videos and a training programme called *Footsteps* for pre- and primary school teachers and childminders. Ask your nursery/childminder/school to obtain a copy from the Road Safety Group.

*Department of the Environment, Transport and Regions (DETR)
This is the government department which deals with road safety and it has a useful website with some interesting ideas; visit it at:
www.roads.detr.gov.uk/roadsafety/index.htm

Chapter 6 - Going Shopping

Shopping with children presents a whole host of new challenges! The needs of the shopper-with-child vary according to the age of the child. With babies, you need to know where to change them and feed them (particularly important if you are breastfeeding as you will unfortunately find you are not always welcome). With toddlers and young children you will need places that they want to go to for fun–partly as a negotiating tactic. This chapter looks at how to make shopping with children easier, and where to go to find clothes, toys and baby equipment in Oxford. See also: *Ch 5 – Getting About* for baby and child transport equipment suppliers.

TYPES OF SHOPPING EXPEDITION

Shopping is one of the first activities that new parents undertake. Out of necessity there is the weekly food shop to cope with; there are also trips to buy things for the baby, new clothes for you THAT FIT and simple indulgence-shopping for recreation which can certainly help beat the baby blues. Be warned – shopping for pleasure becomes increasingly difficult as children get older so make the most of it while you can!

Going shopping

Food Shopping

Supermarkets

It is getting easier to shop in supermarkets with small children. Most big stores now offer adapted trolleys, help with packing and sweet-free tills. Some have parent-and-child parking spaces and cafés. **Tesco** at the Oxford Retail Park, Cowley and **Sainsbury** at Kidlington have a parent and baby room.

The only supermarket in the city centre is Sainsbury's in the Westgate Shopping Centre.
In suburban shopping areas you will find:
Headington: Co-op, Somerfields, Iceland
Cowley Road: Tesco
Templars Square, Cowley: Kwiksave, Co-op, Iceland
Botley: Budgen, Iceland
Summertown: Co-op

Also large **Sainsbury's** on the Eastern Bypass.

Specialist Food Retailers

You can find raw ingredients, herbs and spices for practically any cuisine somewhere in Oxford! Of particular note is the **Lung Wah Choung Chinese Supermarket** on Hythe Bridge Street with an astonishing array of fresh, frozen, dried and tinned ingredients for Chinese, Thai and other Far Eastern cuisines. There is a smaller Chinese supermarket in Windmill Road, Headington. Cowley Road is bursting with shops selling foods from far and wide; from a **Russian delicatessen** to the particularly good **Continental Stores** (opposite Tesco) which has curry spices, oils, legumes and rices in small, medium, large and monster economy catering sizes.

Markets

*Covered Market
Between Cornmarket and the High: Butchers, greengrocers, fishmonger, bakeries, cheese shop, delicatessen as well as clothes, shoes, fancy goods, jewellery and gifts.
Open Mon-Sat.

*Open Air Market
Gloucester Green
Every Wednesday early morning until 4.00. Go with a friend and share the savings of buying in bulk.

*Farmers' Market
Gloucester Green
First Thursday of every month. Go early - all sold out and/or packed up by 3.00. Great for veg, cheese, meat, bread and juices.

Deliveries

The weekly food shop can be reduced in frequency and volume by getting things delivered. See also: *Organic suppliers* and *Chapter 7 - Mail Order and Services*.

Going shopping

*The Co-op Dairy
☎ 790479
Basic foodstuffs.

*Dairy Crest
☎ 243479
Milk and selected other basic foodstuffs – eggs, bread, fruit juice, veg.

*Iceland
☎ 241201 Botley
☎ 762134 Headington

*Gibbons
☎ 241136
Homemade bread in East Oxford.

Supermarkets

You can now shop via the Internet but there is a £5.00 delivery charge.

*Tesco Direct
www.tescodirect.com

*Sainsbury's
www.sainsbury.com

*Waitrose
www.waitrose.com
Minimum order, £50.00.

Organic suppliers

All the main supermarkets sell organic fruit and veg and an ever increasing range of organic products including eggs, flour, dried fruit, biscuits, baked beans etc. All seem to be responding to consumer fears regarding GM foods. For details of the organic box scheme – regular delivery of locally produced organic fruit and veg, contents vary with season – see *Chapter 7 Mail Order and Services*.

*The Co-op
Summertown, Headington, Cowley etc. Good wholefood range and some Fairtrade products. Some stores deliver.

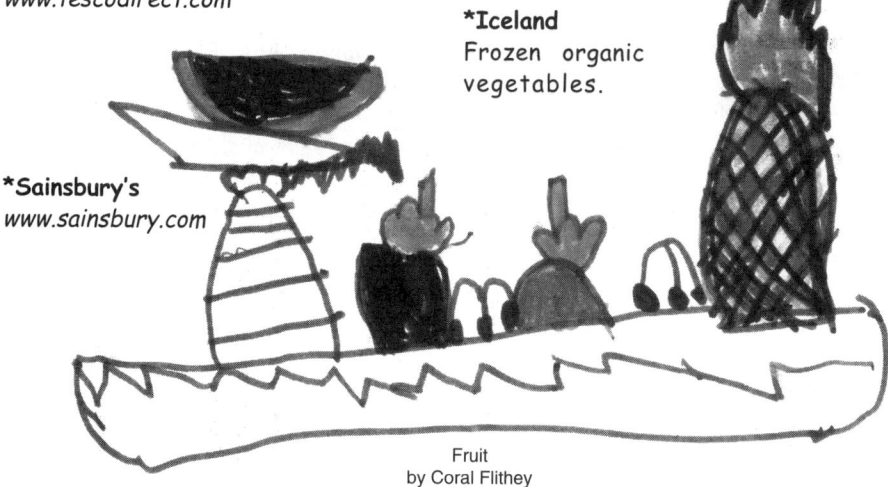

*Iceland
Frozen organic vegetables.

Fruit
by Coral Flithey
aged 4

Going shopping

*Uhuru Wholefoods
Cowley Road (near The Plain)
Oxford's only real wholefood shop stocks organic wheat & yeast-free, fairtrade etc. Does not sell any foods containing GMOs. Local organic vegetables are available on Thursdays. Weekly delivery (also Thurs) of organic bread and cakes from the award winning Village Bakery. Free home delivery on the last Friday of every month. Bulk orders 20% off shelf price.

*Corner Farm
Horton cum Studley
☎ 358933
Open Weds, Thurs, Sat
Organic farm shop selling organic and GM free meat, fish, fruit and veg, breads etc. Home delivery.

*Holland & Barrett,
Golden Cross, Summertown, Headington
Wholefoods & supplements.

*GNC
☎ 249219
17 Westgate Centre
Good range of health and wholefoods.

*M. Feller Son & Daughter
☎ 251164
54-55 Covered Market
Specialist organic butcher. Full range of meats and homemade sausages. Free home delivery for orders over £15.

*Gibbons Bakery
16 Hertford Street
☎ 241136

Small family bakery makes a variety of bread including a delicious organic loaf.

*Quaker Shop
St Giles
Fairtrade dry food (rice, pasta, chocolate etc).

*Queen of Hearts Bakery
Headington, Cowley, Summertown
Range includes organic bread.

SHOPPING IN CENTRAL OXFORD

The introduction of the traffic-free central zone around Cornmarket Street and Broad Street has made it slightly easier for the pedestrian in central Oxford. However, some buses now stop further away from the actual centre.

The main shopping area is centred on Cornmarket Street and Queen Street and their two covered malls; the Westgate and Clarendon Centres. Here you will find most of the big name shops: Marks and Spencer, Boots, Littlewoods, Bhs, ELC, Gap, Allders, Sainsbury's, Waterstones, Boswells, Debenhams and Blackwells dotted around at several sites in Broad Street. The famous and excellent **Covered Market** lies between Cornmarket Street and the High where you will find everything from specialist cheeses to children's clothes; organic meat and vegetables to antiquarian books.

Here is a selection of child-relevant shops in and around the city centre. It is followed by a few tips to help you find the facilities you need when out shopping with children.

Going shopping

Clothes shops

***Adams**
Cornmarket Street
Basic children's clothing.

***Bhs**
Queen Street
Good quality baby and children's clothes.

***Disney Shop**
Westgate Centre
Selection of Disney themed clothing.

Tip: It is often cheaper to buy basic items for 5–8s from the schoolwear ranges of the major stores such as Bhs and M&S.

***Gap and Baby Gap**
Cornmarket Street
Upstairs for Baby Gap. Beautiful clothes at prices to match but some excellent sale bargains.

***Marks and Spencer**
Queen Street
Good quality but not cheap! Nice café and toilets with changing mat in Ladies on first floor (NB they are on opposite sides of the shop, so take small children to the loo first to avoid lengthy trek across the shop half-way through your coffee/tea/meal!)

***Monsoon**
Queen Street
Expensive but great for fabulous girls' clothes such as bridesmaids' dresses. Now has beautiful baby clothes and boy's clothes (0–4yrs). Children's clothes also in Accessorize.

***Two-Foot Nothing**
Covered Market
Expensive, but very nice clothes and a small number of toys. Rocking horse to ride on.

Knitting and Sewing

When you have a baby it may be the only time you wish to knit! There are a few places to buy wool and knitting patterns in Oxford.

***Brambles**
London Road
Headington
Also does needlework supplies, toys and expensive baby clothes.

***Rowan**
Gloucester Green
Trendy and unusual wools. Range of 100 per cent cottons, not cheap!

***Allders**
Westgate Shopping Centre
Wools and needlecraft supplies.

***Busy Bee**
Templars Square
Cowley
Has a policy of only selling patterns if you buy the wool there. Helpful staff. Toy box to amuse toddlers while you are browsing.

Going shopping

*Remnant Kings
New Inn Hall Street
Good range of fabrics, notions, patterns, wools. Fleece fabric by the metre – excellent for cot blankets, scarves, etc – no sewing required as doesn't fray. Also sequins, beads and trimmings. Unfortunately upstairs with no lift.

Shoe Shops

Getting good, well-fitting shoes is important for young feet. If your children have standard feet then Next, Bhs, Adams etc shoes are fine. However, if your child takes an unusual fitting then try Russell and Bromley or Greenwoods for Start-rite shoes.

*Clark's
Cornmarket
Also at **Mothercare World** and **Bicester Village**. Pre-walker shoes are soft but sturdy for when your child first gets to its feet. Children get a photograph of themselves in their first proper pair of shoes at certain branches. Toys and customer loo at Cornmarket branch.

*Michael Greenwood
Summertown
Good range of Clark's, Start-rite and Elephant, all sizes. Toys and rocking horse.

*Russell and Bromley
Ship Street
Start-rite. Will order any size.

Toy shops

*Boswells
Cornmarket Street
Toy department on the first floor. Small lift. Good selection of toys including wooden, trains, Brio, Lego, games.

*Disney Shop
Westgate/Bonn Square
All the Disney merchandise!

*Early Learning Centre
Queen Street
Changing facilities and loo. Tuesday mornings kids can play with toys or join organised activities.

Minnie Mouse at the Disney Store by Alexandra Waring Paynter aged 5

*Oxford Quaker Centre
42 St Giles
☎ 310323
Mon–Sat 12.00–4.00
Wooden toys, children's books, cards. Fair Trade goods.

82

Going shopping

*Restore
Manzil Way, Cowley Road
☎ 790193
Good range of solid, traditional wooden toys, e.g. doll's house, easel, trolley, tops. Also sells cards and organic veg.

Bookshops for children

*The Bookhouse
267 Banbury Road
Summertown
☎ 510887
Good, generally quiet (avoid school pick-up time). Helpful staff.

*Borders
Magdalen Street
☎ 203901
Readings for children 12 noon every Saturday. Organised activities for school-aged children in school holidays. Lift to children's section in basement.

*Blackwells
Broad Street
☎ 792792
Children's department now on first floor of main shop. Extensive children's book selection with knowledgeable staff. Café.

*Inner Bookshop
111 Magdalen Road
☎ 245301
Specialises in books on religious and spiritual titles for adults and children. Mellow atmosphere. The Magic Café nearby has toilets.

*Waterstones
Broad Street
Play area in children's department in basement. Lift. Sound effects, tunnels, nooks, large video screen, engine to sit in and books to look through. Café with space for buggies.

*The Works
Westgate Centre and Cornmarket
Discount books, stationery and art materials. Excellent bargain presents and stocking fillers.

Outdoor equipment shops

*Touchwoods
St Aldates and
Abingdon Road
The Abingdon Road store has a greater range of equipment, e.g. travel cots, children's sleeping bags, swimming aids. Ski-wear and sledges.

*Millets
Queen Street
Waterproofs, outdoor clothes, shoes.

*YHA
St Clements
Outdoor clothing and baby carriers.

FACILITIES IN OXFORD

Baby changing

The following places have baby changing rooms; enquire from an assistant. **Allders**, Bonn Square/Westgate; **Bhs**, Queen Street; **Boots**, Cornmarket;

Going shopping

Blackwells, Broad Street; **Early Learning Centre**, Queen Street; **Littlewoods**, Cornmarket; **Waterstones** Broad Street; **Central Library**, Westgate; **MAO**, Pembroke Street; **Town Hall**, St Aldates; **Wesley Memorial Church Hall**, New Inn Hall Street; **Debenhams**, Magdalen Street.

Loo stops

Public loos can be found in **Market Street**, the **Westgate Centre** (near the escalator), **New Road** (below the Westgate Centre), **Bear Street**, **Gloucester Green** and **Magdalen Street**. These vary in accessibility, cleanliness and facilities. Gloucester Green and Magdalen Street have changing tables.

There are also customer loos in **Debenhams, Allders, Borders, Bhs** and **Littlewoods, M&S, Early Learning Centre** (these are large enough to fit the pushchair and have a loo and changing mat in one room). If caught short elsewhere, ask if you can use the staff loo. Many shops are obliging, and the more of us who ask the more likely they are to consider providing appropriate facilities – after all toddlers are pretty powerful consumers!

Refreshments

See also: Ch 10 - Eating Out
You may need plenty of time to feed your baby or child, especially if you are breastfeeding, so plan ahead if possible! Try the big stores for their restaurants. Otherwise these are child-friendly cafés in and around the city centre.

*The Beat Café
Little Clarendon Street

*The Convocation Coffee House
The High, behind St Mary the Virgin University Church. Access through church or Catte Street.

*Edgar's
Carfax Gardens

*MAO Café
Pembroke Street
Take lift up to museum foyer then another lift down to the café. Good food, vegetarian choices.

*The Magic Café
Magdalen Street (near the Inner Bookshop). Child friendly.

*Rainbow House
(Weds-Fri 10.30-2.00)
New Inn Hall Street
Excellent for pre-school children. Large hall with books, toys, slide and climbing frame. Good low-price food.

*The Nosebag & Saddlebag
St Michael's Street

SECOND HAND SHOPS/SALES

Children want so many clothes, toys and pieces of equipment that you can end up spending a fortune on them. A good way

Going shopping

to save money is to buy and sell second-hand. The best bargains are to be found at **car boot** and **jumble sales**. Look in the Oxford Times and Mail and the free newspapers for times and places. Charity shops usually have children's clothes and equipment. You could also look at *Mr Thrifty's How to Save Money on Absolutely Everything* – available from Hawkins Bazaar (See: *Ch. 7 Mail Order and Services* for details).

Listed below are shops which will buy or sell items.

* * *

*Tip: If you are keen on bargain-hunting, try the **Good Deal Directory** by Noelle Walsh, a country-wide guide to over 2,000 shops and factory outlets for discount clothes, babywear, equipment, home goods, etc.* ☎ *Gloucester (01367) 860016.*

* * *

*Nan's Nearly New
☎ John or Gill 559909

*NCT Nearly New Sales
Usually held at the Cross Street Centre, St Clements. See: Chapter 4 - Meeting People for contacts. Two sales a year, in Spring and Autumn. NCT takes a percentage of the selling price.

*Pass the Parcel
Mrs Sharon Simmonds
End Cottage
West End
Wootton
☎ 01993 812165

By appointment but well worth a visit. Nearly new children's clothes, 0-12 years and maternity wear. 40% commission.

*Revival
60 St Clements
☎ 251005
Dress agency. Fashionable clothes and shoes in tip-top condition only. 50% commission. Childrenswear.

*St Philip and St James School
☎ 557670
Holds a large NCT-style nearly new sale each spring and Autumn. Take 50% of selling price. Usually some interesting items from overseas. You don't need a child at the school to be a seller.

Other schools and nurseries often have nearly new sales. Good for picking up second-hand uniforms. Look out for notices locally.

OUTSIDE THE CITY CENTRE

You may find it convenient to shop outside central Oxford, where it is easier to park and there is a good selection of shops. Children's shops can be found at:

*Botley Road
Toys 'R' Us, warehouse toy store also large baby department (including car seats, buggies, cots etc). Also along Botley Road are **Argos**, **Halfords** and several DIY/furniture stores.

*Headington
Peacocks (good selection of cheap children's clothes), **Brambles** expensive

Going shopping

baby clothes and knitting wools. Also several charity shops, a pet shop and the Co-op. Bury Knowle playground and library close by.

*Summertown
Red House Books, **Michael Greenwood** (Clark's, Start-rite and Elephant shoes), **Shepherd and Woodward** (school clothes and some toys), pet shop.

*Templars Square
Between Towns Road
Cowley
Adams children's clothes, **Oxford Pram Centre** (also sells buggy boards), **Woolworths** (for Ladybird clothes), **Wilkinson's** (kids' crafts and stationery), **WH Smith**, **Dorothy Perkins** for maternity clothes and several charity shops. There are also toilets with changing facilities and an unsupervised play area.

The **John Allen Centre** across the road has **Matalan** (good for kids' clothes and books also has household goods including kids' bedclothes) and **Halfords** (for bikes and car seats).

*Oxford Retail Park
Garsington Road
Cowley
Large **Tesco**, **Burger King**, **Brantano** (shoes), **Boots** (with kids clothes and toys and excellent loo and changing facilities) **Next** (with some lovely, but expensive, kids' clothes) and **Mothercare World** (with parent and child parking spaces and a parent and baby room).

Shopping outside Oxford

You could go even further afield and turn the shopping trip into a real 'day out'. Outlying towns such as Thame, Abingdon, Witney and Wallingford offer some excellent shopping. Try **Thame** for its Tuesday market, **The Bookshop** and **The Pied Pedaller** (toyshop); **Witney** for its famous blanket and teddy bear shops; and **Wallingford** for its market and castle. It's also worth investigating the following larger centres:

*Bicester Village
Signposted from junction 9 of the M40.
☎ 01869 323200
Open 10.00-6.00 daily
Lots of famous brands with discounts of up to 60 per cent. Children's shoes from **Clark's** factory shop (worth phoning to check they have your child's size in stock – new deliveries each day), clothes from **Petit Bateau**, **Jigsaw**, **Benetton**, **Monsoon** etc. **Triumph**, which does excellent and very cheap maternity bras. Outdoor gear from **Helly Hanson** and **Tog 24**. Children's bedding and nightwear from **Descamps**. Book and toy shops.

An excellent children's adventure playground, plenty of parking and safe pedestrianised space for buggies and toddlers. Also a good café, **Pret-a-Manger**, and purpose built changing and feeding facilities. Avoid the weekends here if at all possible, it can get very busy! A a trip to Bicester Village on an empty weekday afternoon is far less stressful.

Going shopping

*Great Western Outlet Village
Swindon, near Junction 16 of the M4, next to STEAM – the GWR museum.
☎ 01793 507600
www.mcarthurglen.com
It's worth phoning for directions from Oxford as it is easy to get lost in the maze of Swindon's roundabouts.

Massive savings on **Gap**, **Next**, **M&S** clothes etc. Interesting and safe outdoor play area. Food section offers a good variety of eateries and space for children and parents to eat.

There is also a **Clark's** factory shop in Swindon in a complex which includes **Asda**, a cinema and a bowling alley.

*High Wycombe
Junction 4 off the M40
Large shopping mall with all the big-name stores such as **Marks and Spencer** All facilities; parking, loos etc.

John Lewis has good changing facilities and great toy department, but no clothes or equipment. Nearest complete John Lewis is in Reading.

Outdoor Play Equipment

*The Active Toy Company
Langley Farm
World's End, Beedon
Newbury, Berks
☎ 01635 248683 for opening times.

*Swings & Things
Appleford
☎ 01235 847620

*Wicken Activity Toys Centre
Whittlebury
☎ 01908 571233 for catalogue.
Weekends and bank holidays 10.00–6.00 or by arrangement.

Clothes shopping
by Coral Flitney
aged 4

Chapter 7 - Mail Order and Services

Oxford is not one of the easiest places to shop with small children. Even with the advent of 'pushchair-friendly' buses and the pedestrianised Cornmarket Street many parents find shopping trips stressful, especially with more than one pre-school child. The combination of crowds, heavy doors and trying to make a decision while consoling a wailing baby/toddler does tend to make the whole experience somewhat taxing.

One solution for many parents, particularly at Christmastime, is to use the vast range of mail order products available. You can buy virtually anything by post these days - clothes, wallpaper, toys, furniture, art materials, organic meat and vegetables, plants, toiletries and so on. The only downside is the added expense of postage and packing - sharing an order with friends can make it cheaper. It is also worth waiting for the catalogue sales in January and July.

We have listed a range of parent/child-oriented mail-order catalogues and where to hire clothing and equipment - please let us know of any additions to this list. Internet shopping is on the increase, so websites are included where relevant and there is a special section on the Internet at the end of the chapter, including children's entertainment - an invaluable service. If you run into any problems with mail ordering, call **Trading Standards** at **Oxfordshire County Council** ☎ 815000.

Mail order and services

Avoid using **Continuous Payment Authorities** when purchasing on the Internet with a credit card. Unlike direct debits and standing orders, or one-off credit card payments, CPAs cannot be cancelled by a phonecall to the bank or card company. Problems can take months to resolve with inefficient or less than upright suppliers.

MATERNITY CLOTHES

*Blooming Marvellous
☎ 0870 751 8944
www.bloomingmarvellous.co.uk
Attractive maternity clothes, plus a good selection of nursery equipment and childrenswear aged 0-3.
Free catalogue

*Jo-Jo Maman Bebe
☎ 0870 241 0560
www.jojomamanbebe.co.uk
Claims to have the most comprehensive mail order collection for pregnant women in the U.K. They also sell stylish post-birth clothes with discreet openings for breastfeeding, nursery equipment and reasonably priced and stylish clothing for 0-5 year olds. They have a child-friendly London shop should you be passing. *Free catalogue*

Tip: When buying breastfeeding bras, check you can manage the cup fastening with one hand – the other hand will usually be supporting the baby!

*Kay Millar
Banbury Road
☎ 554743
Bra fitting service for Bravado breastfeeding bras, available in leopardskin and bright floral designs, as well as black and white. Also sells other useful items e.g. Wilknet slings, pram fleeces.

*Mothercare Direct.
☎ 01923 240365
www.mothercare.com
A range of good maternity wear essentials as well as a wide range of children's clothes, mother and baby products and nursery equipment. Reasonable prices.
Free catalogue

*National Childbirth Trust (NCT)
☎ Mel Minns 516648
Free catalogue: 0141 636 0600
www.nctms.co.uk
See catalogue featuring Mava nursing bras, baby clothes and some useful mother/baby equipment. Local NCT agents can fit bras by appointment or provide a catalogue.

*Next Directory
☎ 0845 600 7000 (8.00-23.00 7 days)
www.next.co.uk
Good quality, fashionable and comfortable maternitywear that is not available in the high street. It is a huge catalogue including clothes for the whole family and a wide range of furnishings, furniture and lighting etc. Worth sharing an order with a friend as the catalogue costs £3 with your first order.

Mail order and services

*The Waiting Room
☎ 01494 866189
Specialises in the hire of maternity wear, particularly useful for special occasion/wedding outfits. Based in Great Missenden.

KIDS' CLOTHES & EQUIPMENT

(See also Maternity Clothes)

*Bishopston Trading Company
☎ 01179 245598
www.bishopstontrading.co.uk
Ethical traders, organic cotton. Adult and child clothes. Small swatches of material sent with catalogue.

*Boots
www.boots.com
An extensive range of mother and baby products and equipment as well as good, reasonably priced clothes for 0-2s.

*Bumblebaby
☎ Rachel Bee 01344 883507
enquiries@bumblebaby.co.uk
Environmentally friendly baby products and wooden toys, washable nappies, toiletries, Daisy Roots shoes, slings, lambskins and Grobags.

*Cheeky Rascals
☎ 01428 682488
www.cheekyrascals.co.uk
Many ingenious ideas and inventions: zip-up swimming waistcoats, disposable bibs-on-roll, inflatable changing mats, buggyboard adaptor fittings for non-standard buggies, etc.

*Cotton-Tails
☎ 744977
www.cotton-tails.co.uk
Local stockists of Grobag-TM sleeping bags and other products, including maternity cushions.

*Great Little Trading Company
☎ 0870 850 6000
www.gltc.co.uk
Innovative products for children and parents. Kitchen, wardrobe and bath accessories, travel, safety aids, etc. Also clothes for children 0-12.
Free catalogue

*Mini Boden
☎ 020 8453 1535
www.boden.co.uk
Trendy, good quality children's clothes but quite pricey. Bargains to be found in the January/July sales but you have to be quick, this catalogue is very popular.
Free catalogue

*Schmidt Natural Clothing
☎ 01342 822169
www.naturalclothing.co.uk
Luxurious reusable nappies plus some unique organic babywear items suitable for babies with eczema.
Free catalogue

*The White Company
☎ 0870 900 9555
www.thewhiteco.com
Offers a good quality, simple range of baby and child 100% cotton bedlinen and wool blankets; so if you are sick of 'cartoon' duvets, this may be for you.

Mail order and services

*Young Explorers
☎ 01789 414791
www.youngexplorers.co.uk
Good stock of swimwear, waterproof clothing, lifejackets and fleeces for all ages. Also Rugbug, a fleecy, weatherproof pouch for prams and buggies.
Free catalogue

TOYS, GIFTS & ART MATERIALS

*Dawson and Son
☎ 08700 367869
www.dawson-and-son.com
Wide selection of wonderful wooden toys and games, musical instruments, action toys, puzzles, unusual baby gifts.
Free catalogue

*Early Learning Centre
☎ 08705 352352
www.elc.co.uk
An extensive mail order service for toys, nursery and outdoor play equipment and all things child-friendly.
Free catalogue

*Escor Toys
☎ 01202 591081
www.escortoys.com
Award-winning range including cars, trains, fairground rides & junior croquet.

*Galt Education
☎ 0161 627 5086
www.galt.co.uk
Produces a huge range of excellent quality toys, furniture, art materials and equipment.

*George and Kay Luck
12 Gastons Lane
Bower Hinton
Somerset TA12 6LN
☎ 01935 822743
Britain's premier wooden puzzle makers with a worldwide market and some impressive design awards to their credit. Send an A4 sae for a catalogue.

*The Green Board Game Co.
☎ 01494 538999
www.greenboardgames.com
Award-winning games and puzzles. Also **Wikki Stix**, twistable, pliable reusable wax sticks for modelling and creating, suitable for 3 years up, especially good for car/plane journeys!
Free catalogue

*Hawkins Bazaar
☎ 01986 782536
www.hawkin.com
Unusual toys and reasonably priced novelties, good for stocking-fillers.
Free catalogue

*Hill Toy Company
☎ 0870 607 1248
www.hilltoy.co.uk
An impressive range of pre-school toys, dressing-up clothes and 'pocket money presents' from £1.95. Popular 'two-in-one' hand puppets – a puffin, a zebra or a giraffe – that come with their own finger puppet baby.
Free catalogue

Mail order and services

*Hopscotch
☎ 01252 717768
www.hopscotchmailorder.co.uk
Traditional, good quality dressing-up clothes for children. Prices for accessories start at £2.50. A good range of animal hats cost £11.95 each – or you could use their ideas to design your own. (Alternatively try **George** at selected Asda stores – nearest one is High Wycombe – for good, reasonably priced dressing-up clothes).
Free catalogue

*Letterbox
☎ 0870 600 7878
www.letterbox.co.uk
Good, colourful selection of children's gifts and stocking fillers, including many personalised items such as bags, dressing-gowns, mugs, chairs and stationery sets. Relatively low prices, some items are cheaper compared to other catalogues. Recommended.
Free catalogue

Mobile by Eloise Huxley aged 4

*Orchard Toys
☎ 0115 937 3547
www.orchardtoys.com
Good range of jigsaws, games and activities for children between the ages of 18 months and 10 years.
Free catalogue

*Owls Educational Direct
☎ 08453 304050
Educational toys, games, puzzles, activities and books. Good colourful floor puzzles for 2-5 year olds.
Free catalogue

*Partyworks
☎ 0870 240 2103
www.partybypost.co.uk
Another catalogue from Bath's Tridias Toys, specialising in party prizes and gifts for under a fiver, activities and games. They sell delights such as 'shark bath gel' and 'dinosaur candles'.
Free catalogue

*Save the Children
☎ 0870 750 7027
www.savethechildrenshop.com
Extensive selection of cards and gifts at Christmas time – with the added bonus of supporting the UK's largest children's charity.

*Tridias Toys By Post
☎ 0870 2402104
www.tridias.co.uk
Interesting and inventive toys e.g. good quality wooden farm/train set/doll's house, science and craft kits, plus a

Mail order and services

wide range of other toys and presents. Some items are expensive compared to other catalogues.
Free catalogue

*Unicef
☎ 0870 075 1000 (24 hour 7 days)
www.unicef.org.uk
Christmas cards, puzzles and gifts.

*Urchin Mail Order
☎ 0800 720 0709
www.urchin.co.uk
Good, unusual range of children's goods, including bike trailers and a good choice of outdoor equipment (eg. backpacks, three-wheeler buggies, waterproof and warm outdoor gear.) Also furniture, bedding, storage, lighting.
Free catalogue

Books

*Amazon
www.amazon.co.uk
Online bookstore. Excellent source of books for children and parenting books. Very reasonable prices, often good discounts (but check postage costs). Prompt delivery, gift message can be included. Also sells videos, toys, music, DVDs, software and electronic and photographic equipment.

*Barefoot Books
☎ 01225 322400 (08:30–18:00 Mon–Fri)
www.barefootbooks.com
Beautifully illustrated, thoughtful books for children aged around three and up. Emphasis on new and traditional myths, tales and poems. Recommended.

*Bloomsbury
☎ 020 7494 2111
www.bloomsburymagazine.com
Innovative range of children's books with the emphasis on exciting works from established and previously unpublished authors and illustrators.

*Books for Children (BFC)
BCA, Guild House, Farnsby Street, Swindon SN99 9XX.
www.booksforchildren.co.uk
Book club which sends monthly catalogues organised by age range. Also offers a small selection of adult books on childcare. Prices are discounted but you have to pay p+p on orders under £30.00 which can reduce the savings.

Introductory offers are usually good value but you do then have to purchase a small number of 'full' price books in the first year of membership.

*Letterbox Library
☎ 020 7503 4801
www.letterboxlibrary.sageweb.co.uk
Specialises in multi-cultural and non-sexist books for children. Book club gives members regular reductions on books. One-off membership fee of £5.
Free catalogue available with no obligation to become a member.

*The Book People
☎ 0870 607 7740
www.thebookpeople.co.uk

Mail order and services

Produces a magazine six times a year featuring greatly reduced, good quality fiction and non-fiction books for children and adults. No membership needed or obligation to buy.

*The Red House
☎ 0870 191 9980
www.redhouse.co.uk
Range of popular titles. Good discounts on many books and special offers.

• •

Tip: Instead of hiring or buying children's videos, try making your own by recording some of the excellent children's schools programmes broadcast during term-time weekday mornings. Try Storytime, Come Outside and Words and Pictures. ☎ BBC Education on 08700 100321 or see www.bbc.co.uk/schools for current schedules

• •

OTHER PRODUCTS AND SERVICES

*Ben Molyneux Photography
☎ 01993 705425.
Specialises in professional black and white portraits of families and children. Friendly, recommended service – good for easy Christmas presents. £20 sitting fee, no obligation to purchase.

*Cash's Name Tapes
Woven name tapes, useful when your child starts school or nursery. Available from Marks and Spencer and Shepherd and Woodward, Summertown. Iron-on ones are available from The White Company, see above.

*Bickiepegs teething biscuits
☎ 01224 790626
Available in Boots. Small mail order leaflet inside offering children's bowls, plates, cups, spoons etc.

*Just Fabrics of Burford
☎ 01993 823391
Good discounts on quality furnishing fabrics. Will send stock fabric cuttings to you. Mail order service available.

*John Lewis High Wycombe
☎ 01494 462666
www.johnlewis.com
Free delivery service to Oxford for larger items (home furnishings/furniture/toys) e.g. children's beds, bedding, storage, dolls houses, outdoor play etc.

*Oxfordshire Children's Information Service
☎ 01993 886933
www.oxoncis.org.uk
Provides local information on childcare and family support. Also gives ideas for holiday and leisure activities. An outreach officer is able to visit parent and toddler groups, NCT groups and health visitor groups to provide information about childcare.

If you would like to book this service, please call OCIS on the number above or email:
enquiries@oxoncis.org.uk

Mail order and services

*Post House Patchwork
8 Iffley Turn
Oxford OX4 1DD
www.post-house-patchwork.co.uk
Quilt kits, patterns, sewing notions and equipment. Good for baby gifts. Send SAE for catalogue.

*Simply Stuck
Barrow Hill Barns
Barrow Hill
Goodworth Clatford
Hants SP11 7RG
☎ 01264 350788
www.simply stuck.com
enquiries@simplystuck.com
Personalised iron-on tapes, washable stickers and clear shoe labels.

Organic & delivery box schemes

*Fellers Butchers
☎ 251164
Covered Market, Oxford.
Offer a home delivery service for all orders over £15. Specialists in organic meat and free-range poultry. Mon-Sat deliveries within Oxford. Phone before 1pm for next day delivery.

*Meat Matters,
2 Blandy's Farm Cottages, Letcombe Regis, Wantage, Oxon OX12 9LJ.
☎ 08080 067426
fax: 01235 772526
Meat Matters can deliver organic meat and vegetables once a week. They have been recommended to us as a friendly firm and the food is good quality.

*Organics Direct
☎ 01604 791911 (09.00-18.00 Mon-Fri)
www.organicsdirect.co.uk
UK's largest organic home delivery service.

*Traidcraft
☎ 0191 4910591
www.traidcraft.co.uk
Fair trade company selling a range of high quality products, including organic sugar, chocolate, coffee & tea. Also fair traded dried fruits, nuts, sugar etc, handbaked Christmas cake and pudding from the Village Bakery (plus handmade cards, beautiful jewellery, clothes, etc.)

*Tollhurst Organic Farm
☎ 0118 9843428
Runs a box scheme with local pickup points. Oxford has 8 drop-off points, some of which have waiting lists. Part of the famous organic Hardwick Estate, Whitchurch-on-Thames (award winning organic farm & farm shop) sells an excellent range of vegetables, meat etc. Worth a visit if you are in the area – and there are happy cows to look at in the farmyard next to the shop!

• •

Tip: Fed up with trying to shop with tired children in tow? Remember that most big supermarkets offer free home delivery of your groceries – phone individual stores for details or try the Internet (see Ch 6 – Shopping).
• •

Mail order and services

Hire Services

It can be very expensive to buy baby equipment, especially as babies quickly grow out of so many items. Also, you may need something temporarily, eg a travel cot. Hiring may be the answer. Below are some hiring options, or alternatively, some baby equipment can be loaned/hired from the Littlemore Sure Start POD Centre.
(See: Ch 3 – Parental Support).

*Baby Borrows
88 Honeybottom Lane
Dry Sandford
Abingdon
☎ 735695
Wide range of quality baby goods to hire, also some to purchase. Buggies (double and single), prams, cots, travel cots, high chairs, car seats, back packs, play pens, fireguards, gates, toys etc.
Also hires out ball-pool and magic maze for children's parties.
 Flexible opening hours. Phone for further details.

*Electric Breast Pump Hire
55 Green Road, Kidlington
☎ Jane Higgs 375667 (evenings)
126 Cumnor Hill
☎ Alison Baker 864812

*Valley Cushion Hire
☎ Nicky Scott 725661
Relief-giving cushions for any mother experiencing problems sitting after labour and delivery.

Buggy and Pram Repair

Most new prams and pushchairs are guaranteed for the first year when bought from a reputable dealer.

*Oxford Pram Centre
Between Towns Road
☎ 778898
Free servicing for the first few months on prams and buggies bought from them. Will lend replacement buggy if repairs take longer than a day.

*John Stoner
43, Home Close
Wootton
☎ 735291 Mob: 07816 962593
Maclaren trained but most makes repaired, subject to availability of parts. Free pushchair loan. Also sells complete Maclaren range at discounted prices. Stocks and fits buggy boards.

Domestic help

The best way to find help with cleaning, ironing and household chores is to advertise locally; local shops, church community centre etc. Check for domestic help offered on noticeboards and in the local press. Try student noticeboards e.g. Oxford Brookes. Also ask friends for their recommendations. Otherwise there are cleaning agencies, but these tend to be an expensive option. They might be worthwhile for a 'one-off' occasion, eg at Christmas. See *Yellow Pages* for numbers.

Mail order and services

*Cookerburra
☎ 714829
www.cookerburra.co.uk
Oven cleaning service.

Car seat fitting

It is estimated that some 7 in 10 children's car seats are incorrectly fitted. The following can check your seat:

*Sitting Tight
Run by the **Oxford County Council Road Safety Group** this service will check seats before or after purchase by trained experts (garages, health visitors and fire officers are part of this county-wide scheme). Free advice and fitting. Advice given about fitting central seatbelts for growing families.
☎ Cathy Welham/Julie Jones
815657/815660
julie.jones@oxfordshire.gov.uk

Magazines

These can provide useful, up-to-date information on mail-order stockists and recommended, tested products for parents and children. Most 'glossies' are available from newsagents. New Parent Network's magazine provides regular updates on local suppliers and services.

Websites

The World Wide Web is such a rapidly developing resource – new sites are constantly expanding and current sites can change very quickly – so these recommendations may soon date. To keep up with developments check out journals and newspapers or ask friends for tips.

But the best thing to do is get online and have fun browsing. Here are a few sites to get you started and give you an idea of the huge range of informative and fun sites currently available.

For Parents

*Babyworld
www.babyworld.co.uk
Expert question and answer pages make this a super site for new parents and anyone thinking of having children.

*National Childbirth Trust
www.nctpregnancyandbabycare.com
Information on pregnancy and parenting.

*Parenthood Web
www.parenthoodweb.com
Wide-ranging information on pregnancy. Lots of useful articles on parenthood in general, an ultrasound library and online chatrooms.

*UKParents
www.ukparents.com
Information and debating forums.

*Under 5s
www.underfives.co.uk
Information on UK early learning goals and other educational subjects, plus advice on finding and choosing childcare.

Mail order and services

For Kids

*CBeebies
www.bbc.co.uk/cbeebies
Links to all their favourite characters – Teletubbies, Tweenies, etc. Fun and games, stories, pictures to print and colour, plus lots more. An excellent starting point for novice surfers.

*Little Animals Activity Centre
www.bbc.co.uk/schools/laac
Best tip on this site – download the entire site and save money on your phone bills. Fun number, letter and music games. Interactive stories will appeal especially to younger users. Fun activities to print out including finger puppets, mazes and dot-to-dot puzzles.

*Fun Brain
www.funbrain.com
Entertaining selection of word, number and memory games for 6 year olds and under.

*Shoo Rayner
www.shoo-rayner.co.uk
This unusual site has been designed by the children's author and illustrator Shoo Rayner.
Play hunt the chameleon or peek-a-boo with Ginger Ninja the cat.

The Teletubbies in their house by Coral Flitney, aged 4.

Mail order and services

The following websites are also recommended.

www.kidsdomain.com
www.childfun.com
www.activityvillage.co.uk
Three sites with games, crafts, themed activities (e.g. seasons, animals etc) some educational stuff and lots of colouring pages to print. For 2+.

www.underfives.co.uk
Colouring pages, themed activities, events and festivals, crafts, songs and rhymes, special needs. A useful UK site for parents and preschool workers.

abcteach.com
Over 5000+ printable pages – activities, flashcards, games, themed units, reading and writing, sign language etc – academic slant, but generally fun. For 3+.

coloringbookfun.com
Lots of subjects – religion, festivals, seasons, animals, TV/book characters, transport, etc – to print out and colour. For all ages.

www.dltk-kids.com
Crafts for kids of all ages.

www.kidsfreeware.com
Many links to downloadable free software for toddlers and older children. Software is mostly 'home created' so is often basic, but still a useful site.

www.howstuffworks.com
Want to know how a telescope works? How beer is made? Where black holes come from? A great site for finding out the answers to all your kids' bizarre questions! Older children should be able to navigate this site easily themselves.

www.ala.org/parentspage/greatsites/amazing.html
Huge listing of websites (mostly US) for kids on various subject areas – e.g. science, language and literature, planet earth etc.

Chapter 8 – Libraries

Even the very smallest of babies get a lot of enjoyment from books and you can get membership of a public library for them as soon as they are born. It is free to join and you can borrow up to ten books at a time, giving you a constant supply of books without it costing a penny.

Don't forget toy libraries which offer loans for a small fee (or even for free). Some have play sessions, give information and advice about play, and are a friendly meeting place for parents and carers. They provide access to a variety of puzzles, games, cassettes and videos. You can find toys to suit the varying interests and abilities of the child.

Public libraries

As well as the main **Central Library** in the Westgate Centre there are several local branches scattered across the city. Membership of one branch gives you borrowing rights at all the others.

Children's libraries

All branches listed have a children's library. Here you will find board books, picture and story books from lots of different children's writers and publishers, as well as factual books for older children – these can be very useful to help with school work. You can keep books for up to three weeks, after which you must return or renew them. There should be no fines for 'under-fives' if books are borrowed on the child's ticket. Most libraries have story tapes, DVDs and children's videos available to borrow for a week at a time. The Central Library also has a selection of children's CD ROMs for hire. There is a small charge for these.

Libraries

The children's sections are very attractive and you don't need to feel as inhibited about noise as in the adult sections. Some libraries hold story and activity sessions for pre-schoolers during term time, and all of them have activities for children during holidays. Ask in good time for free tickets.

If you or your child need toilet facilities while in a library, don't be afraid to ask. There will be either a public toilet or a staff one which you can use. Breastfeeding is allowed in all public libraries in Oxfordshire. The Central Library at Westgate has baby changing facilities. You will find the staff very pleased to help with any questions.

Tip: Public library noticeboards are good sources of community information.

Suggested reading

The libraries have booklists with reading suggestions and there are also books to help you enhance your child's reading. Two recommended titles are: *Babies Need Books* by Dorothy Butler, Penguin, which provides a detailed reading list up to six years, and *Sharing books with babies and toddlers*, by Sue Hale. This is available from the ground level of the Central Library for 99p. Although last published in 1992, it is still a very useful guide to books you and your child might enjoy. An updated leaflet version can be obtained by sending an A4 SAE to:
The Secretary,
Federation of Children's Book Groups,
2 Bridge Wood View
Horsforth
West Yorkshire, LS18 5PE.

Special borrowing rights

If you help to run a pre-school you can borrow 20 books at a time. Some libraries offer story sessions for such groups. There are also special borrowing rights for childminders and foster carers. As always, ask your local librarian. The **Children's Services Librarian** at the County Libraries HQ ☎ 810231 is willing to come and talk to interested groups about books for young children.

Library listing

All the libraries listed have a children's section. For more information visit the OCC website www.oxfordshire.gov.uk

*Central Library (Westgate)
☎ 815509 or Children's Desk 815373
Mon	9.15-7.00
Tue	9.15-7.00
Wed	9.15-7.00
Thu	9.15-7.00
Fri	9.15-5.00
Sat	9.15-5.00

Tip: The Central Library has a good range of foreign language books. Even if your local branch doesn't have titles in the language you want, they can order books in for you.

Libraries

***Blackbird Leys** (Blackbird Leys Road)
☎ 770403
Mon	9.00-12.00, 1.30-5.00
Tue	9.00-12.00
Wed	9.00-12.00, 1.30-5.00
Thu	9.00-12.00, 1.30-5.00
Fri	Closed
Sat	9.30-12.30

***Cowley** (Temple Road)
☎ 777494
Mon	9.15-5.30
Tue	9.15-5.00
Wed	9.15-7.00
Thu	Closed
Fri	9.15-5.30
Sat	9.30-1.00

***Headington** (North Place, Bury Knowle Park) NB Access is up steep stairs.
☎ 762867
Mon	9.15-1.30
Tue	9.15-7.00
Wed	9.15-1.30
Thu	9.15-5.00
Fri	9.15-5.00
Sat	9.15-1.00

***Kidlington** Oxford Road
☎ 373067
Mon	9.30-5.30
Tue	9.30-5.30
Wed	Closed
Thu	9.30-5.30
Fri	9.30-5.00
Sat	9.30-1.00

***Littlemore Peers** (Peers Campus)
☎ 714309
Mon	2.00-7.00
Tue	2.00-4.30
Wed	Closed
Thu	9.30-12.30, 2.00-4.00
Fri	9.30-12.30
Sat	9.30-12.30

***Old Marston** (Oxford Road)
☎ 726823
Mon	Closed
Tue	2.00-5.00, 6.00-7.30
Wed	Closed
Thu	2.00-5.00, 6.00-7.30
Fri	10.00-12.00, 2.00-5.00
Sat	9.30-12.30

***Summertown** (South Parade)
☎ 558290
Mon	9.30-5.30
Tue	9.30-7.00
Wed	Closed
Thu	9.30-5.30
Fri	9.30-5.30
Sat	9.00-1.00

Libraries

*Kennington Library (The Village Hall)
☎ 730763
Mon 2.00-5.00, 6.00-7.30
Tue Closed
Wed 10.00-12.00
Thu Closed
Fri 2.00-5.00, 6.00-7.30
Sat 10.00-12.30

Botley Library (Elms Court)
☎ 248142
Mon 11.30-5.00
Tue 9.30-5.00
Wed Closed
Thu 9.30-5.00
Fri 9.30-7.00
Sat 9.30-1.00

Tip: Most of Oxfordshire's libraries now have free Internet access. Enquire at individual libraries for details.

Mobile libraries

There may be a Mobile Library which stops near you for 20 minutes or so every fortnight. All the vans carry a small stock of children's books which are changed regularly. Prams and buggies must be left outside. For details of the nearest Mobile Library stop, ask at your local library, or ☎ 395445, or visit the Oxfordshire County Council website for stop listing and calendar www.oxfordshire.gov.uk. Click on 'Libraries, Heritage and Countryside'.

TOY LIBRARIES

Sadly, the number of toy libraries in Oxford has continued to fall due to lack of use. This is a great pity as they are an extremely valuable resource for carers of young children. They are usually run by volunteers, so help is always welcomed. If you are interested in starting or running a toy library, contact:

*The National Association of Toy and Leisure Libraries
The NATLL maintains lists of libraries, and has information packs to help in starting one up. They also produce a newsletter and information on fundraising, publicity, training and conferences.
☎ 020 7387 9592
admin@natll.ukfnet
www.natll.org.uk

All the toy libraries listed below offer toys suitable for children 0 to 5 years unless otherwise stated. Some charge a small annual membership fee, and you usually pay 10-50p per toy borrowed. There is good access for pushchairs in all cases.

Cowley

*Temple Cowley Toy Library
Cowley Parish Hall
Between Towns Road
Thur 10-11 Play session.

Libraries

Donnington

*Donnington Doorstep Toy & Book Library
Donnington Doorstep Family Centre
Townsend Square
Donnington Bridge Road
☎ 727721
Fri 10.30–11.30. Term-time only.

Marston

*Marston and Northway Toy Library
Tower Playbase
Maltfield Road
☎ Angela Taylor 742816
First Tue of month 9.30–11.30 term-time, but phone to check. Toys sometimes available at Friday a.m. Toddler Group. Mainly pre-school toys but some suitable for up to 8. Coffee and play.

Barton

*BOD Toy Library
Barton's Open Door Family Centre
Waynflete Road
☎ 764952
Please call to book a time to borrow. Toys can also be borrowed. Ages 0-8.

East Oxford

*Bartlemas Toy Library
Community Room
Bartlemas Nursery School
Cowley Road
☎ school 245768
Thu 11.30–1.00
Toys available to the morning session of the Nursery and the Toddler Group. Term-time only.

Kennington

*Kennington Toy Library
St Swithun's School Community Room
Wed 9.00–10.30 term time.
☎ Katherine 730539
Toys and videos for ages 0-11

Rose Hill, Littlemore & Blackbird Leys

*Rose Hill Toy Library
The Sure-Start Centre
The Oval
☎ 716739
Mon 10.00–12.00 and Fri afternoons.

South Oxford

*South Oxford Toy Library
New Hinksey Primary School
Vicarage Road
☎ school 248159
Wed 2–3.30 term time. Ages 0-9, toys. games, video to borrow, plus music and refreshments.

*Marlborough Road Community Toy Library
St Ebbe's Primary School Hall
Whitehouse Road
☎ school 248863
Mon 2.30–4.00 term time.
Ages 0-9
Refreshments and programme of events.

Libraries

West Oxford and Botley

*West Oxford Toy Library (NAWOTOY)
West Oxford Community Centre
Binsey Lane
Moving to the new Botley Road Community Centre
☎ Sian Baldwin 395639
Fri 9.30-11.00

*Elms Road Nursery Toy Library (NAWOTOY)
Elms Road
☎ Sian Baldwin 395639
Tue 11.15-12.00

*Botley Mother & Toddler Group
St Peter & Paul Church Hall
Westway
☎ Lydia 863214
Thu 9.15-11.15

Wheatley

*Holton Village Hall
☎ Maggie Fyffe 874763
☎ Corinne Miley Smith 873509
Tues 10.00-12.00
Cost: £5.00/year membership. Borrow toys on a weekly or fortnightly basis. Children 0-5.

The following libraries are currently in recess, but the collections of toys remain intact waiting for families to use them and run the library.

*Jericho Toy Library
St Barnabas First School
Cardigan Street
☎ school 557178

*Cutteslowe Toy Library
Cutteslowe Community Centre
Wren Road
☎ Lesley Deacon 311172

*East Oxford Toy Library
East Oxford First School
Union Street
☎ school 240219

*Speedwell First School Toy Library
Sandford Road
Littlemore
☎ school 777659

*Cuddesdon Corner Toy Library
Family Centre
Cuddesdon Way
☎ 773263

PEEP Packs

PEEP groups in Rose Hill, Littlemore and Blackbird Leys and Greater Leys have packs of books and related toys to lend to PEEP group members.

At the time of publication, the PEEP-style groups run by NPN and Florence Park are producing similar

Libraries

Read & Play packs for lending.
☎ 777286. For more information on PEEP, see *Ch. 18 – Off to School*.

OTHER USEFUL GROUPS

*Oxford Children's Book Group
☎ Tizzie Ballard
863043
sue@nealedesign.
freeserve.co.uk
Encourages both parents and children to enjoy children's books.
 Organises two or three events per term.
www.achuka.co.uk

*Advisory Services for the Education of Travellers (ASET)
Room L25, Cricket Road Centre
Cricket Road
☎ 428089
traved@a-s-e-t.demon.co.uk
www.a-s-e-t.demon.co.uk
Available as support to parent travellers (fairground and circus people, people living on the waterways, gypsies) on finding schools and advice, as well as curriculum materials and resources relating to Traveller culture.

*Oxford Development Education Centre (ODEC)
East Oxford Community Centre
Princes Street
☎ Marie Nkolola 790490
Open Tues–Fri.
A multicultural resource for parents, children, and groups with books (many with dual language texts), teaching packs, videos, games from all over the world. Focus on black history.

"I love books"
by Eloise Huxley
aged 4

Chapter 9 – For You

In the busy whirlwind of life with young children, it can be difficult to find time just for yourself, especially if you are a single parent. However, Oxford is full of opportunities to learn a new skill, take part in a sport, 'return to learn' or just give time to yourself. In this section, we look at activities for adults that also offer help with childcare. We cover drop-in crèches, crèches linked to a particular centre or adult activity and courses offering help with childcare or travel costs.

WHAT IS A CRECHE?

Crèches are places where you can leave your baby or child safely under supervision by responsible adults. All crèches which run for longer than two hours must be fully approved by OFSTED. Staff are trained childcare workers who have been subject to police and medical checks. The premises are also checked. A confidential record is kept of each child's details and emergency contacts, so do remember to take all relevant information and phone numbers with you when you first book in your child. Crèches aim to offer stimulating play sessions where children feel happy and secure. Stay with your child for a short while the first time so that they can get used to the new faces and the room before you leave.

Where to go for information

For up-to-date accurate information regarding crèches, childcare and children's activities, contact **Oxfordshire Children's Information Service** ☎ 01993 886933. www.oxoncis.co.uk

The Childcare Development Team at Oxfordshire County Council Early Years and Childcare Service supports the expansion of pre-school places and out of school places in all sectors. If parents feel there is a need for childcare in a particular area, or wish to set up a childcare provision, they should contact the Childcare Development Team on 815215/815277 or email frances.duffy@oxfordshire.gov.uk or norma.thompson@oxfordshire.gov.uk

For you

DROP-IN CRECHES

It is best to book these early although there may be some casual places.

*Donnington Doorstep Crèche
Townsend Square
☎ 727721 to book
Mon 9.45–11.45
£4.50 per session, 6 months–5 years. Crèche also runs alongside various art and craft workshops.

*Sure-Start Family Centre Crèche
Sure-Start Family Centre
Rose Hill
☎ Janice 716739
Wed and Fri, 12.30–3.00pm
Children under 5 welcome
£2.00 a session, £1.50 for siblings. Priority to Rose Hill/Littlemore residents
NB free crèche available for those attending courses run at the centre (such as childcare/healthy living) Phone for details.

*Sure-Start Crèche
Littlemore Community Centre
Fri 12.30–2.30
Priority to Rose Hill/Littlemore residents
☎ Janice 716739

Mobile Crèches

*Oxford Mobile Crèche
Dovecote Centre
Nightingale Avenue
Blackbird Leys
☎ 777751
A mobile crèche based in Oxford providing trained workers, equipment and entertainment (e.g. face-painting) available for business, private or community hire for one-off meetings, events, conferences, weddings etc. Insured and OFSTED approved, it is run as a non-profit making business and prices vary depending on the type of event (business or community) on a sliding scale. Special Needs provision

SPORT AND LEISURE CENTRES

Taking time to exercise regularly can help you relax, improve your fitness and mood, and make you feel more able to cope with the demands of parenting young children.

For you

*Arena Fitness
109 Oxford Road
Cowley
☎ 779115
Daily crèche alongside fitness classes, Pilates, yoga.
Mon–Sat 10.00–11.00
£2.00 per session
Large free car park.

*Kidlington and Gosford Sports Centre
Oxford Road
Kidlington
☎ 376368
Fitness classes, aerobics
Crèche available Mon–Fri 9.30–11.30
Under 2 group and 2 years–5 years group.
£1.60 per hour.
Annual family membership available.

*Aviators
Oxford Airport
Langford Lane
Kidlington
☎ 376600
Fitness classes or gym membership
Babysitting available, 6 weeks–under 5 years.
Mon–Sat mornings, phone for times.
Non-members £2.00 a session, members £1.50, siblings half-price.

*Esporta Health and Racquets Club
St. Edward's School
269c Woodstock Road
☎ 318318
Swimming, fitness classes, sports for all
Extensive childcare facilities and activities run for children aged 6 weeks–17 years.
£3.00 per hour for members only (membership starts at £715 per annum).
An expensive option, but recommended for good organised children's activities.
Advance booking essential.

*White Horse Leisure and Tennis Centre
Audlett Drive
Abingdon
☎ 01235 540700
Definitely worth the 20-minute drive. This is exactly what Oxford *should* have – a council-run, clean, spacious sports centre, large airy swimming pools (children's pools are excellent), aerobics, squash, tennis, café. Ladies tennis and coffee social mornings on Monday and Wednesday. Badminton and coffee social mornings on Thursday.
Pay per session, or family membership available.
Crèche available 9.00–3.00, £2.20 per hour, phone to book.

*The Park Sports Centre
Holton, Wheatley
☎ 872128
Aerobics and fitness classes, gym membership available. One membership covers use at four different centres, including swimming facilities at Thame and Berinsfield.
Crèche available daily in mornings, cost depends on membership 6 weeks–under 5. Phone to book.

For you

NB Sadly, without any consultation and virtually no notice, the crèches at **Temple Cowley Pools** and **Blackbird Leys Leisure Centre** closed down in summer 2003.

Relaxation - but no crèche!

*Blackbird Leys Leisure Centre
Pegasus Road
☎ 467020
Fitness room, exercise classes.

*Brookes Sport
Harcourt Hill
☎ 488379
Membership or pay and play, swimming, tennis, squash, aerobics.

*The Ferry Sports Centre
Summertown
☎ 467060
Swimming, fitness classes, squash.

*Four Pillars Hotels Leisure Clubs
Abingdon Road and Sandford branches.
☎ 0800 374692.
Attractive uncrowded swimming pools, gyms etc. Membership expensive.

*Hinksey Pools
Abingdon Road
☎ 467079
Open only during summer months. Avoid the crowds if you can, it does get very busy in holidays and at weekends. Try a sunny summer evening swim after the children are in bed – a definite perk of Oxford life.

*Oxrad
Marsh Lane
☎ 741336
Gym, fitness classes, children's trampolining.

*Temple Cowley Pools
Temple Road
☎ 467124
Fitness room, exercise classes and pool.

*The Yoga Garden
4 South Parade, Summertown
☎ 311300
Yoga, Pilates, relaxation and fitness classes in clean, purpose-built studios. Pay per course of classes. Nice café next door run by same people. A good 'time out' place.

Crèches linked to art, craft and dance classes

(See also community education, later in this chapter)

*Women and Toddlers Art Group
Ark T Centre
Crowell Road (behind Templars Square shopping centre)
Cowley
☎ 773499/396778 to book
email: ark-t@can-online.org.uk
£3.50 a session
An art group for mothers/carers, children (under 5) play alongside in play area. Sometimes children are involved in the art activities too. Takes place each Wednesday.

For you

*Fusion
Oxford Community Arts Agency
East Oxford Community Centre
Princes Street
☎ 245735
On-site crèche run by Community Centre available for life drawing, dance and movement, mosaics classes, Wed 10.00-1.00, Fri 10.00-12.00. Also available alongside ongoing arts projects, and occasionally for evening classes. Booking number for crèche 792168

*Cuddesdon Corner Family Centre
61-3 Cuddesdon Way
Blackbird Leys
☎ 773263
Free crèche available for most of the adult groups, creative arts and crafts, healthy living, computers for beginners classes. Enquire for times.

RETURN TO LEARN

Oxford is a good city for learning opportunities, whatever your educational background. Discover new skills, refresh and update existing skills or prepare yourself for learning. Even short courses can often give you credits towards a qualification.

For free careers guidance, interview skills and help with your CV, contact the **New Start Adult Guidance Adviser** on 798081.

Try contacting Family Centres and Community Education to check details of local courses.

The courses listed here offer either crèches or help with childcare, depending on circumstances.

*Ruskin Learning Project
Ruskin College
Walton Street
☎ 554331
email: enquiries@ruskin.ac.uk
A small, friendly equal opportunities college, doors open to all adults without higher education. Sometimes called a 'second chance college'. Courses include social work, history, literature, computing, writing, French, art, assertiveness and leadership. Costs subsidised, you may qualify for free courses. Childcare assistance given according to circumstance.

*The Workers Educational Association (WEA)
☎ Pearl Ryall 01993 844886
email: office@ts.wea.org.uk
The WEA runs free or low cost local learning groups all over the city. Topics include assertiveness, computing and parenting. Enquire regarding available crèches.

*ABLE Open Learning Centre
Oxford College of Further Education
Blackbird Leys Precinct
Cuddesdon Way
Blackbird Leys
☎ 776334
email: adultbsu@rmplc.co.uk
Courses free to all. Ongoing flexible learning workshops to improve your basic education - e.g. letter writing,

For you

computer skills, maths and English. Turn up at your convenience between the following times:
Mon,Tues,Thurs 9.30–12.30, 1.30–4.30
Wed 9.30–12.30, 1.30–7.00, closed Fri
Community crèche at Leisure Centre available.

*Adult Basic Skills Unit
☎ 778827
Contact this number to book into specific classes at the Able Learning Centre above.

*Oxford Women's Training Scheme
Northway Centre
Maltfield Road
☎ 741317
www.owts.org.uk
Vocational training and introductory courses to women over 19 who have missed out on an education in the past. Courses offered in computing, IT, woodwork, building skills, painting and decorating, video and media and basic skills. All courses are free with a free onsite crèche, plus help with travel costs.
Crèche based at Tower Playbase, Mon-Fri 9.30–2.45 term-time only
3 months–5 years

*Ethnic Minority Business Service
3 Collins Street
☎ 794431
Free courses, open to everybody regardless of race or gender. Day and evening courses in computers, English, all aspects of running a crèche as a business, starting your own business, first aid, counselling etc. Linked to Abingdon and Witney college.
Crèche available for those studying at EMBS:
Balwadi Crèche
1 Chapel Street
☎ 250237
Open 9.30–12.30, 1.15–3.30 weekdays only. 1–8 year olds welcome.

*Asian Cultural Centre
Manzil Way
☎ 425000
Asian women's activities: Women's Urdu Class Mon 1-3 pm (FREE). For women who want to learn reading, writing and spoken Urdu. Crèche is provided.
Sewing Class. Tues 1.00-3.00pm (FREE). Sewing your own Asian clothes with experienced sewing tutor. Crèche is provided.
Women's Lunch Club, Mon 12.00-1.00. Women meet and socialise. Lunch Club caters for vegetarian.
Swimming for women 12.00-1.00. Phone for crèche availability.

English Language classes

There are several free English as a second language classes running in Oxford. These are open to permanent UK residents, some EU citizens, refugees and asylum-seekers. Free crèche places provided where available. For more information or an appointment to discuss your learning, contact:

For you

*The Community English School
(ESOL)
Education Complex
Union Street
Oxford
☎ 728688

Community Education

Community Education provides a huge range of evening and day classes on subjects ranging from cookery, car maintenance and computer courses to foreign languages, yoga and art. Some daytime courses have crèches. Each August a new list of classes is available from local Community Education offices. Check at local libraries for information.

*North and West Oxford Community Education Office
The Ferry Centre
Diamond Place
Summertown
☎ 511757
nawocec@oxfordshire.gov.uk

*Headington Area Community Education Office
Northway Centre, Dora Carr Close
Headington
☎ 768359
headingtoncec@oxfordshire.gov.uk

*Cumnor and Kennington Community Education Centre
Matthew Arnold School
Arnold's Way
Cumnor
☎ 862009
cumnorcec@oxfordshire.gov.uk

*East and South Oxford Community Education
Littlemore CEC Office
Peers Campus
Sandy Lane West
Littlemore
☎ 712094
easocec@oxfordshire.gov.uk

Sources of information

For further information on evening and day classes contact the following:

*Oxford University Department of Continuing Education
Rewley House
☎ 270360
www.conted.ox.ac.uk
A wide and interesting range of weekly evening classes, day and weekend schools, diplomas and certificates available, taught at Rewley House or Ewart Place in Summertown. Recommended, especially the day conferences. Open to all.

*Oxford College of Further Education
Oxpens
☎ 269396 for careers help and guidance.
☎ 269269 for course enquiries

*Workers' Educational Association (WEA) Thames and Solent
☎ 246270

For you

QUIET TIME

Time by yourself to reflect and think is hard to find when you are a parent of young children – but making time to do this can help family life run more peacefully. Sometimes it can help to go to your local place of worship – most offer an open door during the week or weekends after services when all is quiet. You may need a chance to reflect/pray or just to sit quietly. For quiet time away, try a day/residential retreat. Although retreats are normally run by religious communities, you do not have to be 'religious' to go. Some charge modest fees, others are free or ask for a donation. They all offer the opportunity for peace, quiet and reflection.

*The Abbey
Sutton Courteney
☎ 01235 847401
www.theabbey.uk.com
Recommended. Open to all regardless of beliefs. Small charge per 24 hours. Phone for details.

*Stanton House
Pound Lane, Stanton St.John
☎ 358807
Retreat house owned by Christian charitable trust. Provides place for peace and quiet, day groups welcome or residential. No structured programme.

*Charney Manor
Nr. Wantage
☎ 01235 868206

*Carmelite Priory
Boars Hill
☎ 730183

DATES FOR YOUR DIARY

*The Oxford Literary Festival
☎ 305305
www.SundayTimes-oxfordliteraryfestival.com
Takes place annually at the beginning of April with a wide range of authors and illustrators speaking about their work, debates, children's events, bookshop and café. Great for children and adults. Check in the *Oxford Times* and notices in local bookshops for the festival itinerary.

*Oxford International Women's Festival
☎ Ann Mobbs 553755 .
www.oxfordwomen.co.uk
This usually takes place during the first two weeks of March. The festival celebrates the creativity of women through theatre, music, talks, exhibitions, workshops, discussion groups, dance performance and social activities.

It aims to highlight women's local, national and international issues, to support women and organisations who are campaigning for equal rights and to celebrate women's achievements.

Chapter 10 – Eating Out

"how long can we hide under here, do you think?"

If you need a snack when out shopping with your children or are planning a meal out with your family then this chapter is for you. Eating out with children can be stressful, especially if the venue is not welcoming to youngsters, so we have put together a list of places to eat which we have found to be child-friendly. The list is based on recommendations sent in by you, so please keep them coming in, using the form at the end of the book. Please note that the turnover of and changes in pubs and restaurants and their management seems to be more rapid than ever, so it is always worth double-checking before setting off on a long or specific journey to one of the establishments listed.

Bon appetit!

TYPES OF PLACES TO EAT

There is a great variety of places out there and thankfully, more are becoming family-friendly – witness the number of pubs which now have family rooms. Here is a selection of eateries, to suit all pockets, worth visiting in the Oxford area. We have also included some suggestions for picnic sites outside Oxford.

Eating out

Smoke Free?
The Oxfordshire Smoke-Free Eating Guide is available free from Social & Cultural Services, Vale of White Horse District Council, Abbey House, Abingdon, OX14 3JE, ☎ 01235 520202. It lists cafés, tearooms, restaurants, hotels, guest houses, B&Bs, pubs, leisure centres and motorway services that are either entirely smoke-free or have smoke-free areas. It indicates whether wheelchair access and baby changing facilities are available and if breastfeeding is welcome. It was compiled in 2001 so some entries are out of date and it is by no means exhaustive, but it makes a good starting point!

Drop-in centres
These are your cheapest option for eating out. They serve adult lunches for under £1 and the sort of food that most children will eat. Breastfeeding is never a problem. There are nappy-changing facilities, high chairs and toys. The main drawback is that some are not open at weekends.

*Rainbow House
Wesley Memorial Church Hall
New Inn Hall Street
Weds–Fri 10.30–2.00
Good, simple, child-friendly, home-cooked food (pizza, soup etc.) toys and play area.

*Jericho Family Lunch Club
St Barnabas Centre
Canal Street
☎ 557902/557249
Thu 11.45–2.00
Playroom for children.

Family centres
These provide opportunities to meet with other parents in your area. They all serve lunch at midday and refreshments at other times. See: Chapter 4 - Meeting People for a full listing.

*BOD (Barton's Open Door)
Waynflete Road
☎ 764952
Bring and share lunch every Monday. Inexpensive refreshments all day.

*Cuddesdon Corner
61-3 Cuddesdon Way
Blackbird Leys
☎ 773263 Fax 747415
pc@cuddcorn.freeserve.co.uk

*Donnington Doorstep
Townsend Square
(off Donnington Bridge Road)
☎ 727721
Mon–Fri 10–4.00 Drop-in.
Cheap refreshments throughout the day and excellent home-cooked lunch from 12.00, varied menu, usually with vegetarian option.

*Florence Park Family Centre
Rymers Lane
☎ 777286
Open access drop-in Mon, Thurs and Fri 10.00–3.00.
Cheap lunches, or bring your own.

Eating out

*Kaleidoscope Centre for Families
Oxford Road
Kidlington
☎ 372591

*Littlemore Community Centre
Giles Road
Littlemore
☎ 771764
Holds drop-in 'snack and play' sessions.

*Sure Start Family Centre
The Oval
Rose Hill
☎ 716739
Mon-Fri 10.30–3.00.
Cheap refreshments and excellent, varied, home-cooked lunch, with vegetarian option, at 12.00.

Cafés

These are all good for coffee, lunch or afternoon tea. See also: *Chapter 6 - Going Shopping* for more café ideas.

*Ashmolean Museum Café
For well behaved children only. Good facilities (lift, changing etc.) but food not particularly appealing to children.

*Borders
☎ 248559
Handy Starbucks coffee bar in bookshop. Good central place for meeting friends as plenty to amuse the children while waiting (children's books, headphones in music dept). Toilets with changing tables not very spacious – those with double buggies, beware!

*The Vaults (Convocation Coffee House)
University Church, High Street
Good escape from crowds in town. Light lunches, coffee.

*Covered Market
Between High St and Market St.
Lots of eateries from Cornish pasties to ice cream, under the cover of the market roof and away from the traffic.

Tip: Farmers' Markets are great for bread, cakes and for trying samples of cheese, fish, meat and fruit juices. There's always someone selling bacon or sausage butties!

*Edgar's Café
Carfax Gardens
☎ 790622
Outdoor cafe (with indoor area) tucked away under the trees beside Carfax Tower. Child-friendly food, will warm bottles and baby food. Breastfeeding acceptable. Toilets. Easy access.

*George and Davis
Little Clarendon Street
Older kids love sitting on the high stools for the wonderful (but expensive) ice creams.

*Gino's
Gloucester Green
Not specifically catering for children but very accommodating and child-friendly. High chairs, children's menu/portions

Eating out

Eating out by Hebe York aged 4

*The Good Bean Coffee Co.
Above Blackwells main shop
Broad Street
Lift for pushchairs. Light lunches, good coffee, comfy sofas and books!

*The Magic Café
110 Magdalen Road
☎ 794604
Mon-Sat 10.00-6.00
Fri 10.00-10.00pm
Vegetarian lunches, drinks and cakes. Friendly atmosphere, reasonable prices. Children very welcome. Breastfeeding is fine. Great for a break after visiting the Goldfish Bowl (aquarium shop) See: Ch. 11 - Out and About in Oxford.

*Modern Art Oxford (formerly MOMA)
30 Pembroke Street
☎ 722733
www.modernartoxford.org.uk
Tues-Sat 10.00-5.00, Sun 12.00-5.00
Child-friendly café. No special children's food but happy to warm bottles and baby food. No high chairs but low tables. Nice comfy low benches all along one side to breastfeed and there are changing facilities. MOMA would like both children and parents to feel comfortable in the café. Access either down stairs (with help) or up lift, through shop and down by internal lift.

*New Road Baptist Church Coffee House
Bonn Square
☎ 250134
Central, pleasant café for a snack lunch. High chairs but no changing facilities, loos are small. Access via stairs but you can sit downstairs and ring for service.

*St Aldates Church Coffee House
94 St Aldates
☎ 245952
Reasonably priced homemade food, delicious cakes and light lunches. High chairs available. Children welcome.

*Starbucks
Several in Oxford:
6 Cornmarket ☎ 249675
127 High Street ☎ 244874
Magdalen Street (at back of Borders Bookshop – see above) ☎ 248559
Cornmarket branch has a small corner for children with megablocks on a child's table. Loo on ground floor.

Restaurants

If you are looking for something a bit more substantial for lunch then the following restaurants welcome families.

Eating out

*Aqua Vitae
Folly Bridge, Abingdon Road
☎ 247775
Not child-oriented but surprisingly child friendly; no high chairs but will provide if you call ahead.

*Aziz
230 Cowley Road
☎ 794945
Award-winning curry house. Children welcome.

Tip: Any place will be more child-friendly if you choose a quiet time to go so staff are more relaxed and have more leisure to attend to your children

*Bar Meze
London Road, Headington
Turkish cuisine, meze menu has child-friendly dishes such as houmous and pitta bread. Pleasant staff.

*Blue Palms
South Parade, Summertown
☎ 559653
Pizza and pasta always a hit; a more upmarket place to go with kids.

*Branca
111 Walton Street
☎ 556111
Recommended by several quite different mums. Not cheap, but goes the extra mile to keep children happy. Worth visiting just to see the fabulous loos with gorgeous mirrors!

*Brookes Restaurant
Oxford Brookes University
Gypsy Lane
☎ 483803
www.brookes.ac.uk
Brookes University training restaurant for its hotel and catering students provides superb weekday lunches. in term-time. A major treat for both eye and palate. You will rarely encounter such a perfect level of warm, friendly helpful but unobtrusive service. All customers, including children, welcomed. Not cheap but excellent value – essential to book. High chairs.

*Browns
5-11 Woodstock Road
☎ 311415
www.browns-restaurants.com
Mon–Sat 11.00–late; Sun 12.00–late.
Listed by Egon Ronay as one of *the* family restaurants of the year. Children's menu, plastic bibs, high chairs, buggy-parking, non-smoking. Breastfeeding fine. Changing facilities in the disabled loo. Easy access.

*Café Coco
23 Cowley Road near The Plain
☎ 200232
Relaxed atmosphere but can get smoky in the evening. High chair, changing table in downstairs toilet.

*Café Rouge
Little Clarendon Street
☎ 310194
Child-friendly. Crayons and paper for kids. Downstairs loo. But can get smoky.

119

Eating out

*Chiang Mai
130a High Street (down one of those little side alleys)
☎ 202233
Independent, local, family-run, Thai restaurant. Extremely popular with everyone, including families, advance booking usually essential. Food superb (and all given chilli-ratings for heat!). Excellent vegetarian menu with lots of choice. Pineapple rice served in a fresh pineapple is fun. Non-smoking section. Nice clean loos but quite small, no changing facilities.

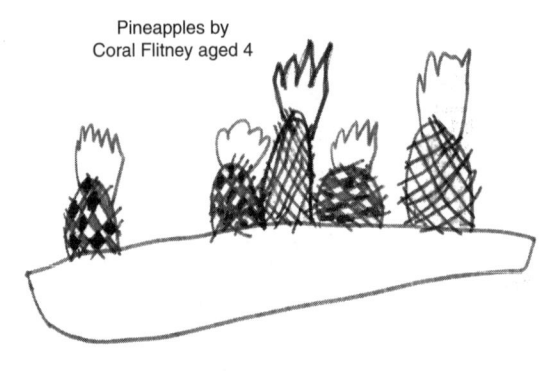

Pineapples by Coral Flitney aged 4

*Edamame (Japanese)
15 Holywell Street
☎ 246916
Owners understand children's needs. Serves only Japanese food but young children often love the noodles not to mention the 'edamame' itself - fresh green soya beans. Lovely food at very reasonable prices, nice atmosphere. Drawbacks: small, you can't book. Tends to close completely for holidays, so phone to check it's open before you go.

*Fisher's Restaurant
35 St Clements
☎ 243003
Informal, good for fresh fish and chips. Welcomes children, crayons provided. High chairs and children's menu.

*The Flame (Persian)
Windmill Road, Headington
Nice food, not too spicy for small children. Child-friendly staff.

*Kazbar
27 Cowley Road
☎ 202920
Often does a bargain lunch with lots of little starters. Lots of space to lounge or scramble around on big bench seats with masses of cushions. Very laid back, welcomes children, though no special (eg changing) facilities. NB gets really crowded and smoky in the evening but is expanding into next-door building.

*Liaison (Chinese)
29 Castle Street
☎ 242944
High chairs, great food, very helpful staff who will willingly entertain bored small children!

Tip: Take some small amusements with you – a finger puppet, a tiny pad or a few sheets of paper, a few crayons, a small jigsaw or puzzle book – to prevent boredom while you are waiting to be served.

Eating out

*Le Manoir aux Quat' Saisons
Church Road, Great Milton
☎ 01844 278881
No guide to Oxford would be complete without mention of this famous restaurant! Brilliant place for a really special family lunch. Although expensive, it isn't stuffy, and the set lunch isn't as dear as you might expect. The restaurant is genuinely child friendly (children are sometimes invited into the kitchens to choose their own pudding!). The gardens are a dream. If you go for lunch no one seems to mind if you stay until early evening. Even the loos are worth a visit! Not everybody's cup of tea, but it really is possible with well-behaved kids.

*Moonlight Tandoori
58 Cowley Road
☎ 240275
Consistently good curry house offering wide range of dishes. Children welcome.

*Moya (Eastern European)
St Clements
☎ 200111
Varied menu. Not too spicy for small children. Excellent milkshakes and non-alcoholic cocktails. High chair available. Large downstairs disabled toilet with changing facilities.

*Nando's
Cowley Road
☎ 203357
Grilled spatchcock chicken, either plain or hot and spicy. Also healthy takeaway option, with fresh salad and rolls. Baby change in disabled loo.

*Old Orleans Restaurant
George Street
☎ 792718
Children's menu, high chairs, non-smoking area, crayons and colour-in menu, changing facilities in the disabled toilet. Children's entertainment at Christmas time. Easy access.

*Le Petit Blanc
71-72 Walton Street
☎ 510999
For a major treat, Le Petit Blanc (Raymond Blanc's 'cheap' alternative to Le Manoir) really is pretty child friendly: they provide crayons and paper model 2CVs to make while you're waiting for the food, and the children's menu is not much more expensive than the usual nuggets and chips variety – but includes eg smoked salmon, good pasta dishes and really nice ice cream. High chairs, and staff are patient with kids.

*Red Star Noodle Bar
Cowley Road (opposite Zodiac)
☎ 251248
Open 12.00-2.30 and 6.00-11.00
No specifically child-friendly facilities, but the food's good and inexpensive and older children have fun eating with chopsticks. Bench seats

Tip: Many places - especially on the Cowley Road - now do economical fixed price 'banquets' and Sunday lunches, with children half price.

Eating out

*Rice Box
178 Cowley Road
☎ 202138
You can eat here for £5 a head, everyone likes something on the menu. Open 12.00-2.00 and 5.00-midnight. (Also does home delivery from 5.30.) Bench seats.

Burger and Pizza Restaurants

Burger and pizza chains are usually well geared up for children and a visit can be a good negotiating tactic with bored kids!

*Burger King
25 Cornmarket ☎ 245151
Retail Park, Cowley ☎ 711837.
High chairs, children's menu.

*Gourmet Pizza
2 The Gallery
Gloucester Green
☎ 793146
Children's menu with games (crayons provided), high chairs, changing facilities, non-smoking area, space to park buggies and carrycots.

*Mama Mia
South Parade
Summertown
☎ 514141
Very popular with families and deservedly so. Worth booking ahead at busy times. Child-friendly Italian staff. Wooden Tripp Trapp toddler seats. Pizza, pasta, ice cream. Nice clean loos but no special changing facilities.

*Mario's
103 Cowley Road
☎ 722955
12.00-2.00 (Tue-Sat), 6.30-11.00 (Tue-Sun)
Popular, independent, family-run establishment: the original Mario, a blacksmith, even made all the chairs and metalwork. His son now provides pizza, pasta, and other Italian food in a relaxed atmosphere. Child-friendly food in children's portions. One high chair, no changing facilities, no non-smoking area. Breastfeeding fine.

*McDonald's Restaurant
Cornmarket Street ☎ 794736, Carpenter's Arms, Botley Road ☎ 793263 and London Road, Headington Roundabout ☎ 744849
All the usual child-oriented facilities.

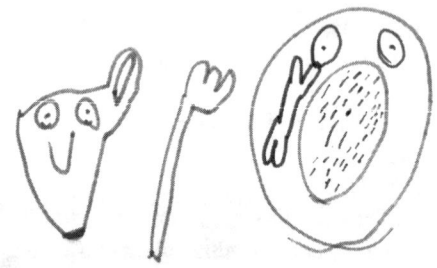

*Pizza Express
8 Golden Cross
Cornmarket Street
☎ 790442
Child friendly. Leave pushchairs downstairs. High chairs. Particularly good at lunchtime. Don't seem to mind how many children you take or how much mess they make!

Happy meal by Coral Flitney aged 4

Eating out

*Pizza Hut
61-3 George Street
☎ 790089
Children's menu, high chair, changing and breastfeeding facilities, non-smoking area. Easy access.

*Pizza Hut
10-12 High Street
☎ 724473
Children's menu, high chairs, large no-smoking area. Games and colouring (crayons provided), pond with fish. Space to park buggies and some tables will accommodate a carrycot. No changing facilities. Downstairs entrance and no lift but staff willing to assist.

• •

Tip: Even if restaurants don't have special facilities for children, don't be put off. Eating early in the evenings can often mean staff have more time to be friendly and you are less likely to be seated in the corner by the kitchen.

• •

Shop restaurants

City centre department stores and larger shops offer children's facilities. Bhs, Debenhams and Marks & Spencer do 'lunch in a box' for kids where they can choose a selection of items for a fixed price, including cheese and fruit. All are open Mon–Sun.

*Allders
Westgate
☎ 304700
Breastfeeding is acceptable in self-service restaurant. Children's menu, bottle-warming facility and high chairs. Changing facilities in store. Lift access.

*Bhs
Queen Street
☎ 242661
The café is next to the children's clothes section on the first floor and is generally child-friendly.

*Debenhams
Magdalen Street
☎ 243161
Debenhams cafés are usually child friendly with children's/infants' food and staff willing to help struggling parents. Low table with bead toy. Good, spacious baby-change close by.

*Littlewoods
52 Cornmarket
☎ 201845
Children's meals and lunch boxes, baby food and drinks, warming facilities, high chairs and non-smoking area. Staff are willing to help struggling parents, e.g. with buggies, trays, etc. Changing facilities next to women's toilets on second floor. Access via lift.

*Marks & Spencer
Queen Street
☎ 248075
Relatively new restaurant on first floor. Special child packs available. Toilets

Eating out

with changing mat in Ladies on first floor (NB they are on the opposite side of the shop to the café, so take small children to the loo first to avoid lengthy trek across the shop half-way through your coffee/tea/meal!)

*Marks & Spencer
Banbury Road
Summertown
Child-friendly. Story books, paper and crayons, pictures displayed. Wooden toddler seats. Well-spaced tables. Ladies' loos have disabled access and changing station.

Tea in the country

Looking for a rural afternoon tea or even lunch? Try the following:

*Blooms
Garden/aquatic centre on the Oxford Road just outside Bicester
☎ 01869 242248
Nice cakes, highchairs. Just one unisex loo! Lovely wooden toys for sale, huge range of plants, thousands of tropical fish and some big outdoor varieties, splashy water features, and the best outdoor play equipment area ever. (Not strictly speaking a playground, but display area for the range of equipment!) Good place to spend half a day or more.

*Burford Garden Centre
Just off A40 by turning for Burford
☎ 01993 823285/823117
Great teas. Indoor toys, so good for meeting other families with children on a rainy day.

*Godwins' Ice-Cream Farm
Manor Farm
Weston-on-the-Green
near Bicester
☎ 01869 351647
neil@westononthegreen.freeserve.co.uk
Signposted from the A34 and very easy to find. Open all year 9.00-5.00. Teas (with wonderful home-made cakes) and breakfasts as well as ice cream made on the farm with cream from their own cows. Always 22 flavours available daily in the summer, from Apple Strudel, Almond, Banana and Banoffi through Cinnamon & Date, Honeycomb and Mince Pie to Strawberry Yogurt Ripple, Tutti Frutti and Vanilla. Eat some there and take some home for the freezer. Also do children's parties and sometimes have special events/attractions at the weekends. Cows, horses, rabbits and tractors to look at.

*Millets Farm Shop
See Ch 12: Days Out

*Notcutts Garden Centre
Nuneham Courtenay
☎ 343454
Restaurant has high chairs, food's good and cheap, and there's lots to see inside (animals, noisy parrot, fish, books, real and plastic flowers) and outside (lots of plants plus overpriced playhouses, summer houses, sheds etc).

*Oxfordshire Museum
Woodstock
☎ 01993 811456
Small modern café in the centre of

Eating out

Woodstock. Sit on the patio while children play in enclosed gardens. Steps, grassy slope, benches, sculpture, flowers. Modern, spacious toilets across the garden from the café. Access to the museum is free: from Roman remains and stuffed trout to hands-on science/innovation exhibits and children's toys (some can be played with).

*Royal Oak Farm Tea Room
Beckley (on the B4027)
☎ 351246
Weekends and bank holidays only (Easter–Sept). Tea room is behind the farm shop and has both indoor and outdoor seating. Really good cakes and light snacks. Very child friendly. Lots of animals to feed and stroke. Tractor to play on. Toilets. Great for Christmas supplies from turkeys and puddings to Christmas trees and mistletoe.

*Waterperry House Tea Room
☎ 01844 338087/339226
Follow the signs to Waterperry from A40 at Wheatley. Drive right to end of village and into the car-park.
Mar–Oct 10.00–5.30 (weekdays)
10.00–6.00 (weekends)
Nov–Feb 10.00–5.00
Lovely in the summer as you can eat on the lawn and the children can run around playing hide-and-seek in the bushes. Follow up with a free visit to the garden centre greenhouses to see the cacti and tropical plants or pay to go into the gardens. Lovely tea room with home-made cakes. High chairs and baby changing. Worth a trip out.

Pubs

In England, pubs can now apply for a children's certificate where, in the absence of a family room, children are allowed into certain areas of the pub deemed suitable. In practice, however, many publicans are turning a blind eye to the legislation and welcome families. In any case, pub legislation looks set to change again, with restrictions being relaxed even further.

We can recommend the following pubs where families can relax and have a meal or drink together.
(NS=No-smoking area)

Central Oxford

*Chequers (NS)
off High Street
☎ 726904
Large pub accessed down small alleyway off the High. Upstairs room where families are welcome during the day for meals.

*Far from the Madding Crowd (NS)
☎ 240900 or 792200
Friar's Entry off Magdalen Street between Borders and Gloucester Green. New pub with good food menu. Well-behaved children welcome. Large non-smoking area, fairtrade coffee and tea.

*Head of the River
Folly Bridge
☎ 721600
Large pub just on the edge of the city centre with patio areas overlooking the

Eating out

Thames (no fencing between patio and river). Ideal for watching all the activity on the river.

*King's Arms (NS)
Holywell Street and Parks Road
☎ 242369
Big, busy, and boisterous pub with six different drinking areas. Definitely adult rather than family atmosphere, but children welcome, particularly in the coffee room.

*Turf Tavern
Bath Place, off Holywell St and Pembroke Street
☎ 243235
Children allowed in back bar and three courtyards of this popular pub. Have fun trying to find it from Holywell Street or New College Lane! Look out for the medieval city walls. The patios can be covered and there are patio heaters for cold days.

*Waterman's Arms
South Street,
Osney Island (off Botley Road)
☎ 248832
Some tables outside with potential area to spill onto riverside. No parking. Small garden where children are made welcome by friendly landlady. Very near Osney Lock which is of interest to young and old alike.

*The White House
2 Botley Road
☎ 242823
Near the railway station. Nice enclosed rear garden, small car park. Excellent (adult) menu. Child friendly, high chairs.

Out of town
Some of these pubs are chosen because you can comfortably eat indoors with your children; others because they have large and/or safe gardens where your children can run around and play, leaving you to eat in peace! Pubs all have different opening hours, and many serve food only on certain days or at certain times. It is always best to phone to check before you set out. A few of these pubs are really outstanding, both in terms of the excellent facilities they provide for children and their attractions for adults: these are marked with a double star **.

Inside the Ring Road

*Angel and Greyhound
St Clements
☎ 242660
Large friendly pub with board games, bar billiards and electronic games. Children welcome in back part of pub and small garden at rear. NCP parking behind pub, next to Angel and Greyhound Meadow, great for picnics.

*Bricklayers Arms**
Old Marston
☎ 250177
Everything you could wish for: baby change in disabled loo, high chairs, children's menu (or half-portions of Sunday lunch), nice range of adult food,

Eating out

enclosed garden, large car park, excellent playground in good condition. Shady position, great on a hot day. Follow signs to St Nicholas church.

*The Fishes Inn (NS)
North Hinksey Village
☎ 249796
Child friendly staff and a relaxed atmosphere, children can sit in the conservatory. Garden, parking. Not ideal for very small children because of the proximity of the river.

*Gardener's Arms
39 Plantation Road
☎ 559814
Small enclosed garden at rear. No special facilities for children. Unusual entirely vegetarian menu.

*General Elliot
Manor Road
South Hinksey
☎ 739369
Reached by car off the ring road or on foot across the Devil's Backbone from Hinksey Park. Garden, small play area. Family-friendly pub with good food served until 9.00pm but be warned, there's often no food available on Sundays.

*The Isis Tavern
Riverside,
Iffley Lock
☎ 247006
On towpath between Donnington Bridge and Iffley Lock. Garden with swings. Boats and ducks to watch. NB very close to water's edge.

*The Perch
Binsey
☎ 728891
Delightful country pub but in the heart of the city, adjacent to Port Meadow and the Thames. Reached via Binsey Lane off Botley Road or by foot across Port Meadow. There is a fine garden (where the first public reading of Alice in Wonderland was heard) extending down to the river, with a play area and giant chess set. The lamb's quite tasty too!

*Plasterer's Arms
9 Marston Road
☎ 247114
Enclosed grassy garden at rear directly accessibly through gate beside pub. Standard pub food, often special offers mid-week, big bowls of chips. Spacious clean loos accessible from garden.

*The Plough
Wolvercote
Non-smoking room decorated as a library for families to eat in. Reasonably good, reasonably priced middle-of-the-road food. No garden, but an outside area to sit in that backs onto the grassy common. Very near (within sight of) a play area with swings and slides and the railway and canal (not near enough for the children to fall in).

*Port Mahon
82 St Clements
☎ 202067
No special facilities for children, loos not good for nappy changing, but landlady loves little ones and makes them wel-

Eating out

come. (NPN has its pub nights in the function room here.) Large enclosed area at rear with wooden decking. Home-cooked food includes West Indian dishes.

*The Prince of Wales
Church Way
Iffley Village
☎ 778543
Pub in the heart of picturesque Iffley Village, not far from Iffley Lock and a beautiful Norman church. Food served lunchtime and evenings, every day. Patios to side and rear. Excellent pub to cycle/walk to although car-parking is available.

*Somerset House
241 Marston Road
☎ 243687
Enclosed garden at rear with climbing frame, often has bouncy castle during summer. Loos very small, not good for changing nappies!

*The Trout
Godstow Road
Wolvercote
☎ 302071
Beautiful location right by bridge and river. Garden with peacocks, rabbits and weir to watch. Good nearby walks around Godstow Nunnery and along the river. Many people have reported that the pub itself, however, is not very child friendly, so you may prefer to enjoy a quick drink in the gardens, and eat elsewhere!

*Victoria Arms (NS)
Mill Lane
Marston
☎ 241382
One mile north of University Parks along towpath. Big garden with climbing frame, which leads to the Cherwell. Children also welcome inside. Family room. You can punt to this pub from the Cherwell Boat House, Bardwell Road. Accessible by bike – a good cycle path runs between Marston and Summertown. Large car park so you can drive through the pretty village of Old Marston

Outside the Ring Road

*Bat and Ball Inn
Cuddesdon
☎ 874379
Crammed with cricketing memorabilia.

*Bishop Blaize Inn
Burdrop, Sibford Gower (off B4035)
☎ 01295 780323
www.bishopblaize.co.uk
All facilities (including nappy changing in disabled loo) in this oakbeamed inglenooked 17th century inn, children welcome, home-cooked food, utterly fabulous views from the garden (which has a couple of swings) – a very good reason for a pleasant drive out in the country!

*Boat Inn**
Thrup
Just north of Kidlington. Large enclosed garden with play area. Excellent nappy changing facilities in disabled loo. High

Eating out

chairs, children's portions and separate children's menu. Parking. Great for canalside walks past pretty narrow boats, to bridge that you can pull up with a rope!

*Clifden Arms**
☎ 01844 339273
Clifden Road, Worminghall (on the road from Stanton St John to Long Crendon) This place is a real find! Huge enclosed garden with large grassy area for ball games, swings, climbing frames, large wooden train and giant boot slide, also Aunt Sally. Superb adult food with nice sauces, fresh fish and vegetarian dishes, also children's menu. Also does amazing value mid-week specials, varying from time to time, eg curry nights or two-for-price-of-one meals – phone for details. Beautiful old thatched pub with plenty of tables for eating al fresco, and friendly service. Highly recommended.

*Crown**
Lower Basildon
☎ 01491 671262/671262
just by entrance to Beale Park – a great end to a family day out
Everything a family pub should be and have – large garden with grass, trees, play equipment, picnic tables, stunning views over glorious countryside, great food for adults and children, baby change in the disabled loos, lots of high chairs, even some toys. In summer evenings you can even eavesdrop on the open air concerts at the National Trust's Basildon House across the road!

*Deddington Arms
☎ 01869 338364
Pub has nice restaurant with helpful staff, high chairs, welcoming to families with children.

*The Ferryman Inn (NS)
Bablock Hythe
☎ 880028.
Try the approach by ferry.

*George Inn
5 Sandford Road, Littlemore
☎ 779341
Large grassy garden at rear with play equipment. Standard pub food includes nuggets and chips style children's menu.

*The Golden Cross
Wycombe Road,
Saunderton (this side of West Wycombe)
☎ 01494 565974
Voted Best Family Pub in the Wycombe District in the 2002 Village Pub competition. Separate dining area; high chairs; garden with play equipment; suits of armour in the loos! Very convenient for before/after visiting the Hell-fire caves or the Home of Rest for Horses (See Ch. 12 – Days Out).

*The King's Arms (NS)
Church Road
Sandford-on-Thames
☎ 777095
Two miles south of Donnington Bridge along towpath. Outdoor children's play area. Next to pretty Sandford Lock.

129

Eating out

*Maybush Inn
Newbridge
☎ 300624
Opposite the Rose Revived with garden by river.

*The Nut Tree Inn
Murcott, Nr Kidlington
☎ 331253
Charming pub, lovely garden and duck pond. Excellent food. Children welcome.

*Olde Leatherne Bottle
Lewknor, just off M40, J6
☎ 01844 351482
400 year old country inn, quick & easy to find in village just off motorway, with excellent food, non-smoking family room and large (unfenced) garden with plenty of play equipment in good order. Very convenient en route home from London!

*Plough
Garsington
☎ 361370
Large grassy garden with good wooden obstacle course and metal helicopter climbing frame, lots of wooden picnic tables, great views across the fields to Oxford. Simple food served lunchtimes only (no evening meals), plus Sunday roast. Spacious clean carpeted loos. Children welcome outdoors or until 7.00 pm indoors (but rooms are small and smoky). In the summer, you might even hear the famous Garsington outdoor opera wafting across the fields!

*Plough Inn (NS)
Long Wittenham
☎ 407738
Long garden down to the Thames, with hills good for rolling down.

*The Plough
Sutton Courtenay
☎ 01235 848801

*Red Lion
Cassington Road, Yarnton
☎ 373556
Has a garden with swings and two or three wooden climbing frames.

*Red Lion Hotel
Long Compton, near Chipping Norton
☎ 01608 684221
Friendly village inn in beautiful countryside, on A3400 to Stratford, close to Rollright Stones. Plenty of parking, large garden with playground equipment, eat indoors or out, good quality bar food lunchtime and evening seven days a week.

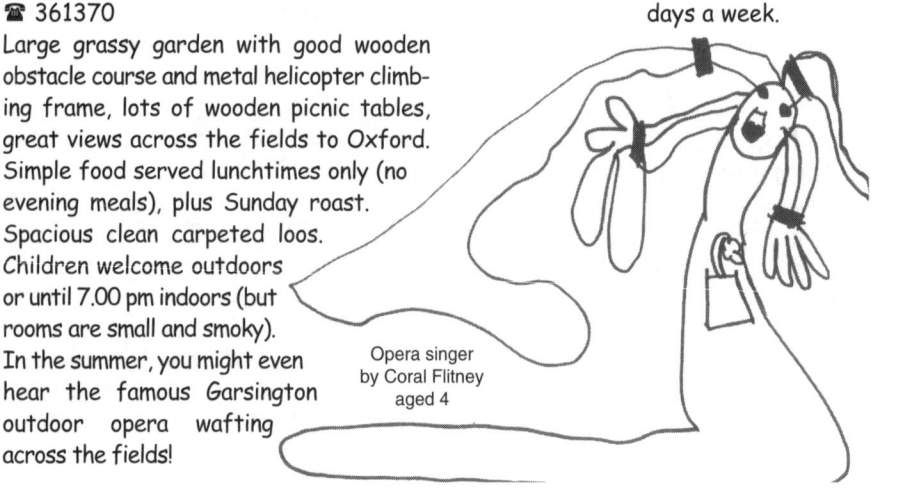

Opera singer by Coral Flitney aged 4

Eating out

*Rose Revived Inn (NS)
Newbridge
☎ 300221
Kids' menu. Superb riverside location.

*Seven Stars
Marsh Baldon
☎ 343255
Family room. Very welcoming to children. Large pleasant grassy garden, friendly staff, good choice of food.

*The Star Inn (NS)
Stanton St-John
☎ 351277
Kids' menu. Children allowed in back room and garden with play equipment.

*Swan
Sutton Courtenay
☎ 01235 847446
Large enclosed grassy garden, swings, playhouse, toy cars. Non-smoking dining area, high chairs, nappy change in ladies. No food Sunday eves. NB Sutton Courtenay has several pubs with gardens.

*The Three Horseshoes (NS)
Garsington
☎ 361395

*The White Hart (NS)
Fyfield
☎ 390585
Medieval inn, sheltered garden/play area.

Picnic places

Picnics are a great way to eat out with the family. Here are some picnic site suggestions.

*Angel and Greyhound Meadow
Strip of sward by the river running from Magdalen Bridge behind St Clements. Access from St Clements car park. Loos in car park.

*Botanical Gardens
Near Magdalen Bridge off the High. Good loos.

*Christ Church Meadow
An easy pushchair walk from the centre of town. Access through large gates on St Aldates. Picnic by the river; nice walk past boathouses.

*Hinksey Parks
Playground and boats, ducks!

*Shotover Park
Headington
Sandpit. Access at the top Old Road. Plenty of parking. Woods.

*South Parks
Fabulous views of Oxford from the top of the hill. Playground.

*University Parks
Try walking from Ferry Road, Marston. Otherwise access from Parks Road. Ducks, river, bridge and weir.

*Wolvercote
Godstow Road
Lower Wolvercote
Grassy spot by shallow area of river used as bathing place in summer. Barbecue equipment for public use.

Chapter 11 - Out and About in Oxford

Fed up with being cooped up with the children – want to know where to take them? Run out of ideas?
In this chapter we look at a range of places to go and activities to do with young children within the ring road. You may be looking for something just to while away a couple of hours or you might want something to fill up a whole day. Hopefully, whatever your interest, you'll find something in the following pages. For more information on days out further afield, see: *Ch. 12 - Days Out.*

PARKS AND PLAYGROUNDS

Always a winner, and free! There are over 100 play areas in the city, ranging from the smaller enclosed safe spaces for children to run around, to the much bigger parks with lots of activities and well-equipped playgrounds. The City Council has been slowly improving play areas and if you encounter any damaged or vandalised equipment, or have any worries about the safety of your playground, please ring the **Parks Office** ☎ 467267 and let them know. The following is a list of the main playgrounds and parks in the city, but do investigate locally as there are several small nature reserves, such as Rock Edge in Headington, and other areas of green to be explored as well.

Out and about in Oxford

Parks

*Angel and Greyhound Meadow
Access from St Clements car park, Alan Bullock Close and Bath Street. Grassed area with pleasant walks next to the river Cherwell. Great for picnics. Small, enclosed play area. Nearest loos in St Clements car park.

*Botley Road Recreation Ground
Access from Botley Road (just by Osney Bridge, beside the community centre) or Henry Road. Large grassy area with playground, including large paddling pool. Close to town centre. A refreshing break from shopping on a hot day! No loos.

*Trees
by Hebe York
aged 4*

*Bury Knowle
Access from London Road in Headington or from North Place just off the High Street. Small car park at North Place (free) or at Somerfield's supermarket (pay and display). Large area of grass with big trees, good for conkers! Tennis courts and crazy golf at one end with ice-cream and drinks for sale in the summer. Large enclosed play area with equipment for young and older children. Safe and interesting. Unisex cubicle loos on London Road. Headington Library in the park at North Place.

*Cutteslowe Park
Access from Harbord Road, off Banbury Road or Elsfield Way (Northern By-pass); car park at both points.
Lots of space in which to let off steam. Rabbits and caged birds, duck pond, enclosed paddling pool, putting green. Tennis, bowls, football and cricket to watch. Miniature steam train rides Easter-Oct, Sun 2.00-5.30 (4.30 in Oct). Large, enclosed, interesting and safe play area. Ice cream for sale in the summer. Loos near the birds.

*Florence Park
Access from Florence Park Road, Rymers Lane, Cornwallis Road, and paths running from Boundary Brook Road, Henley Avenue and Oxford (Cowley) Road.

Formally laid-out park with lots of long straight paths, great for exploring and learning to ride a bike! Easy for

Out and about in Oxford

buggies. Bowls, tennis courts, table-tennis and crazy golf. Enclosed, safe, imaginative play area with some recently updated equipment. Loos by the bowling green. Ice-cream and drinks for sale in the summer.

*Headington Hill Park
Access from Headington Hill or Marston Road. Loos next to Headington Hill entrance. Lovely trees, grass and a paved path all the way round. Tree trunks to climb. Long straight paths good for cycling.

*Hinksey Park
Access from Abingdon Road, Lake Street and Marlborough Road. Car park at Abingdon Road entrance. Oxford's Blackpool in summer with lovely open-air swimming pool complete with fountains and a gently sloping edge perfect for little ones. (See: Ch. 15 - *Activities for Kids*). There is also a children's boating pond and a paddling pool but this is scheduled for conversion to a water feature, and an enclosed, safe children's playground with interesting and fun equipment. Loos next to playground. Another large lake has remote controlled yachts on Sunday mornings. Good for train spotting; a bridge goes over the lake and then the railway line. If you want a good walk follow the path (the 'Devil's Backbone') over the field to South Hinksey. Lots more signposted walks in fields around the village. Path comes out next to The General Elliot pub which has a small play area.

*Mesopotamia
Access from University Parks, Kings Mill Lane off Marston Road (opposite new Brookes University site), or cycle path from Marston. NB No cycling in park.

Paved wooded path between two rivers. Easy for pushchairs. Weir by mill. Ducks, geese, moorhens, coots, swans. Horses at the end of Ferry Road.

*South Park
Access from the bottom of Morrell Avenue, Warneford Lane, Cheney Lane and Headington Hill.

Open hilly grassland with clumps of trees (good for kites and toboggans). Great views of Oxford's spires. Picnic tables under the trees and a safe, enclosed play area by Warneford Lane entrance with some excellent equipment. The grassland area gets quite muddy and boggy when it's wet so not good for buggies. No loos.

*University Parks
Access from Parks Road, South Parks Road or Norham Gardens. This makes a good end to a walk from Marston. Follow the paths at the end of Edgeway Road or off Cherwell Drive, next to where the bicycle track starts.

Pleasant park next to the River Cherwell. Tennis and cricket to watch. Good toddler stop when shopping in town or after visiting the University Museum. Loos in the centre of the park. Restrictions include no cycling. Easy for buggies.

Out and about in Oxford

College grounds

Most colleges are open to visitors in the afternoons. Opening times are displayed at the gates of each college. Entrance is often free. Some colleges are closed to visitors in the summer.

*Christchurch Meadows
Access through Christ Church at the bottom of St Aldates, through Merton Walk (opposite Magpie Lane) or from Rose Lane next to the Botanic Garden. Beware though, because you can only get through the gates at Merton Walk and Rose Lane by collapsing your buggy! Pleasant round walk around the meadows by the Thames. Small farm.

*Magdalen College
High Street (next to Magdalen Bridge) Open afternoons until dusk.
Through the cloisters to the deer park. Turn right over the bridge for a pretty walk next to the two branches of the River Cherwell. Cows, mill and rare spring flowers. No dogs allowed.
NB **Punting** from wharf by the college and Magdalen Bridge.

*University Botanic Garden
Entrance from High Street, opposite Magdalen College.
☎ 286690
Daily 9.00–4.30 (last entry)
Late opening Thurs to 7.30.
Glasshouses open daily 2.00–4.00.
Admission free in winter but 1 April– 30 Sept £2.50, unless you are university staff or student (Oxford or Brookes or OUP). You can buy a season ticket for £5.00. Children under 12 free.

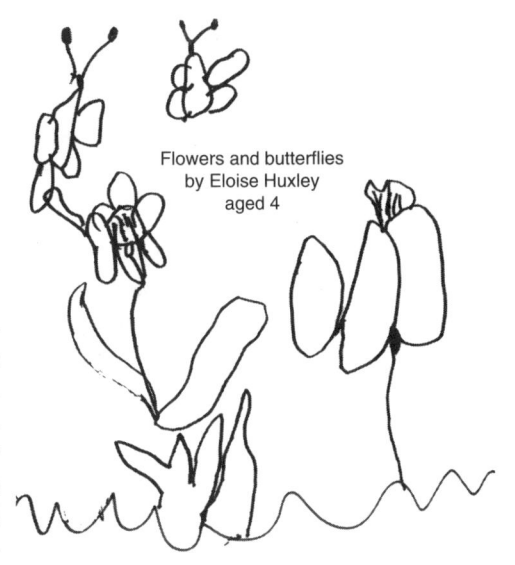

Not strictly a college, but part of the University and a great place for summer picnics or winter visits to the lovely warm hothouses to see jungly plants, lemon and banana trees and cacti.

Paths round the garden are easy for buggies and a good short walk for toddlers or reluctant walkers! Ducks on the Cherwell which runs alongside the gardens. Just outside the entrance there is a small hedged maze-style rose garden, great for small children.

*Worcester College
Bottom of Beaumont Street.
Steps from quad lead into attractive gardens with lake and huge trees. An oasis of calm in the centre of town.

Flowers and butterflies
by Eloise Huxley
aged 4

Out and about in Oxford

Countryside sites

There are nearly thirty countryside sites in Oxford. The **City Council Countryside Service** looks after them so that we can all enjoy the wildlife and natural spaces right on our doorstep. It also runs numerous events throughout the year suitable for young families, such as working woodland days, fossil hunts, dusk walks, mini-beast safaris and holiday fun days. Look out for their free maps and leaflets or contact them on ☎ 715830.

*C.S. Lewis Nature Reserve
Lewis Close, off Kiln Lane, Risinghurst. A hidden world where C. S. Lewis and J.R.R. Tolkien dreamt up Narnia and Middlearth. Exciting walkways take you past a massive pond and up through the woods. Not feasible for pushchairs.

*Happy Valley
Wyevale Garden Centre, sliproad off the Southern Bypass.
A smallish nature reserve with an interesting round walk, just long enough for most 3-5 year olds. Babies are better carried than in a buggy. Start at the beginning of Chilswell Path, on the sliproad to the garden centre, up a steep hill, left into a reed marsh (look out for lizards and lots of wild flowers) and carry on through wooded valley to end of wood. Carry on up Boar's Hill for a longer walk, or turn right up to a great picnic spot. Or finish off with tea at the coffee shop in the garden centre.

*Iffley Lock and Iffley Church
Reached via towpath from Donnington Bridge or from Mill Lane, Iffley.
Busy lock (spring-autumn), a great place to watch boats and feed ducks. The *Isis* pub with garden, open all day, is nearby. Cross the lock and weir, follow lane and turn right for the romanesque church. Lots of animal sculpture, stained glass and pleasant churchyard. Community-run shop in the village and a kiosk at the lock sells ice creams, teas etc.

*Iffley Meadow and Long Bridges
A nice walk, starting from the lock and along the towpath. Turn left just after the *Isis* pub, go through the gate and walk across Iffley Meadows, managed by BBONT as a traditional meadow (cows sometimes in the field). Rare snakeshead fritillary flowers in spring.

Walk back to the towpath, turn left along the bank and beyond Donnington Bridge until you come to Long Bridges Nature Park. Good for blackberries, watching boats and feeding ducks.

*Port Meadow
Numerous access points but the best known are from Walton Well Road, Aristotle Lane and Godstow Road.

Vast, flat, rural common by the River Thames. Horses, cattle, geese, ducks and boats. Watch the bats in the evening! For a longer walk follow road from *The Perch* to Binsey church where the mysterious St Margaret's Well can be found in the churchyard. Or take the towpath from *The Perch*, past the ruins

Out and about in Oxford

of Godstow Nunnery to *The Trout* on the other side of the river near Wolvercote. Good for buggies in summer, more difficult when wet. Old bathing place, Godstow Road, worth a visit in itself. Shallows under bridge, good for sailing boats. Picnic tables, public barbecue equipment and ice cream for sale in summer.

*Raleigh Park
Access from Westminster Way, Raleigh Park Road and Harcourt Hill, Botley. Rough, grassy hillside with some woodland and a pond – great for pond-dipping. No good for buggies.

*Rock Edge
Access from Old Road, Headington Quarry, just past Windmill Road. Old quarry good for fossil hunting! 160 million years ago Oxford was covered by a warm, shallow sea, so look out for coral, shellfish and sea urchins; but please don't dig out the rock face.

*Shotover Country Park
Numerous pedestrian points of access but only one car park at Shotover Plain at the very end of Old Road. Woodland with signposted walks, some possible with a buggy. Trail leaflets available from the **Countryside Service**. who also organise (mostly free) events such as *Give a Bird a Home*, *Bluebells of Brasenose*, *Where's the Water* (divining and dowsing), *Tell Tales* (local storyteller) bats and treasure hunts.

The main attraction for children is a natural sandpit with a small stream on the lower slopes of Shotover Hill, near the trail marked by red posts. Great for family picnics; you can rest while they build dams and get filthy. But be warned, the sand can stain, so go in old clothes, and don't forget your bucket and spade!

MUSEUMS

*Ashmolean Museum
Beaumont Street
☎ 278000
education.service@ashmus.ox.ac.uk
www.ashmole.ox.ac.uk
Tues–Sat 10.00–5.00, Sun 2.00–5.00
Free, although donations welcome.
Egyptian mummies, Viking relics and beautiful paintings. Drop-in activity sessions for children 5–11 and parents one Saturday each month ☎ 278015. Shop with some children's goods. Pleasant café downstairs via lift, but not cheap, and food not very small-child friendly.

*Curioxity
Old Fire Station (2nd floor)
40 George Street
☎ 247004
Open weekends, half-term and school holidays 10.00–4.00. Adult £2.50, Child 3+ £2.20
A hands-on science and technology gallery aimed at 3–13 year olds. New maths puzzle corner. Good fun. Allow only about an hour for a visit as it's

137

Out and about in Oxford

quite small.
On second floor of Fire Station.
No lift.

Modern Art Oxford (formerly MOMA)
Pembroke Street
☎ 722733 or 813830
www.modernartoxford.org.uk
Tues-Sat 10.00-5.00, Sun 12.00-5.00
Free entry.
Children's activities and workshops, also mostly free. Child-friendly café.
See: Ch. 10 Eating Out and Ch 13 Holiday Times.

Museum of Oxford
St Aldates
☎ 252761
museum@oxford.gov.uk
www.oxford.gov.uk/museum
www.aliceinoxford.net
Tue-Fri 10.00-4.30
Sat 10.00-5.00, Sun 12.00-4.00.
Adult £2.00, Child 5-16 50p, U5s free.
NB Access up several stone steps so difficult for buggies and wheelchairs.

Exhibits 'tell the story of Oxford' and range from a mammoth's tooth to a working Morris car engine (push the button!).

Six Oxford displays show various rooms through time e.g., a Victorian kitchen, and an Elizabethan Inn. Wonderful 'Guess the smell' game. Plenty of room for buggies but lots of stairs and no lift. Some displays well above child eye-level. Also included

'Alice in Wonderland' exhibition.

No toilets inside, nearest ones just outside in Blue Boar Street. Shop, audio tour, and regular temporary exhibitions, some child-orientated. Join 'Kids' Club' (free) to receive events listings. Phone for details.

Pitt-Rivers Museum
Entrance through University Museum.
On three floors.
☎ 270927
www.prm.ox.ac.uk
Mon-Sat 12.00-4.30, Sun 2.00-4.30
Free, although donations welcome.
Aladdin's cave of treasure and curios, including

Out and about in Oxford

Inuit suits, a totem pole, a huge range of masks and a gruesome collection of shrunken heads! Activities for families on the first Saturday of each month, phone for details.

*Oxford University Museum of Natural History
Parks Road
www.oum.ox.ac.uk
☎ 272950
Open daily 12.00–5.00 (but days and times vary at Christmas and Easter) Stepped entrance but also disabled access. Free, donations welcome. Great to spend an afternoon in this wonderful building, its stone and glass roof arching over the dinosaur skeletons like a giant ribcage. The *T. rex* is a cast, but all the dinosaur bones in the cases were found locally. Play stepping stones on the life-size casts of local 170-million-year-old Megalosaurus footprints on the front lawn. Skeletons, fossils and stuffed animals, including a reconstruction of a dodo. Children's activities every Sunday 2.00–4.00. Small shop has books, dinosaur kits, fossils, puzzles etc. Baby change in disabled loo. Watch out for the temporary BBC Wildlife Photographer of the Year exhibition – the big prints are great for children. Check for dates as it varies each year.

TOWERS

If you think your children would like a bird's-eye view of Oxford, and you won't have a heart attack worrying about them falling over the edge, try the following. Hold on tight!

*Carfax Tower
Carfax
☎ 790522
NB No children under 7 years.
Daily 10.00–5.30 (Apr–Oct)
10.00–3.30 (Nov–Mar) except Dec 25th–1st Jan.
Adult £1.40, child (7-15) 70p

*St Michael at the Northgate
Cornmarket
☎ 240940
Daily 10.00–5.00 Apr–Oct
10.00–4.00 Nov–March
Adults £1.50, children 80p
Café open alternate Saturdays 11.00–1.00
High wall at top, restricted view for little ones.

Out and about in Oxford

*University Church of St Mary the Virgin
High Street
☎ 279111
Daily 9.00–5.00 (July-Aug 9.00–7.00)
Adult £1.60, child (5+) 80p. U5s free.
Spiral staircase is difficult, especially if you've got more than one child to hold on to. Best on a weekday out of the tourist season. Best of the three for little ones. Gaps in balustrade all covered with thick metal mesh – excellent views, and safe.

OXFORD'S OTHER ATTRACTIONS

*The Goldfish Bowl
Magdalen Road
East Oxford
Aquarium supplier. Just great! Children love it. Large and varied collection of tropical and coldwater fish. No pressure on you to buy but please make sure your children are well supervised.

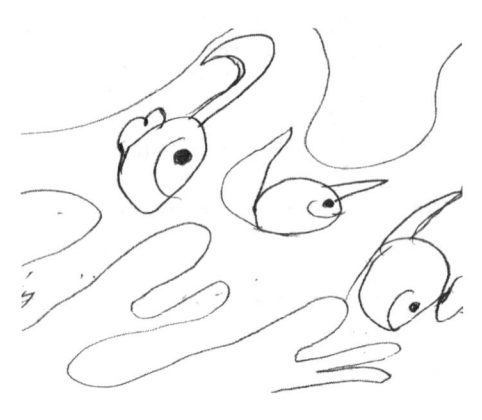

The Goldfish Bowl by Coral Flitney, aged 4

*The Oxford Story
6 Broad Street
☎ 728822
www.oxfordstory.co.uk
Mon–Fri 10.00–4.30. Sun 11.00–4.30 (Sept to June)
Daily 9.30–5.00 (July–Aug))
Adult £6.75, child (4-16) £5.25,
U4s free.
Sight, smell and sound journey through the history of Oxford. Not all that suitable for under-5s, but they might enjoy the exciting ride if you were taking older brothers and sisters. Children's commentary available. Loos.

*Lung Wah Choung Chinese Supermarket
41-2 Hythe Bridge Street
☎ 790703
Daily 10.00–7.00.
Lots of interesting food and sweets to smell, look at (and buy!), cooking implements. Good for kitting out a playhouse with plastic bowls and chopsticks.

Bus Tours

Some children might enjoy zooming around Oxford looking at the sights on an open-top bus. You can choose to be fully guided or hear a taped commentary. Catch bus outside Queen's College on the High Street or from the starting point (see below) or anywhere along the route. Tickets are valid all day and you can get on and off at stops all round Oxford.

Out and about in Oxford

***Guide Friday – City Sightseeing Tour**
☎ 790522
First bus leaves the railway station at 9.30 and then about every 15-20 minutes, (more frequent in the summer) last bus varies with season, phone to check. Whole tour lasts about an hour. Adult £9.00, child (5+) £3.00, U5s free.

Walking Tours

You will find many guides advertising their tours on Broad Street or High Street. Children don't always enjoy being herded but Lord of the Rings fans might like the Tolkien Tour (currently Weds 11.45) organised by Blackwells ☎ 333606. They also organise Civil War Tours email oxford@blackwell.co.uk. At time of press they are starting 1.5 hour Children's Writers Tours, Fri 2.00 focused on writers old and new from Lewis Carroll through Kenneth Grahame and Shirley Hughes to Philip Pullman. Adult £6.50, child (4+) £3.50. U4s free. Phone in advance or turn up 15 minutes early.

River Trips

*Salter's Steamers
Folly Bridge (bottom of St Aldates)
☎ 243421
www.salterssteamers.co.uk
info@salterssteamers.co.uk
Regular daily Thames cruises May-Sept from Folly Bridge to Iffley or Abingdon. Iffley trip: leaves every hour from 11.00 until 5.00; 40 minute round trip. Adult £4.70, child (5+) £2.50, U5s free Abingdon trip, Leaves at 9.15 and 2.30, 2 hours each way. Return: Adult £12.00, child (5+) £7.20, U5s free (or get a single and return by bus).

*Boat hire
Boats and punts can be hired from Magdalen Bridge, Folly Bridge and the Cherwell Boathouse (Bardwell Road).

DIARY OF REGULAR EVENTS

This is by no means an exhaustive list. There is always something to do in Oxford. Check the free papers for what's on. See also Ch 13 – *Holiday Times* for schedule of annual **Fun in the Parks**. There are also **Film in the Parks** (free showings of family features) between June and August and **Pomp in the Parks** (silver and brass bands). For general information on Oxford City events ☎ 467259 (Events Officer), ☎ 0800 052 1455 freephone. Email events@oxford.co.uk.

Feb-May

*Lambing
Many farms open their lambing sheds to the public at this time of year (e.g. Hill Farm ☎ 407792 in Little Wittenham, Farmer Gow's near Cumnor, also Cogges Museum has lambing weekends). Check the local press for details.

*Eggstravaganza
Egg-rolling and painted egg competitions at Shotover on Easter Monday.

Out and about in Oxford

*University boat races
Torpids (February or March) and Eights (5th week of University summer term, usually the last week in May when each boat has to bump the one in front). The races take place over several days in the afternoons, and start at Donnington Bridge.

● ● ● ● ● ● ● ● ● ● ● ● ● ● ● ● ● ● ● ●
Tip: Watch out for the pushbikes when the gun goes off!
● ● ● ● ● ● ● ● ● ● ● ● ● ● ● ● ● ● ● ●

March

*Science Week
Normally about the second week in March. ☎ 247004 for local Family Science programme of events.

*Oxford Literary Festival
The range of children's events (over 2s) includes poetry and rhyme readings, stories and picnics with established children's authors. Book through the Oxford Playhouse ☎ 305305 www.oxfordplayhouse.com

*International Women's Day
☎ Ann Mobbs 553755
ann@amobbs.freeserve.co.uk
www.oxfordwomen.co.uk
Celebration usually covers the first two weeks of March. Most events exclusively for women but generally family friendly.

May

*May Day
If you can bear to wake them that early, you might like try to get to Magdalen Bridge at 6.00 a.m. on May 1st to hear the Magdalen choristers sing from the top of the college tower to welcome in the summer. You can then wander the streets listening to live music and watching Morris men dance. Many pubs and cafés open for breakfast but you may have to book. It's an experience! NB The authorities have been closing or restricting access to the bridge in recent years because of fears of collapse and to stop people jumping into the river, so if you want to end up on the town side of the bridge, check in advance or don't approach from The Plain.

*May fly
The first of the series of Fun in the Parks events; see *Ch. 13 Holiday Times*.

*Lord Mayor's Parade
Watch the parade of floats leave the town centre and make its way to South Park, where the usual funfair and entertainments can be found.

*Artweeks
See local press for dates. Free guide for listings available in art and bookshops and libraries. Hundreds of exhibitions in homes, galleries, schools, artists' studios and buildings not normally open to the public all over the Oxford area. Some are more suitable

Out and about in Oxford

for children than others, such as allotment art at Elder Stubbs, off Rymers Lane, children's art workshops by local illustrator, Korky Paul, and an amazing multimedia tent in South Park.

*****The Oxford Balloon Fiesta**
Fun fair and hot air balloons in all shapes and sizes (giant strawberries and licorice allsorts men) tethered in Cutteslowe or South Park over a couple of days. Definitely worth trying to see them launch/land at dawn and dusk. Details from www.oxford.gov.uk

June/July/August

*****Sheriffe of Oxford's Races**
Horse races on Port Meadow. There is also a small dog show, a few stalls, a beer tent, and on-course betting!

*****Oxford Canal Festival**
See *Chapter 13 Holiday Times* for Fun in the Parks details.

*****Cowley Road Carnival**
Big, colourful, lively multicultural community event. Carnival procession followed by varied programme of activities. Two stages, in Manzil Way Gardens, with music and dancing, children's activities, etc. Dress: bright, wild, wacky, anything goes!

*****Elder Stubbs Allotment Festival**
Large annual community event held in partnership with and in aid of local mental health charity, RESTORE. Incredible how many stalls, events and activities they can cram in between the plots of onions, marrow, sweetcorn and marigolds. Access is from Rymers Lane, through a marvellous area of imaginative wicker sculptures. You'll find music, crafts, children's games, activities and competitions, poetry, art, sculpture, dancing, animal rides, hot and cold food – and, of course, lots of vegetables, fruit and flowers! One of the best, and least expensive, family days out in Oxford. Look out for posters, or ask at Restore in Manzil Way.

Horse riding at Elder Stubbs by Coral Flitney aged 4

Watch out for City Council children's events throughout the summer holidays. Contact **Recreation** ☎ 252826 for the free booklet *Play for All* which gives you all the details you need. You can also get updated information from Oxfordshire Children's Information Service, ☎ 01993 886933, www.oxoncis.org.uk

September

*****St Giles' Fair**
The whole of St Giles from Broad Street up to the branching of Banbury and Woodstock Roads, is transformed into a world of candy floss, helter-skelters, hot dogs and dodgems for two

Out and about in Oxford

days (the first Monday and Tuesday after the first Sunday in September). Fabulous views from the top of the Big Wheel! Great fun, but hold on to small hands and purses tightly!

October/November

*Round Table Fireworks Display
South Park
Usually on the last weekend in October, before Bonfire Night. If your children like fireworks this is well worth a visit. The fireworks are superb and there's always a huge bonfire, live music and food stalls.

*Wolfson College Fireworks
Usually the Saturday after the Round Table display. Beautiful setting: fireworks are reflected in the lake. Funds collected for charity.

*Mushroom Hunt
Shotover
☎ 715830
Annual mushrooming event. Expert on hand to identify the edible ones! Ends with a big fry-up.

Christmas tree
by Eloise Huxley
aged 4

December

*Father Christmas
Can be found in his grotto at Allders, also Yarnton Nurseries and Wellplace zoo (take warm footwear for the queue), or aboard a steam train on the steaming days at the **Didcot** or **Buckinghamshire Railway Centres**.
See: *Ch. 12 - Days Out* and check local papers for other Santa events and appearances.

*Children's church services
A lot of churches do crib services especially for children. The town centre services at the University Church and St Michael at the North Gate, where the whole church is lit by candlelight, are recommended. Also, look out for Christingle, nativity and carol services.

*Quarry (Morris) Men
On Boxing Day morning this Morris team performs its traditional Christmas mummers play in front of the pubs in Headington Quarry moving from pub to pub and ending up at the Mason's Arms. It's great fun, if a little rowdy. Phone the pubs for timings (The Chequers Inn ☎ 762543, The Six Bells ☎ 308573, The Mason's Arms ☎ 764579).

Chapter 12 - Days Out

Farmyard Visits. Outings.

Feel like a day out? Listed below are some tried and tested outings you can enjoy with your children. Some places are fairly near to Oxford, others are further afield; some are free, some you have to pay for, but all provide a day's entertainment for young children.

OTHER SOURCES OF INFORMATION

Let's Go with the Children for Berks, Bucks and Oxon is an excellent publication produced annually and costing around £3.50 www.cubepublications.co.uk ☎ 01425 279001, proceeds go to Great Ormond Street Hospital Children's Charity.

Another good annual publication is the *National Gardens Scheme Book*, about £5.00 for the UK and 45p for the Oxfordshire booklet. These are available in the spring in garden centres and book shops and list all the private gardens that are open through the summer, usually on Sundays. If you read the descriptions of the gardens carefully, you can often spot if they are suitable for children. They usually sell tea and cakes as well. All the gardens are opened for charity.

NB prices were correct at time of research, but are likely to increase. Most venues do offer concessions and family tickets so please phone them for current charges.

Days out

OUTSIDE AREAS

If the weather is fine, get out and about to one of these great locations. Take some food with you; it's surprising how far a child will walk with the promise of a treat at the end.

*Abbey Meadow
Abingdon
Free. Great in summer, through a lovely park with old ruins and pretty flowers. On the banks of the River Thames with swans and boats to watch. A large, fenced-off, dog-free area with water activity features, play ground and outdoor swimming pool.

*Blenheim Palace
Woodstock
Entrances on A34 and in Woodstock.
☎ 01993 811325
administrator@blenheimpalace.com
www.blenheimpalace.com
Park open daily 9.00–4.45 (except Christmas day)
Cost: £7.50 per car including access to the park, herb gardens, butterfly house, adventure playground, pleasure gardens and the miniature train to reach these attractions. If you use the good bus service to Woodstock, pedestrian entry is £2.50/adult and £1.00 for 5-15s.

The pleasure gardens include lots of intriguing small mazes, a big hedge maze, free pitch and putt, giant chess and draughts and large climbing apparatus with sandpit are open mid-March–end October. November–mid-March only the park is open. Entry charges are reduced to £5.00/car or £1.00/pedestrian (50p per child). Under 5s are free.

Walk round the magnificent grounds to let the kids burn off some energy. But note that no cycling, skating or scooters are permitted. Sheep, ducks, geese, café, excellent ice cream and picnic areas are other attractions.

*Brill Hill
Brill Windmill
Turn right at Boarstall onto the B4011, take the first road left into the village. Oxfordshire's very own Teletubby land! A windmill (sometimes open) and lovely grassy mounds. Good for picnics. Fantastic views over Otmoor. No loos. Pub with garden nearby. Free.

*Broughton Castle
Near Banbury
No charge for the grounds which offer good views of north Oxfordshire.

Broughton Castle
by Leon Quelch
aged 4

146

Days out

*Chiltern Sculpture Trail
Cowlease Wood, north of Christmas Common
Free
M40 to junction 6, left onto the B4009, first right (A40 Stokenchurch), first right again (bridge over M40) wood is on your left after about a mile.
Numerous forest trails which lead to unusual (and sometimes easy to miss!) sculptures. Look out for trees full of fish, tree trunks with legs wearing ankle socks and shoes and big brass bells which ring when bashed with a stick! No toilets. Picnic area with unusually arty tables. Great bluebells in May.

*Cotswold Water Park
South of Cirencester
www.waterpark.org
Network of 132 lakes, including Keynes Country Park. Two children's swimming 'beaches', play equipment, barbecue hire, boat hire, bike hire (including tagalongs, trailers, children's), Wildlife walks, bird hides, wooden sculpture trail.

*Country Lanes
Moreton-in-Marsh
☎ 01608 650065
Bicycle hire company. Also hires out trailers for children, child seats and helmets. A good day out, involving a half-hour train journey to Moreton-in-Marsh. *Country Lanes* office at station.

*Farmoor Reservoir
Cumnor Road
Farmoor
Enter at gate no. 3
Walk around the reservoir, watch the sailing. Dinghy racing Sunday mornings.

*Harcourt Arboretum
Nuneham Courtney
(May–Oct) Daily 10.00–5.00
(Nov–April) Weekdays only 10.00–4.30
Closed Christmas and Easter.
☎ 343501
Free. Parking £2.00/day or £5.00 for a full year's pass. (NB Take £1.00 coins) Park inside the grounds. Paths mostly accessible by buggy. Look out for the peacocks. Carpets of bluebells in May, lots of rhododendrons in June, conkers and acorns in October. Perfect for picnics with crawling babies. No dogs.

*Hell-Fire Caves
West Wycombe
☎ 01494 533739
1 Mar–31 Oct open daily 11.00–5.30
Nov–Feb open weekends and school holidays only. Last admission 5.00.
Cost: Adult £3.75, 3–16s £2.50
Fairly scary caves that seem to go down and down! Includes life-size models which make it even scarier! Not for sensitive children. Surrounding countryside, West Wycombe Hill, is good for picnics and walks (to calm your nerves!)

*Jarn Mound
Boar's Hill
Free
A good Sunday morning outing. Climb the mound to view Oxford and then

147

Days out

explore the nooks and crannies of the 'wild' garden. Lots to stimulate the imagination. No toilets.

*Minster Lovell
Near Witney
Free
Marvellous ruins by the River Windrush, perfect for paddling, picnicking and exploring. Visit the palatial dovecote just across the field.

*Northleigh Roman Villa
Stonesfield/Northleigh
Free
Park in Stonesfield village. About one mile's walk to Roman villa, down a steep hill, across a shallow stream (catch minnows in a jam jar from the footbridge, or have fun wading across—shoes advisable), then across field to villa. Or walk through glorious woodland, or, with a buggy, down a steep rough road. Large mosaic installed in a building with glass wall for viewing.

*Wallingford Castle
Wallingford
Free
Good ruined castle, mostly grassed over. Ramparts, a mound with a path spiralling up and a bridge over the old moat. Good running about and exploring for 4-8 year olds.

*Westonbirt Arboretum
off A433 near Tetbury
☎ 01666 880220
www.westonbirtarboretum.com

westonbirt@forestry.gsi.gov.uk
Open daily 10.00-8.00 (or dusk). Adult £6.00, Child (5-15) £1.00, under 5s free. (Additional £1.50 for adults during summer festival).Worth an hour's drive to see the beautiful blooms in spring and the autumn colours of the National Arboretum. Most magical of all is the illuminations in December with dramatic lighting effects and carols in the woods. Excellent facilities, wheelchair accessible, baby changing, buggy-friendly paths.

*White Horse Hill
Near Uffington
Free
See the White Horse cut out of the chalk. Good for kite-flying and hearing skylarks. Very exposed.

*Wittenham Clumps and Little Wittenham Nature Reserve
Near Dorchester
Take the A423 out of Oxford. Dorchester is on a bus route.
Free
Either park on the southern side of the clumps for quick ascent or in Little Wittenham for quick access to walk.

The Clumps are the highest point in an otherwise very flat part of southern Oxfordshire. They give fantastic views for relatively little climb. Usual hill activities abound; kite-flying, remote-control glider flying and sledging.

The woodland at the side of the hill is lovely to walk in. It includes a bird hide on stilts at the side of a large

Days out

pond, which is well worth finding. Also in Little Wittenham is Days Lock, famous for Pooh Sticks (the national championships are held here on New Year's Day). It is possible to walk to Little Wittenham from Dorchester across the fields, if your buggy can handle it.

ACTIVITY SWIMMING POOLS

*Aqua Vale
Park Street
Aylesbury
☎ 01296 488555
Mon-Fri 9.30 a..m.–10.00 p.m.
Sat/Sun 8.30 am.–10.00 p.m.
Adult: £3.95, Child £2.20
Delightful set of pools for all the family, includes connected indoor and outdoor leisure and swimming pools. Outdoor pool open all year round! Several spa/jacuzzi places indoors and out, a flume, water slides, wild water and large shallow water play area for toddlers. Water and indoor air pleasantly warm. Good family changing with playpens and change tables.

*Coral Reef
Nine Mile Ride
Bracknell, Berkshire
☎ 01344 862525/862484 (24 hour)
www.bracknell-forest.gov.uk/coralreef
Follow the A322 out of Bracknell town centre, cross two roundabouts and at the third, turn right on to Nine Mile Ride (A3095 to Crowthorne) pool and big car park is on the right.
Mon-Fri 10.30-late (7.00 Wed and Fri), slides open from 3.30 term-time, all day during school holidays.
Sat-Sun 9.00-5.45, slides open all day (sessions limited to 2 hours).
Cost: Weekdays term-time 10.30-3.30 Adult/Child (4-15) £3.20. Under 4s free.
Other times: Adult £5.70, Child (4-15) £4.00. Under 4s free.
A long drive (avoid rush hour) but well worth it. A really exciting swimming

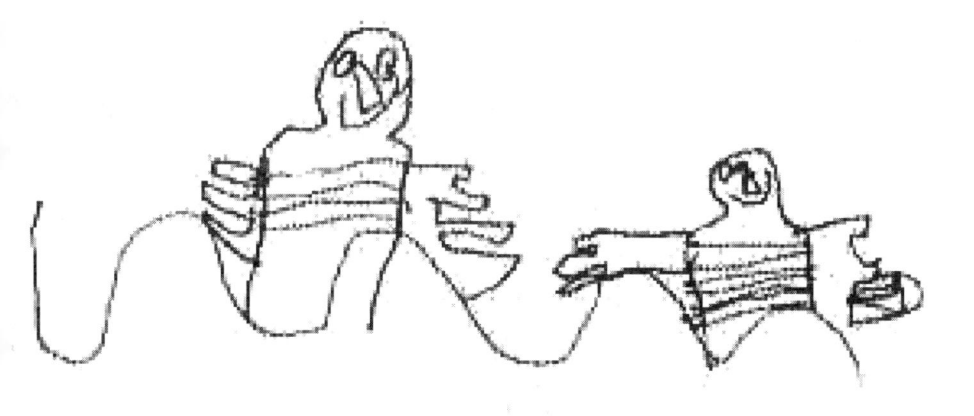

Days out

pool for confident under-5s to child-at-heart adults. Huge pirate ship with 'spouting cannons', slides, currents and waterfalls. No more than two under-8s allowed per adult. Café overlooking the pool. Fabulous value midweek term-time, £3.20 for one adult with two pre-school children, otherwise expensive, but a great day out.

*Didcot Wave Leisure Pool
Newlands Avenue
Didcot
☎ 01235 819888
Signposted from the main shopping street in Didcot.
6.30 am (7.00 a.m. Sat–Sun) – late.
Cost: Adult £3.00, Child (4+) £2.10, under 4s free.
Leisure pool with swimming lanes and wave machine, underwater geysers and bubbles, a shallow beach area and big slide (for competent swimmers only). Phone for session times.

*Windsor Leisure Centre
Clewer Mead, Stovell Road
Windsor
☎ 01753 850004
www.rbwm.gov.uk
Sat 10.00–7.00, Sun 9.00–600
Weekdays 10.00–6.00 school holidays
Term time weekdays from 12.00–6.15 (closing time varies, phone for details)
Cost: Adult £3.50 Child (5+), £2.35, under 5s free.
Absolutely the perfect first activity pool for babies, toddlers and young children. Enormous light airy glass dome with doors opening directly out to grassy area and playground in summer. Good acoustics - quiet. Huge, extremely shallow (a few inches) beach area for crawling, splashing and enjoying waves. Two flumes: babies and toddlers can ride on parents' laps. Little slides, water cannon, water umbrella, 'wild water'. And two superb hot jacuzzis to warm them up if need be. Also has a 6-lane, 25m pool with movable floor, plenty of space to sit beside the pool, free hairdryers, good changing facilities, café. Quick drive from Oxford. Easy to find.

*Wood Green Leisure Centre
Banbury
☎ 01295 262742
Mon–Fri 11.00–6.00
Sat, Sun 10.00–6.00
Cost: Adult £2.75, Child (5+) £1.75, under 5s free.
Superb, open air Olympic-sized swimming pool. Flume. Toys and inflatables allowed in the shallow end. Diving board at deep end. Toddler paddling pool. Grassy lawn and picnic tables. Good changing facilities, large lockers, plenty of free parking. Everything we ought to have at Hinksey! Worth the 50 minute drive.

INDOOR ACTIVITY/SOFT PLAY

For the energetic child it can be difficult to get enough runaround time when the weather is bad. Try some of the following.

Days out

*Activity World
Beech Road
High Wycombe
☎ 01494 464410
www.activityworld.co.uk
Daily 9.30-6.00.
Cost: Adult free, Child (5-12) £4.30, Child (0-5) £3.50. Height limit, 5 feet. Difficult to find – take your mobile phone to check directions! – but well worth it. Enormous warehouse crammed with loads of things to climb, pedal, slide, ride and swing on and jump into, for kids of all ages. Separate toddler area in view of café (burger & fries type food).

*Chunky Monkeys
Berrick Salome
☎ Kerry 891982 or Louise 400425
Mon 9.30-3.30, Fri 9.30-12.00
Cost: Adult free, Child £3, sibling £1.50.
Bouncy castle, slides, ball pit, baby area, ride-on toys, parents' coffee area, in village hall. Also, birthday parties (see Chapter 14 Parties and Treats).

*Crazy Colosseum
Kidlington & Gosford Sports Centre
Kidlington
☎ 376368
Mon-Fri 11.00-5.00
Sat, Sun 10.00-12.00 (0-5 yrs), 1.00-4.00 (0-8 yrs)
Cost: Adult free, Child (5-10) £2.80, Child (0-4) £2.30
Small floor space, but filled to high ceiling: three floors, ball pit, ball cannon. Roman theme. Not much room for parents. Café elsewhere in the centre.

*Fundays
Bourton on the Water
☎ 01451 822999
www.fundaysplaybarn.com
Daily 10.00-6.00
Cost: Adult £1, Child (4-11) £4/£4.50, Child (1-4) £3/£4.20, Child (under 1) £1, U1 free weekdays term time or if with older child.
Big light airy space for older children, dominated by several enormous bump and drop slides. Lots to climb. Lovely toddler area, with ball pit, warm air stream to levitate balls, playhouse style layout with rooms and stairs and windows, visible from pleasant café. Website has puzzles and games. Two-tier price structure for weekdays/weekends and holidays.

TIP: Dress children in long sleeves and leggings or trousers, to avoid friction burns

*Funtasia
9-15 Warwick Road
Banbury
☎ 01295 250866
www.funtasia.uk.com
Tues-Fri 3.00-6.00
Sat, Sun, holidays 10.00-6.00
Cost: Adult free, Child (4-12) £3.75, Child (0-4) £2.75, pre-walking free.
Huge warehouse, two enormous bouncy castles (one with climbing wall), two

Days out

floor Indian tunnel house with large deep ball pit, several sizes of drop slide, some space-rocket-style interconnecting climbing frames, ride on toys, large separate enclosed toddler area, all in view of café.

*Kinderkids
Witney
☎ 01993 700125
www.kindergarten.co.uk
info@kindergarten/uk.co.uk
Mon-Sat 2.00-6.00 (9.30-1.30 as crèche)
Sun 11.00-6.00
Cost: Adult free, Child (9 months +) £2.50 for 1 hour, £3.25 for 90 minutes, more if using crèche facility.
A pleasant, well maintained soft play space with some ride on toys, for younger children only. Operates as a crèche in the mornings. Very safety conscious - no hot drinks allowed in the building.

*Moonbase
Wycombe Sports Centre, Marlow Hill
High Wycombe
☎ 01494 688105
www.wll.co.uk
Daily 10.00-5.00
Cost: Adult free, Child (5-8) £3.50, Child (2-5) £2.50, Child (0-2) £1.35, pre-walking: free
Compact, great atmosphere (lots of bright colours and lunar space artwork), well maintained, very thoroughly padded, three levels of soft play, small area for 0-2s. Space for parents to sit,

cheap hot drinks, friendly helpful staff. Quick to reach, easy to find: head towards High Wycombe from the M40 and it's the first turn on the right after the roundabout.

TIP: A needle in a haystack is nothing to a sock in a ballpit – dress tiny tots in babygrows or tights

*Tumble Towers
Witney
☎ 01993 700789
www.tumbletowers.com
Mon-Sat 9.00-6.00
Sun 10.00-6.00
Cost: Adult free, Child (4+) £3.25, Child (1-4) £2 weekdays before 12.00 including squash and biscuits, £2.25 after 12.00 and at weekends, under 1 free.
Soft play area makes maximal use of a comparatively small space: lots to do. Separate area for tiny tots. Activities in the mornings, as well as the soft play. Nice café with real kids food (cheese on toast, marmite fingers, fresh fruit!). Crayons, paper, stencils etc always freely available by tables. Conveniently situated at end of car park by main street and shopping centre; easily accessible from Oxford by bus.

*Snakes and Ladders (previously Wiggy's World)
Abingdon
☎ 01235 522227
Daily 10.00-6.00 (last admission 5.00-5.30)

152

Days out

Cost: Child (over 5) £5.00, child (under 5) £4.00, child (under 2) £3.00.
£1.00 reduction per child after 4.30.
Height restriction 4ft 8in.
Huge warehouse with compartments for different activities.
Battery operated motorbikes.
Coffee shop overlooking play area. Prices vary for mornings, afternoons, weekends, holidays.

*Xscape – Indoor Skiing
Milton Keynes
☎ 01908 230260
Daily 9.00–11.00, peak rates apply 5.00–11.00 and weekends
Cost: for one hour's ski tuition for parent and toddler (3–5 years), peak or off-peak: £25.00.
Going skiing abroad? Prepare for the real slopes here and make the most of your holiday abroad! Recreational skiing, tobogganing, snowbiking also available.

ANIMALS AND PLANTS

In this section we look at places where you can see and/or touch animals or Pick Your Own fruit and vegetables.
Also, look in local papers for **agricultural shows**. Thame Show ☎ 01844 212737 and Otmoor Show are held in the late summer/early autumn.

*Birdland Park Ltd
Rissington Road
Bourton-on-the-Water
☎ 01451 820480

April–Oct 10.00–6.00 (last entry 5.00)
Nov–March 10.00–4.00 (last entry 3.00)
Cost: Adults £4.75. Child (4–14) £2.65, under 4s free.
Open all year apart from Christmas Day.
Seven acres of parkland, gardens, lakes and waterways.

*Bucks Goat Centre
Old Risborough Road
Stoke Mandeville, Bucks
☎ 01296 612983
10.00–5.00 daily
Cost: Adult £3.50, Child (2–15) £2.50, under 2s free.
A bit rough and ready but good on a wet day as it has shelter. It includes a toddlers playroom and a full-size trampoline. As well as lots of goats there are also hens, ducks, llamas, owls, reptiles, wallabies. Shop, café, picnic area and loos with baby change.

*Beale Park
Beside the A329 to Reading at Upper Basildon.

Chicken
by Georgia Saldanha
aged 4

Days out

☎ 01189 845 172
1 Mar-31 Oct daily 10.00-6.00
Nov-Feb daily 10-5.00
Adult £5.50, Child (3-15) £4.00,
U3s free.
Lots of exotic birds, a pets' corner, rare breeds of farm animals. Take your swimming togs and buckets and spades as there are paddling pools and a giant sandpit. Plus a small steam train, model boat museum, extensive and marvellous adventure and ro-play playgrounds and café. Good loos and baby change. NB Take cash/chequebook – the park does not take credit or debit cards.

*Cogges Manor Farm Museum
Nine miles west of Oxford on A40, Witney exit.
☎ 01993 772602
www.semuseums.org.uk/cogges
There is a regular bus service from Oxford to Witney with a bus-stop near the Farm Museum.
Open April-Dec, closed Dec-Mar.
Tues-Fri and Bank Holiday Mondays 10.30-5.30
Sat and Sun 12.00-5.30
Cost: Adult £4.40, child (3-16) £2.30, U3s free.
Working Victorian farm museum with lots of traditional farm animals to see and daily demonstrations e.g. hand milking, baking, lacemaking. Lots of room to run about. Children's activities in farmhouse. Good programme of special events and activities throughout the summer. Picnic area and café, loos with baby change.

*Cotswold Farm Park
Guiting Power
Stow-on-the-Wold
☎ 01451 850307
Open March-mid Sept 10.30-5.00 daily
Mid-September-end Oct, weekends 10.30-4.00
Cost: Adult £4.80, child (3-16) £3.30, U3s free.
Rare breeds of farm animals in beautiful undulating Cotswold countryside. Perfect for picnics. Excellent hands-on activities for children. Especially good in the spring/early summer for lambing and chicks hatching. Bottle feeding lambs, shearing, milking. Adventure playground to suit all ages of children, from babyswings to flying fox. Battery-powered and pedal tractors. Audio tour for adults on history of farm animals through the ages. Loos, baby change, café, shop with really good toys. Allow a whole day.

*Cotswold Wildlife Park
Beside the A361 just outside Burford.
☎ 01993 823006
www.cotswoldwildlifepark.co.uk
Daily from 10.00-4.30 (last admission)
Cost: Adult £7.50, child (3-16) £5.00, U3s free.
Lots of 'wild' animals in spacious parkland and landscaped gardens. Farm animal corner, railway, superb adventure playground, café and picnic area. So much to see and do, you need at least a full day. At £115, the family season ticket will give very good value.

Days out

*Farmer Gow's Activity Farm
Eaton Road, Appleton
☎ 863472
enquiries@farmergows.co.uk
www.farmergows.co.uk
Wed–Sun 10.00–5.00. Also open Mon/Tues during Spring lambing, half-terms and holidays, and in December (for Xmas trees). Closed Christmas to mid-March.
Cost: Adult £4.00, child (3–16) £3.35, U3s free.
Glorious place in showers and shine. Lots of activities both outdoors and under-cover, Lambs, sheep, goats, free-range piglets in idyllic woodland. Pedal/ride-on milk tankers, tractors; hay-bales with tunnels, mountain bikes, sandpit, picnic area, loo and baby change. All rubbish to be taken home.

Elephants
by Georgia Saldanha
aged 4

*Home of Rest for Horses
Princes Risborough
☎ 01494 488464
Daily 2.00–4.00
Free
Bring a bag of carrots (NO apples please!) and feed these retired horses, ponies and donkeys. Each has its own story. Excellent small museum brings word 'horsepower' to life.

*Living Rainforest
Hampstead Norreys
Berkshire
3 miles northeast of A34/M4 junction.
☎ 01635 202444
Daily 10.00–5.00
Cost: Adult £4.95, Child (5–14) £3.25, Child (3–4) £1.95, U3s free.
Big greenhouses full of jungle plants with paths, ponds, bridges and a few animals e.g. monkeys and poisonous frogs. A good wet-weather outing. Café and shop, including plants for sale. Children's activities at weekends and holidays. Baby change in disabled loos.

*Millets Pick-Your-Own Farm
At Frilford on the A415, east of Kingston Bagpuize.
☎ 01865 392200
www.milletsfarmcentre.com
Free
A good place to visit all year round. As well as pick-your-own vegetables, up-market gourmet farm shop with bakery and frozen food and a garden centre, there are rabbits, pigs, goats, sheep, guinea-pigs and other animals.

155

Days out

Children can play in the sandpit and in the playground, while you watch them from the terrace of the coffee shop. Remember their buckets and spades. In July to September, come and try out the Maize Maze—quite a challenge! Also go-karts, swingboats, squirters, small train, bouncy castle, etc. in summer holidays.

*Oak Farm Rare Breeds Park
Aylesbury off A41
☎ 01296 415709
www.pebblesculpt.co.uk/oakfarm
Open Easter–Oct, daily 10.00–5.00 (weather permitting, phone to check). Cost: Adult £3.00, child (18mts+) £2.00
Lots of different types of animals, some of which you can feed and handle. Picnic areas inside and out. Modest play areas. Baby change.

*Odds Farm Park
Wooburn Common
High Wycombe, Junction 2 on M40
☎ 01628 520188
www.oddsfarm.co.uk
April–mid Sept and school holidays: daily 10.00–5.30. Last admission 4.30 (or 5.00–5.30 June–Aug).
Mid Sept–Mar daily 10.00–4.00
Cost: Adult £5.50, child (2+) £4.50, U2s free.
Farm park which has really been designed with children in mind. Particularly good for toddlers/pre-schoolers. Lots of hands-on activities throughout the day: feeding, milking, egg collecting etc. Tractor and trailer rides. Play areas for under and over 5s with logs, hay bales, real made-safe tractors etc to climb on. Café, shop and picnic areas. Loos with low level basins and loos, baby change. Voted the best family attraction in Bucks three years running.

*Rectory Farm Pick-Your-Own
Stanton St-John
☎ 351677
Free
Seasonal fruit and veg. Asparagus in May. Raspberries and strawberries most popular with children. Large sand-pit, bouncy castle, adventure playground and picnic area.

*St Tiggywinkle's
Haddenham
☎ 01844 292292
mail@sttiggywinkles.org.uk
Open daily, 10.00–4.00, weekdays only, Sept–Easter.
Cost: Adult £3.80, Child (5-16) £2,80, U5s free.
Hospital for wildlife (NOT pets), including deer, foxes, swans and, of course, hedgehogs! Also Hedgehog World, a staggeringly comprehensive museum of the hedgehog, from ancient historical to fashion, mythological, military and seafaring aspects.

*Water Fowl Sanctuary and Children's Animal Centre
Wigginton Heath
☎ 01608 730252
Daily (except Christmas day)

Days out

10.00–5.30 or dusk.
Cost: Adult £3.50, Child £2.50.
Between Bloxham and Hook Norton
Follow signs from the A361 or B4035.
A haven for unwanted pets. Children are encouraged to handle and feed them. Also 'Baby Barn' with baby pigs, goats, lambs, etc. Play area with a renovated 'Thomas', baby change in pipeline.

*Waterperry Gardens
See: *Chapter 10 - Eating Out*

*Wellplace Zoo
Ipsden, off A4074 near Wallingford.
☎ 01491 680473
Easter–Sept: Daily 10.00–5.00
Oct–Easter: weekends only.10.00–4.00.
Cost: Adult: £2.50, child (2-14) £1.00,
U 2s free.
Large collection of birds and animals. Great for toddlers, lots to see in a small area, free range guinea pigs on the grass. Rabbits, penguins, ponies, goats, sheep, parrots, monkeys and kookaburras. Many you are allowed to feed. Bags of food available to buy at the entrance. Safe play area for children and plenty of picnic space. Coffee shop. Loos (borrow changing mat from kiosk). Also free brollies to borrow on rainy days. Fabulous Santa and grotto at Xmas.

*Yarnton Nurseries Garden Centre
Sandy Lane
Yarnton
☎ 372124
Open Mon-Sat 9.00–5.30
Sun 10.30–4.30
Usual garden centre facilities plus a Reptile House with snakes, lizards, chameleons as well as spiders. Also a Pet and Aquatic Centre. Oasis coffee house, outdoor loos. Good Christmas grotto.

MUSEUMS AND THEMED PARKS

Transport

If your child prefers things that go 'VROOM' to things that go MOO then try some of the following. Also look out in late September for the **Shillingford Ploughing Competition**. Masses of tractors doing their stuff!

*Banbury Museum and Tooley's Boatyard
Spiceball Park
Banbury
☎ 01295 259855
banburymuseum@cherwell-dc.gov.uk
Mon–Sat 9.30-5.30
Sun, Bank Hol. 13.00–4.30
Free
Modern museum in Castle Quay Shopping Centre. Hands-on activities, events. Overlooks historic boatyard. Watch canal boats being repaired. For boatyard tours ☎ 07817 542208.

*Buckinghamshire Railway Centre
Quainton Road Station
Quainton, Nr Aylesbury
☎ 01296 655720 or 655450 for recorded info.
www.bucksrailcentre.org.uk
Cost: Adult £3.00-7.00, child (5+) £2.00-5.00, U5s free.

Days out

Travel back in time to a Victorian country station. Unlimited free rides on some days. Varied programme of steaming open days, diesel days, special events throughout the year. Phone for timetable. Fascinating collection of locomotives, carriages and wagons. Also miniature railway and Thomas the Tank Engine events. The old Oxford Station has been transported here and preserved in all its sunlit, glass-roofed glory! Exemplary facilities for all. Shop with 'Thomas' merchandise.

*Didcot Railway Centre
Behind British Rail Didcot Parkway Station
☎ 01235 817200
www.didcotrailwaycentre.org.uk
Cost: Adult £4.00-7.00, child (3-15) £2.50-7.00, U3s free.
Every weekend but limited facilities Oct-Apr. Daily 11.00-5.00 (May-Sept). Great for Thomas the Tank Engine fans. Rides on trains (steam on first and last Sunday in the month, more in summer: phone for details). Children can climb into drivers' cabs even on 'static' days. Museum, café and a picnic area. Excellent shop with 'Thomas' merchandise. Special events throughout the summer and Thomas meets Santa Steaming at Christmas. The £24.00 family membership is extraordinarily good value, giving free access to all events throughout the year, except children at the Christmas Special.

*Heritage Motor Centre
Gaydon
Just off M40 J12
☎ 01926 641182
Daily 10.00-5.00
Cost: Adult £8.00, Child (5-16) £6.00, U5s free.
Timeroad of motor transport, from the very first wonderfully ingenious Victorian contraptions to the latest hi-tech models. Lots to see and do, for all the family. Experiment with car design using magnetic Mini body panels, or make a Landrover from cardboard cut-outs. Go-karts (for over 8s) and electric cars (3-7s) weekends and school holidays (extra charge).

*Long Hanborough Bus Museum
Long Hanborough
☎ 01993 883617 (Sundays only)
Sundays 10.30-4.30 all year and bank holidays.

Chitty Chitty Bang Bang
by Leon Quelch
aged 4

Days out

August only: daily 1.30–4.30
Cost: Adult £2.50, child (5+) £1.50, U5s free.
A large collection of old buses and trams some of which children can climb on. Free bus rides first Sunday of each month from April to October. Special events throughout the year. Contact the Museum for details.

*Museum of Berkshire Aviation
Woodley
Reading
☎ 01189 448089
Apr–Oct Sat, Sun, Wed 10.30–5.00
Nov–Mar Sun 12.00–4.00
Cost: Adult £2.50, Child (5+) £1.50, U5s free.
Collection of aircraft and photographs. Children can climb into the cockpit of a Dakota fuselage front-end.

*Railway Outings
Trips on steam trains are frequently run by local enthusiast groups in Cholsey on the **Cholsey and Wallingford Railway** ☎ 01491 835067 and Chinnor, on the **Chinnor and Princes Risborough Railway** ☎ 01844 353535 (M40 J6, then B4009). Phone for opening times and details of special events.

If you want to go further afield to find a heritage railway, you can try the following:

*Great Whipsnade Railway
Whipsnade Wild Animal Park
Dunstable
☎ 01582 872171

*Hollycombe Steam Collection
Iron hill, Hollycombe
nr Liphook, Hants
☎ 01428 724900

*Leighton Buzzard Railway
Pages Park
Leighton Buzzard
☎ 01525 373888

*Mid-Hants Railway
Alton, Alresford
☎ 01962 733810

*Swindon and Cricklade Railway
Blunsdon
☎ 01793 771615 (weekends)

*STEAM
Museum of the Great Western Railway.
Kemble Drive, Swindon
☎ 01793 466646
www.steam-museum.org.uk
Cost: Adult £5.95, child (5-16) £ 3.80, under 5s free.
No rides, but a very hands-on museum: build your own bridge, work the signals, shunt the wagons and drive your own steam train (simulation!).

Models and Theme Parks

All the theme parks listed are roughly an hour's drive from Oxford, and each offers at least a full day's worth of activities. To save time *and* money, take a picnic. To minimise time queueing at the most popular parks, avoid weekends and school holidays if you can. The

Days out

other model museums are closer and could be seen in half a day.

Tip: You can get to lots of places – and add some adventure – by train. For times and fares, call National Rail Enquiries (24hrs) 08457 484950.

*Bekonscott Model Village
Warwick Road
Beaconsfield, Bucks
☎ 01494 672919
Junction 2 on M40.
Daily 10.00–5.00 (Spring half term to Autumn half term)
Cost: Adult £4.80, Child (3+) £3.00, U3s free.
Model village depicting life in the 1930s with gauge 1 model railway. Delight for all the family. Refreshments, shop, picnic areas, playground and elevated walkway. Sit-on railway operates weekends and holidays, 50p extra. Loos, baby change.

*Chessington World of Adventures
M40, M25
☎ 0870 4447777
www.chessington.com
Times and prices vary, phone to check. Formerly Chessington Zoo. A great day out for all the family, from toddler up. More than you can do in a day. Still many zoo animals (gorillas, monkeys, large cats, reptile house). Monorail. Meet Dennis the Menace in Beanoland, ordrive Mr Toad's car through Toytown. Shows, rides, roller coasters and roundabouts.

*Legoland
Windsor
Family theme park two miles from Windsor on B3022 Bracknell to Ascot road. Well signposted from motorways.
☎ 08705 040404 (recorded information)
www.legoland.co.uk
Times vary throughout year. Phone to check.
Charges include all attractions. Activity areas, live shows, rides, Duplo playtown, adventure play area, children's driving school, Miniland, amazing Lego model of Europe, puppet theatres, a train, etc. Lots of places to eat and shops selling Lego, Duplo, etc. A very expensive day out but good fun; one to save for a real treat. Allow a full day to enjoy it.

*Miniature World
High Street
Bourton-on-the-Water
☎ 01451 810121
Cost: Adult £2.95, child (2–12) £2.00, U2s free.
Superb indoor fantasy world of miniature scenes and exhibits, each accurate to the finest detail.

*Paulton's Park
A34, M3, M27 J2
Ower, near Romsey
☎ 02380 814455/814442
www.paultonspark.co.uk
Open daily 10.00–6.00, last admission 4.00. Rides close 5.00.
Cost: Adult £12.50, Child (under 14) £11.50, children under 1 metre, free.
Lovely park set in beautiful (flat) gar-

Days out

dens. Particularly aimed at under 8s rather than older children. Most rides suitable for toddlers and pre-schoolers. Very atmospheric boardwalk through 'prehistoric' garden with life-size model dinosaurs and sound effects. Lots of extra free activities you would expect to pay for elsewhere.

*Pendon Museum of Miniature Landscape and Transport
Right at end of road at Long Wittenham.
☎ 407365
Every weekend 2.00–5.00
Cost: Adult £4.00, child (7-17) £2.00, U6s free.
Scale model of the Vale of the White Horse as it was in the 1930s, with lots of model trains. Great for enthusiasts and older children. Viewing galleries are narrow so no pushchairs are allowed.

*Thorpe Park
M40, M25
☎ 0870 4444466
www.thorpepark.com
Times and prices vary, phone to check.
Great place for hot sunny days. Lots of water and splashy rides. Man-made sandy beach by a large shallow pool with tot-sized flumes and slides. All the fun of the fair, or cross the lake by boat to the farm animals.

Museums & Hands-on Science

*Explore @Bristol
☎ 0845 345 1235
www.at-bristol.org.uk
Daily 10.00–6.00
Hands-on science centre. IMAX theatre and 'Living Rainforest' at same site.

*Lookout Discovery Centre
(opposite Coral Reef Pool)
Nine Mile Ride
Bracknell
☎ 01344 354400
Cost: Adult £4.65, child (4-15) £3.10, U3s free.
Hands-on science and nature museum. Launch a rocket, hot-air balloon, crawl

Days out

through a mole hole. Café, picnic area and adventure playground.

*Roald Dahl Children's Gallery
Bucks County Museum
Church Street, Aylesbury
Daily 10.00–5.00,
Restricted to 3.00–5.00 weekdays in term time.
☎ 01296 331441
www.buckscc.gov.uk/museum
Cost: Adult £3.50, Child (3-16) £2.75, U3s free.
Great fun, especially if you are a *Charlie and the Chocolate Factory* fan. Very popular, often need to book an hour's slot in advance. NB the County Museum next door is free, family friendly and well worth a visit. Plenty of hands-on activities.

London

With the capital only some 50 miles away there is endless scope for days out in London. Here we have listed a handful of museum attractions that are usually guaranteed winners with kids. Remember, holidays and weekends are the busy times for these venues so you might consider going on a quieter weekday if you have children still under school-age.

*London Aquarium
Westminster Bridge Road
Nearest tube stations: Westminster, Waterloo.
☎ 020 7967 8000
www.londonaquarium.co.uk
Daily 10.00–6.00 last admission 5.00
Cost: Adult £8.75, child (3-14) £5.25, U3s free.
Very impressive aquarium. Huge, two-storey tank with many different fish. Includes a beach area where you can stroke a ray!

*Tip: Take the coach to London. It is much cheaper and more frequent than the train. Look out for special deals for children in holiday times.
Tel: 772250 (Oxford Stagecoach)
Tel: 785400 (Oxford Bus Company)*

*Natural History Museum
Cromwell Road
☎ 020 7942 4000
www.nhm.ac.uk
Nearest tube: South Kensington. District and Circle lines from Victoria, Circle line from Paddington, Piccadilly line from Park Royal (Oxford Tube request stop).
Daily 10.00–6.00
Free
Dinosaurs feature strongly with skeletons and life-sized animatronics. Check out the refurbished Earth Galleries complete with earthquake and new gallery for children in basement.

*Victoria and Albert Museum
Brompton Road
☎ 020 7942 2000

www.vam.ac.uk

Days out

Free
Tube: South Kensington (see above)
Museum of decorative arts with a great costume section – probably more suitable for older children. But look out for temporary exhibitions that might be of interest.

* *

Tip: When visiting busy venues dress your child in something distinctive – it can help you spot them in a crowd.

* *

*Science Museum
Exhibition Road
☎ 020 7942 4000
www.nmsi.ac.uk
Daily 10.00–6.00
Free
Nearest tube: South Kensington
(See above)
Lots of hands-on activities. Try *The Garden* (3-6 year olds) and for older kids, *The Launchpad*. Cafés and picnic areas scattered through the museum.

*National Maritime Museum
Greenwich
☎ 020 8858 4422
www.nmm.ac.uk
British Rail to Maze Hill, Greenwich, Docklands Light Railway to Cutty Sark Station, or boat from Westminster Pier. Recently refurbished with lots of new galleries. Always something special for children. In the same area there is also the Royal Observatory, the Queen's House, a great park and the *Cutty Sark* as well as a great market and plenty of eateries. A long trip from Oxford, but lots to do when you get there.

Ship
by Leon Quelch
aged 4

Chapter 13 - Holiday Times

Does your local toddler group close down for the summer? Perhaps your older children are about to break up from school and you haven't a clue as to how you are going to keep them entertained. Do you need to work and your usual term-time arrangements have ended? Or are you on a low income but would like to get away? In this section, we hope to offer you some solutions to all these difficulties, as well as give you lots of ideas on how to keep you and your children happy in the holidays.

PLAY FOR ALL

Remember to look out in early summer for the leaflet produced by the City Council's **Play Development Team** called *Play For All*. This is a great guide to all the activities going on in the summer holidays: ☎ 252179, or the City Council Helpline 249811 for a copy. Information is also available from the Oxfordshire Children's Information Service frequently updated database, ☎ 01993 886933/email enquiries@oxoncis.org.uk.

PLACES TO GO

There are plenty of places in Oxford to simply drop into with children during holiday times. Here are just a few ideas, both outdoor and indoor. See also: *Chapter 15 - Activities for Kids*

Adventure playgrounds

Children are free to come and go as they please and places are on a first come, first served basis. Otherwise, they offer a similar range of activities to playschemes.

*Blackbird Leys Adventure Playground
Cuddesdon Way
Ages 7-16

Holiday times

*South Oxford Adventure Playground
Whitehouse Road
For 5-15s

Family centres

All the family centres stay open in the holidays and most offer special holiday activities for older children as well as those usually available. For more details on family centres, see Ch. 4 - Meeting People.

Swimming & leisure centres

Timetables change during the holidays so that for most of the day the various facilities are open to the general public. Many of the centres offer holiday playschemes and sports activities/coaching for children.

*Temple Cowley Pools ☎ 467110
email: tcpools@oxford.gov.uk
*Ferry Sports Centre ☎ 467060
email: ferrysc@oxford.gov.uk
*Blackbird Leys Pool ☎ 467040
email: bblpool@oxford.gov.uk
All offer intensive swimming courses in the school holidays.

*Kidlington & Gosford Sports Centre
Oxford Road
Kidlington
☎ 376368
Offers weekly courses including swimming, football, fencing and cycling proficiency. These are usually for children aged 8+. Places need to be booked well in advance in person at reception at the sports centre. There is also a new soft play area, the **Crazy Colosseum**, which is popular with younger children.

Fun in the Parks

The City Council Events Team (☎ 467259 email events@oxford.gov.uk) organises lots of events throughout Oxford, including **Fun in the Parks**. Events details are also listed on the City Council website: www.oxford.gov.uk

Fun in the Parks events take place on Saturdays or over weekends between May and September and are opportunities for the whole community to get involved. Admission is mostly free and there is usually music, live entertainment, food and drink, and art and craft stalls. Events include:

*Florence Park Open Day
Horticultural theme with flowers and produce from around the area as well as gardening advice and workshops. Always includes competitions for young gardeners.

*Every Dog Has its Day
Florence Park or Cutteslowe Park
Another annual fun day with classes to enter pets into and an exemption dog show.

*Oxford Canal Festival
Aristotle Lane Recreation Ground
Traditional arts and crafts and the chance to look round and ride on traditional canal boats.

Holiday times

*Festival of Sport
Cutteslowe Park
Football team challenge and other sports to play including tennis, bowls, petanque, crazy golf, pitch & putt.

*Playing football
by Louis Rogers
aged 4*

*May Fly
Usually South Park
Radio roadshow, live stage and dance tent with trade and charity stalls, bouncy castle, entertainers.

*Oxford Balloon Festival
Cutteslowe or South Park
Early morning and evening mass balloon launches, mediaeval combat displays and activities, entertainers, arts & crafts. There is an admission charge for this event.

*West Oxford Fun Day
Botley Park and West Oxford Community Centre
Music, dance and general family entertainment.

*Leys Fair
Blackbird Leys Park
Local entertainers, performers and music plus the fair!

*Jazz in the Parks
South Park
Family day out for listening and dancing to jazz musicians.

Libraries and Museums

Most library branches as well as the **University Museum**, the **Museum of Oxford**, and the **Pitt Rivers Museum** offer story times, activity sessions, quizzes and special exhibitions in the school holidays (including some half-terms). These are free and it is often best to book a place well in advance. Phone them for a timetable of events. See: *Ch. 8 Libraries* and *Chapter 11 Out and About in Oxford* for contact details. Also look out for the **Museum of Oxford**'s tours of Oxford Castle mound.

THINGS TO DO

Arts activities

*Donnington Doorstep
☎ 727721
Free or low-cost art and craft workshops for under- and over-5s in the May half-term and summer holidays. Phone for details or look out for adverts.

Holiday times

*Oxford Playhouse
11-12 Beaumont Street
☎ Rupert Rowbotham 305366
rupert.rowbotham@oxfordplayhouse.com
www.oxfordplayhouse.co.uk
Holiday workshops in school holidays, including some half-terms, for example in puppetry. Three years upwards, but younger children must be accompanied by an adult. There is usually a charge.

*Modern Art Oxford
Pembroke Street
☎ 722733
24-hour infoline 813830
www.modernartoxford.org.uk
Runs workshops for 8-12s in the half-terms and holidays, mostly free, but there may be a charge for materials. Booking in advance necessary for some workshops. Children's art activities in the entrance area every weekend and drop-in family workshops on selected Sunday afternoons. Both free.

*Holiday clay workshops
Potter **Janet Crombie** ☎ 722429 often runs children's holiday workshops.

*Holiday art courses
255 Iffley Road
☎ Joanne Acty – home 250400 or work 794368
Mon-Fri 10.00–3.00 for 7-17s
After School Club for 7-8 year olds on Mondays and Tuesdays, 4.00–6.00
Also Saturday sessions.
£24.00/day, £16.00/session

*Janet Crombie
☎ 722429
Summer one-week art course for 6-16 year-olds. £140.00/week.

Countryside events

The City Council's **Countryside Service**
☎ 715830
email countryside@oxford.gov.uk
sometimes organises children's events in the holidays. They usually have an environmental theme. Under-8s must be accompanied by an adult. *Play For All* gives full details.

Oxford Play Day

Play Day happens every August, often in and around **Blackbird Leys Leisure Centre** ☎ 467020. There are lots of free activities on offer, from music workshops to pond-dipping, arts and crafts to story-telling. Aimed at 5 to 13-year-olds but younger children also welcome if accompanied by an adult.
Playbus - see *Ch 15 – Activities for Kids* for details of Oxfordshire Playbus Association ☎ 256809

Sports activities

The City Council's **Sports Development Team** ☎ 467269 is excellent at organising summer sports activities for children all over the city, although these are mainly aimed at the over-11s.

Holiday times

However, they do usually take *Top Sport* (free multi-sport activity sessions for 7-12s) into various Oxford parks. Check the *Play for All* leaflet

Football

Oxford United runs four-day-long football courses for boys and girls aged 6-13 of all abilities in the school holidays (including half-terms) at various venues in and around Oxford. About £32 per course. Look out for information at your child's school or phone the **Sports Development Team** ☎ 467269

Tennis

☎ **Sports Development** 467269
Weekly tennis coaching for 5-16s in parks across the city, June-Sept. £1.50 per week. Rackets and balls provided.

Playing tennis
by Francesca Burrell
aged 7

General sports activities

*Esporta Health and Rackets Club
St Edward's School
☎ 318300/318318
Call for a holiday course brochure.

Holiday Camps

*Supercamps
☎ 01367 718362
Activity holidays for children aged 4-14. Call for details.

Playschemes

Playschemes can help relieve children's boredom in the holidays and give you a break or a chance to go out to work (although not always for a full day).

A playscheme is a programme of events, activities, and outings organised by a voluntary committee who employ trained staff to work with the children. A fee is charged and children usually stay for the day (some playschemes finish between 3.00 and 4.30 and some operate on a sessional basis).

There are playschemes running all over the city during the summer holidays. Some run for the full six weeks and some run at Easter too. Most are for children aged 5-12, but usually there are one or two which take younger children, such as the **Barton Early Years Playscheme**, **Dovecote Playscheme** and **Chinese Playscheme**.

168

Holiday times

If you want your child to go to a playscheme, get hold of the *Play For All* leaflet which has a helpful map. Alternatively, you can get a printout from the **Oxfordshire Children's Information Service** database which is updated fortnightly ☎ 01993 886933. It is important to register your child early as these are very popular.

Private playschemes

There are also a number of private holiday playschemes in Oxford, often held in private schools such as Radley, Josca's, Headington, Oxford High School and St Edward's. They are generally advertised in the local press, or you can get current details from the Oxfordshire Children's Information Service ☎ 01993 886933. They are expensive (sometimes over £100 a week) but may offer a wider range of activities and longer hours (8.00 until 6.00 in some cases).

*Kangaroo Club Summer Playscheme
3-5s Playgroup
Oxford School
Glanville Road
One week afternoon playscheme for 3-5s. £15.00 for week. Write for details.

Disabled Children

See: *Chapter 15 - Activities for Kids* for details of **Parasol**, a project that integrates children with special needs into activities and playschemes.

Getting away

Bringing up children can sometimes be stressful and lonely, particularly if you are a single parent. A holiday can make all the difference. However, if you don't have very much money or have other difficulties, it may seem impossible. A useful information manual, whether you are a lone parent or not, is produced by the **National Council for One Parent Families** www.ncopf.org.uk ☎ 0800 018 5026. In the holiday section of the manual there is a wealth of suggestions for cheap holidays, tips and information on financial help for families. You can look through the manual at **Donnington Doorstep Family Centre** (See: *Chapter 4 - Meeting People*).

*The Holiday Care Service
Second Floor
Imperial buildings
Victoria Road
Horley
Surrey RH6 7PZ
☎ 01293 774535
Provides support and information for people whose circumstances make having a holiday difficult. Send an sae for free information sheets.

Here are some holiday ideas for getting away from it all with the kids.

Cottages

Hiring a cottage with friends can be a good way of keeping down accommoda-

Holiday times

tion costs on holiday, you can also share the childcare.

Below are just two of the many companies offering this type of accommodation. Prices vary according to the size and location and season.

It is worth trying to rent cottages directly from the owners—try the internet or the classifieds of magazines such as *The Lady*.

*English Country Cottages
☎ 08700 781100
www.english-country-cottages.co.uk/ecc_homepage.html
email: ecc.enquiry@holidaycottages-group.com

*Welcome Holidays Ltd
☎ 01756 799999
www.easycottages.com/index.htm

Camping

Camping can be a cheap and fun option for holidays with kids. Check out the following for an all-inclusive deal.

*Keycamp holidays
☎ 0870 7000 123
fax 0870 7000 733
www.keycamp.com
email bkrequest@keycamp.com
Luxury camping and mobile home self-drive holidays in Europe. 'Supertents' are large, pre-erected and come with well-equipped kitchens, sprung beds and mattresses, electric lights. Cots, high chairs and all-terrain pushchairs are included and most sites provide baby baths and washing machines and dryer, and have free children's clubs for ages 4-12. Some offer toddler clubs and teenage activities too.

If you prefer to take your own equipment and find camping sites yourself, try *www.uk-sites.com* (complete directory of all UK caravan and camping sites) or *www.ukcampsite.co.uk* for information on sites in the UK, Eire, France and Spain.

If you're wondering how to get all that equipment into a small car, you can hire a roof box from the Wantage Motorist Centre Ltd ☎ 01235 765793 from about £2 per day.

Farm holidays

Pig on the farm
by Alexandra Waring Paynter
aged 5

170

Holiday times

Rural locations, bed and breakfast or self-catering accommodation and in some cases, the chance to get involved in life on the farm mean that farm holidays are becoming increasingly popular. Do give a farm holiday a try - kids love being able to collect eggs, feed the animals and drink milk from cows they have met. Farm stays are often much cheaper and more luxurious than much of the B+B or hotel accommodation on offer. Many farms charge only £20.00 per adult per night for 4-star, en-suite room with breakfast.

*Farmstay UK
01271 336141
http://212.134.55.132/farmstayuk/index.html
email info@farmstay.co.uk
Free brochure.
Farmstay UK is a network of over 1000 farms providing bed and breakfast or self catering accommodation throughout the UK. Members are inspected for hygiene and service standards by Farmstay UK and the National Tourist Organisation, and are given star ratings on the same lines as hotels.

Organic holidays

*Organic Holidays
Tranfield House
Tranfield Gardens
Guiseley
Leeds LS20 8PZ
☎ 01943 870791
fax: 01943 871468

http://www.organicplacestostay.com
email: lindamoss@organicholidays.com
Information on accommodation at organic farms and smallholdings plus guesthouses and B & Bs where organic produce is used. There are nearly 400 locations in UK and Eire plus lots in Europe and worldwide (including India, USA, S. Africa and Morocco). Organic certification (Soil Association).

Home exchange holidays

Exchanging is a great way to enjoy a cheap holiday. It gives you a holiday base with all the comforts, space and privacy of home and with no accommodation charges. Register with a home exchange agency and you will receive a directory containing hundreds of 'listings', including house photographs describing the homes and holiday preferences of members seeking a home-swap holiday during the current year. Arrange to swap your home with another member of the register – you stay in their home while they stay in yours.

• •

Tip: Swapping with another family with children of similar ages means you don't have to lug travel cots, highchairs, pushchairs etc as they are already there.

• •

*HomeLink
www.homelink.org.uk
☎ 01344 842 642

Holiday times

Email exchange@homelink.org.uk
The world's largest and oldest home exchange organisation. Based in UK, but members are worldwide.

*Home Base Holidays
☎ 020 8 886 8752
www.homebase-hols.com
email info@homebase-hols.com

*NCT Houseswap Register
Run charitably and raises money for the NCT. Members are mostly UK-based. email Denise Tupman at: thetupmans@yahoo.co.uk for information.

Hotels

You might be lucky and find a hotel that offers proper facilities for families and children. Here are a couple recommended by NPN members, to give you an idea of what is available if money is no object. But check with local Tourist Boards.

• •

Tip: When you book, check what your price includes—children's clubs and activities, room service, cooked breakfasts, baby listening service can be extra!

• • • • • • • • • • • • • • • • • • • •

*Knoll House Hotel
Studland Bay
Dorset BH19 3AH
☎ 01929 450450
Fax: 01929 450423
email: office@knollhouse.co.uk
www.knollhouse.co.uk
Separate dining room for under-8s, playroom, adventure playground and a kitchen with 24-hour access to parents for sterilising baby equipment, making food etc. Evening baby listening service. Cost: Full-board starts at £100 per adult per night, prices for children are on a sliding scale according to age and needs.

*Bedruthan Steps Hotel
Mawgan Porth
Cornwall, TR8 4BU
☎ 01637 860555
Reservations only: 01637 860860
Fax: 01637 860714
email: office@bedruthan.com
www.bedruthan.com
Range of holiday activity clubs for children 0-15 years, art and craft activities, separate dining room for under 7s, baby listening service, adventure playground and assault course, soft play area. Equipment such as off-road pushchairs, sterilisers, baby baths available for hire.
Cost: Half-board only starts at £40 per night/adult in the winter up to £90 in high season. Prices for children are on a sliding scale according to age.

Holiday Parks

*Center Parcs
☎ 08705 200 300
www.centerparcs.com

Holiday times

Short break holidays targeted at the family market with ample provision for babies and children. There are four holiday centres in the UK, situated in a rural 'forest' location. There is an extensive range of indoor and outdoor sports and leisure facilities and each holiday village has a Subtropical Swimming Paradise, beneath a transparent dome which houses water activities including a wave pool, river slides and rides, children's pools, jacuzzis and saunas. Good for those frequent rainy days!

Accommodation is in self-catering villas. There are different themed restaurants on each site plus supermarkets and shops. Baby-sitting service available.

Elveden Forest, Brandon, Suffolk
☎ 01842 894000
Longleat Forest, Warminster, Wiltshire
☎ 01985 848000

Sherwood Forest, Rufford, Newark, Nottinghamshire ☎ 01623 827400
Oasis Whinfell Forest, Temple Sowerby, Penrith, Cumbria. This is the newest of the UK holiday centres.

Center Parcs has a number of other holiday villages in the Netherlands, Belgium, France and Germany.

*Haven Holidays
(sister company British Holidays)
Family breaks in about 40 'holiday parks' across the UK. Accommodation is self-catering, mostly in static caravans, chalets and apartments, situated in complexes with sports and leisure facilities, bars and restaurants. Accommodation and facilities vary with location. Prices include membership of kids' clubs, use of sports facilities and pools plus entertainment. You can book online at:
http://online.haven-holidays.co.uk

Going on holiday
by Francesca Burrell
aged 7

Chapter 14 – Parties and Treats

Want to do something different for a special occasion or child's birthday? Stuck for ideas? Here is a selection of places to go in and around Oxford for party supplies and food and to host children's parties. You can also check out your local library, bookshop, or supermarket for a range of books on the subject. *Kids' Parties*, published by the Australian Women's Weekly Home Library, is particularly good.

CHILDREN'S PARTIES

Party bits and pieces

Supermarkets and newsagents often have a reasonable selection of party stationery, games and gifts; here are some specialist shops in Oxford:

*Baby Borrows
☎ 735695
Ballpool and magic maze for hire. Excellent for under 5s parties.

Parties and treats

*Birthdays
Queen Street
☎ 202455

*Celebrations
Turl Street and Market Street corner
☎ 202608

*Honest Stationery
151 Cowley Road
☎ 242524
Good for presents, invitations, acceptances and party bags.

*Partymania
179 Kingston Road
☎ 513397
Party goods including piñatas – giant hollow, papier maché models that you fill with small treats and sweets, and suspend in the air for children to bash with a stick until the contents spill out.

*Party Plus
188 Cowley Road
☎ 793878

*Party Pieces
FREEPOST RG910
Childs Court Farm
Ashampstead Common, Reading
Berks, RG8 8QT
☎ 01635 201844
Free mail-order catalogue of party goods.

*Party Works
☎ 0870 2402103
Free mail-order catalogue with range of party goods.

Food and birthday cakes

*A Piece of Cake
18 Upper High Street
Thame
☎ 01844 213428
Cake decorations and supplies. Also mail order.

*The Cake Shop
101 Avenue 3
The Covered Market
☎ 248691
Imaginative range of cakes to order plus edible and non-edible decorations to liven up your own cake. Cake tins to hire.

*Cake Expectations
69 Botley Road
☎ 250450
Sell and hire cake-making equipment, tins, icing, food colours and decorations. Bake and decorate birthday cakes.

*Truly Scrumptious
Unit 12
Oxford Business Centre
Osney Lane
☎ 790769
Party food to order and some cakes, including individual party boxes for each child.

Tip: Check Yellow Pages and local papers for caterers and companies hiring out bouncy castles, ball pits, tables and chairs etc.

Parties and treats

Children's Entertainers

Look in the Yellow Pages or the local papers for magicians, clowns and puppet shows who will come to your home.

*Bryan Down Oldtime Entertainment
☎ 873544
www.oxfly.co.uk
Bouncy castles, children's games, children's fairground rides.

*Colonel Custard
☎ 01296 434727
www.colonelcustard.com
Magic, juggling, balloons etc.

*Derek and Christie
☎ 01491 873990/07836 537722
Magic, puppets, games, discos etc.

*Nigel the Clown
☎ 776291
fax: 711633
Ring for prices. Also supplies and operates bouncy castles.

*Magic Martin
☎ 01295 788206
Magic show and games. Rabbits!

*Uncle Wiggy
☎ 01235 522227
Half or whole hour including magic show and Punch and Judy.
Ring for prices.

Places to hire

Can't bear to have a party at home? The following can be booked for a party, some with activities, for a price! Church halls and community centres are often a good choice and some pubs have private rooms for hire.

*Barton Neighbourhood Centre
Underhill Circus
☎ 761987
Hall £35.00 for two hours, plus setting up time. Bouncy castle included.

*Blackbird Leys Leisure Centre
Pegasus Road
☎ 467020
There are two options:
A ballpond party for 6-7s and younger. 1.5 hours with the ballpond, soft shapes and play mats for £34.00, maximum 20. For older children you can choose one hour of supervised play with bouncy castle, football, soft play, basketball and party games, followed by one hour in the Griffin Suite for tea. They can also do the catering (phone for menu and prices). Cost £42.00 plus food.

Parties and treats

*Blackbird Leys Pool
Blackbird Leys Road
☎ 467040
Sat 1.00–2.00, 2.30–3.30, 4.00–5.00
Sun 1.00–2.00. £40.00.
Inflatable crocodile available. You can have your birthday cake in reception or at the poolside. Lifeguards provided. They suggest 20–30 children. Could be combined with adjacent adventure playground which has its own hall.

*Brookes Sport Centre
Harcourt Hill
☎ 253575
One hour in sports hall (football, unihoc, relays, or adventure games for under 5s) followed by half-an-hour in pool (for over 5s) supervised by staff. Room next to pool available for food. Bring your own. £55.00 for hall only or £72.50 with swim. Up to 16 children.

*Chunky Monkeys
Berrick Salome Village hall (or in similar hall)
☎ Kerry 891982 or Louise 400425
Parties by arrangement for up to 30 children, from £30.00 upwards. See *Chapter 12 Days Out*. Bouncy castle, slides, ballpit, ride-on toys, baby area.

*Designaway
Asthall Manor
Asthall (off A40 to Witney)
☎ 01993 824445 Mob: 07714 797366
Mon–Sat 10.00–3.00
£3.00 studio fee.
Children's pottery and painting parties. Painting mugs, bowls, plates, tiles, anything – in the studio, at home, or away. Items painted at home taken for firing and returned.

*Ferry Pool
Marston Ferry Road
☎ 476060
Sports hall available on Saturdays. Pool available Sat 5.15–7.15, Sun 1.00–3.00. Viewing area for tea and games (provided by you). Prices on request.

*Jardine's Club (10-pin bowling)
Friar's Square Shopping Centre
Aylesbury
☎ 01296 415698
Birthday package £6.99 per child, all ages (ramp and gutter bumpers provided for small children). Bring your own cake, but food, balloons etc. provided.

*Kidlington and Gosford Sports Centre
Gosford Hill
☎ 376368
Swimming parties: Sat, Sun. Up to 30 children. Lifeguards provided.
Activity hall parties: Sat, Sun. bouncy castle, climbing frames etc.
Sports parties: Sat, Sun, Basketball, football, multi-sports.
Crazy Colosseum parties, various days. Large 3-tier soft-play area including ball pit, slide.
Phone for prices.

*Laserquest
Gloucester Green
☎ 200233

Parties and treats

Party packages minimum 6 children, age 6+. 2x20 minute games plus drinks and food provided with room.
£10.00 per child.

*McDonald's Restaurant
Headington Roundabout
☎ 744849
Party room to hire, Sat/Sun 12.00-1.30 Monday to Thursday 2.00-3.30. £4.99 per child including meal, party bags, present for the birthday child, and two assistants.

*The Moon Base
High Wycombe Sports Centre
☎ 01494 688105
Small but very well equipped play area with soft play, ball pits, etc. Try combining this with a visit to the Sports Centre Pool and hiring the centre's party room for food. Prices start at £4.50/head depending on age.

*North Oxford Association
☎ Mrs Sears 552295 (9.00-12.30)
Three rooms for hire: Cutteslowe Pavilion at Cutteslowe Park, and at the Ferry Centre, Marston Ferry Road.

*Oxford Ice Rink
Oxpens Road
☎ 467000/467002
£60.00 for up to 12 children (extras pay normal price) to skate for 2 hours. Room provided before, during and after party. Bring own food or order in pizzas etc. Skating 'steward' available for £20.00.

*Oxford Silver Band Hall
Cowley
Opposite Temple Cowley Pool
☎ Jackie 01869 240618
Hall for hire at low hourly rate. Use of playgroup toys. Kitchen facilities, parking.

*Oxsrad Sports and Leisure Centre
Marsh Lane
☎ 741336
www.oxsrad.org.uk
Sports parties: football, basketball, trampolining, multi-activity at various times on Sat and Sun. Phone for details.

*Peers Sports and Arts Centre
Sandy Lane West
Littlemore
☎ 467095
Pool available Sat 2.45-3.30. Max. 20. Fully supervised by two lifeguards. Tyres, rafts, etc. £45.00 including room for birthday tea provided by you. Peers also provides bouncy castle parties Sat 12.30-2.30 and 3.00-5.00 for £58.

Staff supervise, set out other gym equipment and organise games. Tables are set up in hall for birthday tea provided by you.

*St Matthews Church Hall
Marlborough Road
☎ 798587
Meeting rooms and kitchen facilities suitable for children's parties. £12.00 per hour. Toys can be hired.

Parties and treats

*Snozone@Xscape
602 Marlborough Gate
Avebury Boulevard
Central Milton Keynes
☎ 01908 230260
For older children, birthday packages include tobogganing, skiing, snowboarding. Food can be provided.
Also in Xscape building, **Silvertrek**, climbing wall parties for 6yrs +.
☎ 01908 200388.

*Temple Cowley Swimming Pool
Temple Road
Cowley
☎ 467111
Sat/Sun various two-hour sessions including one hour in the pool and one hour in the party room (bring your own food). Age 3-6 in the learner pool, or age 5+ in the main pool with obstacle course. Prices start from £46.00 for 25 children. Phone for package details.

*Tumble Towers
Wesley Walk
High Street
Witney
☎ 01993 700789
www.tumbletowers.com
Big soft-play area with ballpits, climbing tower etc. Birthday packages every day. Two-hour slots. £4.00-5.00 for toddlers, £7.50/ child for older children. Food provided.

*Wheatley Park Sports Centre
☎ 872128
Pre-school age party Sun 1.00-3.00, 90 minutes, soft-play equipment, small bouncy castle, supervised by staff. £50.00. Bring own food. Parties for age 5-8s Sat and Sun, from 12.00, 2.00 and 4.00. One hour in sports hall, 45 minutes to eat.

Bouncy castle, parachute, sports equipment. Specific sports can be organised including roller-skating. £60.00. Bring own food.

*Snakes and Ladders (formerly Wiggy's World)
Audlett Drive
Abingdon
From Oxford take the A34 to Abingdon turn left onto Oxford Road (A4183) for approx two miles, turn left into Radley Road and right into Audlett Drive.
☎ 01235 522227
Play apparatus suitable for all ages from toddlers to age 12 including soft play, climbing frames and race track with go-karts. 90 minutes in play centre plus 30 minutes in party room for hot or cold food. Bring your own cake, but party bags etc otherwise provided. Prices around £8.00 per child, depending on requirements.

Farm Parties

For a party with a difference, the following locations offer activities such as tractor rides, treasure hunts, animal attractions and so on.

Children usually love a visit to the farm, so these can be great alternative party venues.

Parties and treats

*Farmer Gow's Activity Farm
Appleton
☎ 863472
www.farmergows.co.uk
email: enquiries@farmergows.co.uk
Also miniature ride-on tractors, adventure playground. Please call for details of party packages. Food can be provided.

*Sandy Lane Farm
Tiddington
☎ 01844 338503

*Gubbins Farm
Marsh Gibbon
☎ 863817

*Cotswold Farm Park
Bemborough
Near Guiting Power
Gloucs.
☎ 01451 850307
Also offers organised games if required. Food can be provided.

*Odds Farm Park
Wooburn Common
High Wycombe
Bucks
☎ 01628 520188
www.oddsfarm.co.uk

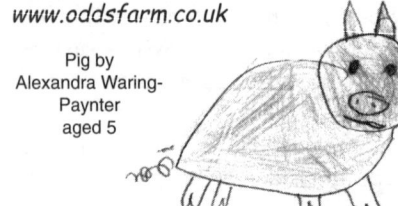

Pig by Alexandra Waring-Paynter aged 5

OTHER TREATS

Theatres, cinemas & concerts

Theatres and cinemas often have children's shows, especially at holiday times. Try the **Hexagon Theatre**, Reading, Chipping Norton's **The Theatre** (famous for its pantomimes), **Aylesbury Civic Centre** and the **Corn Exchange** and **Watermill Theatres**, Newbury. Also look out for City Council sponsored children's theatre in various community centres throughout the year.

*ABC Cinemas
George Street
☎ 723911
Magdalen Street
☎ 725305

*Aylesbury Civic Centre
☎ 01296 585527
Children's day one Saturday each month. Fun from 11.30, including face painting, craft activities, etc and hour-long studio performance at 2.00, usually with puppets, music and mime. Suitable for 3+. Call for dates.

*Music at Oxford
☎ 242865
Box office 08707 500659
www.musicatoxford.com
Some classical concerts suitable for children.

Parties and treats

*New Theatre, Oxford
(Formerly the Apollo)
George Street
☎ 243041
☎ 0870 6063500 (booking)
Ballets and seasonal shows at Christmas.

At the ballet
by Eloise Huxley
Aged 4

*Old Fire Station
George Street
☎ 297170

*Oxford Ice Rink
Oxpens Road
☎ 467002
Usually has a show on ice at Christmas.

*Oxford Playhouse
Beaumont Street
☎ 305305

www.oxfordplayhouse.com
Some shows suitable for 2+, plus Christmas pantomime. Workshops suitable for 6+

*The Phoenix
Walton Street
☎ 512526 after 2.00pm
Saturday 'Kids Club' pre-film activities from 1.15. Film at 2.00. Aimed at 5-11 year olds but some films may be suitable for under-5s. Birthday package of film plus games and party food afterwards in room upstairs.

Ideas for Themed Parties

Themed birthday parties can be fun and memorable occasions, without great expense. For ideas and suggestions, try typing 'children's birthday parties' into an Internet search engine and you'll access an enormous selection of resources. One particularly good site is: www.birthdaypartyideas.com which has a huge list of party themes and ideas emailed in by parents, full of extraordinary tried and tested party suggestions, e.g.: Batman, Barbie, Backwards parties, Cinderella, Christmas Cookie, Indoor Beach and mermaid parties, through to Willie Wonka and Zorro parties, complete with details of how to produce clever invitations, cakes, costumes, games, food etc on these themes. Also consider Piñata parties (see Partymania, above) if you've space, and collaborative treasure hunts with group prizes.

Chapter 15 - Activities for Kids

Activities.... drama, art, music, holiday courses

Would you like to try out an activity with your baby or toddler? There are lots of organised groups for under-5s in the Oxford area and all of them offer a chance to develop basic skills. A trip to the local playground or singing nursery rhymes together will do just as well. But it can be very enjoyable to do something with others. You can both make new friends and your child will learn how to get on with other children. As your child becomes more independent, he or she will often want to go along to a group alone, so you will also find here lots of ideas for the over-5s.

NB This is a very difficult section to compile. Groups' details change continuously, so please bear with us if you find something that's wrong. Do let us know of any changes, corrections or new groups, using the form at the end of the book or email oxfordforunder8s@oxoncis.org.uk

OXFORD CITY COUNCIL

The Council's website *www.oxford.gov.uk* gives details of times and current prices of swimming, sports and leisure activities, or you can ring your nearest leisure centre (numbers below). The Council also runs several schemes relevant to children and recreation. A guide is available to help you find the sport you are interested in

Activities for kids

and show you where to go. These include training for play workers as well as play opportunities for young children such as Playdays, After School Clubs and crèches. For general enquiries on play provision in Oxford, ☎252179 or email jphillips@oxford.gov.uk or write to Joey Phillips, Play Development, Oxford City Council, St Aldates Chambers, Oxford OX1 1DS. Also try Oxfordshire Children's Information Service ☎ 01993 886933 www.oxoncis.org.uk

Oxford Slice Card

This is an easy-to-use passport to sport, leisure and ice activities in Oxford. Pick up an application form at the City Council's Sports Centres. It will save you money if you go twice a week or more. Prices start at £24/month for adults, £12/month for children (3-16) or £48/month for families for an AquaSlice card giving unlimited swimming. People on benefits are entitled to a BonusSlice card giving big discounts on many sports and leisure activities. Ask about reductions on Aquababies and other classes.

Special needs

If your child has special needs don't be put off from participating in the following activities. Although it might be wise to contact the groups beforehand to check on their facilities, most should welcome your child. You could also contact the City Council's **Parasol** project which promotes the inclusion of disabled children and young people into mainstream recreational and social activities. It provides helpers to work alongside children and give support appropriate to their needs to enable them to participate as fully as possible.

For more information please contact **Dan Norey** on ☎ 742816.

OUTDOOR & SPORTS ACTIVITIES

Swimming

Most children find swimming fun and they can start young. Local pools recommend that babies be six months old (this is not compulsory – see *Baby Swimming*, below) and up-to-date with their vaccinations before they start (although the NHS says that there is no need to wait for immunisation before swimming). Remember, babies do get cold quickly, so it is best to keep the session short and choose a warm pool. Learner pools are usually much warmer than the main pool. You can take your baby along by yourself or try one of the special sessions listed below.

Young children, even if they are normally potty or toilet trained, often have 'accidents' in pools due to being wet and excited. Using aquanappies for some time after they are normally 'dry' can save both you and your child from a lot of embarrassment (e.g. from the whole pool being evacuated). The reusable ones available from stores such as Boots, Jenners Pharmacy, Mothercare,

Activities for kids

Toys 'R' Us and Touchwood Sports feel more like swimming trunks than nappies, and are extremely effective!

Tip: Reusable swimming nappies for babies and pre-school children are much cheaper than disposables if you swim often.

Children may get swimming lessons at school but it's good to go swimming regularly with your child (remember under-8s must always be accompanied) or, if you can afford it, send them to swimming lessons. All pools offer lessons to children over 5 and some run courses for under-5s. Crash swimming courses for over-5s are available in school holidays and half-terms. Pools also offer family sessions and fun swims with.

North Oxford

*Ferry Sports Centre
Diamond Place
Summertown
☎ 467060
Warm learner pool with shallow steps at one end. Floats at poolside.
Water Babies and Ducklings:
£3.70 for one adult and one child.
Family fun and toddler splash sessions
Junior lessons: from age 4.5

*Abacus Swim School
☎ 863055
Offers term-time lessons and intensive weeks in school holidays with small groups. Based in North Oxford. Ages 4+
Cost: £96.00 for 12-lesson course.

East Oxford and Cowley

*Temple Cowley Pool
Temple Road
☎ 467110 (times) 467124 (bookings)
Warm learner pool, with shallow steps at one end. Armbands and floats available at poolside.
Aquababies: Instructed classes, for babies 6-18 months. .
Ducklings: Water confidence for the under 5s.
Booking advisable for both as classes are often full
Cost: Both classes £3.50 for one adult and one child.

Blackbird Leys

*Blackbird Leys Pool
Blackbird Leys Road
☎ 467040
Parent and baby/toddler session:
Thurs 12.00-1.00
Cost: £3.50 for one adult and one child.
Lessons for 5 years up also available.

Littlemore

*Peers Sports Centre
Sandy Lane West
☎ 467095
No learner pool, but the water is warm. Armbands available.
Junior lessons (5+): Tue, Wed and Sun only.

Activities for kids

Botley

*Westminster Leisure Centre
Westminster College
Harcourt Hill
☎ 253575
Parent and toddler: Mon 2.30-4.00
Cost: £3.00 for one adult and one child.
Duckling session planned from Easter 2003.

Abingdon

*White Horse Leisure and Tennis Centre
Audlett Drive
☎ 01235 540700
www.whitehorsedc.gov.uk
New pools and sports centre.
Adult and child classes: 4-48 months
Junior lessons: (3+)
Booking required.

Kidlington

*Kidlington and Gosford Sports Centre
Gosford Hill School
☎ 376368 Booking required
Ducklings and Junior lessons (4+).

Playing in the pool
by Eloise Huxley
aged 4

Baby Swimming

Underwater swimming classes for 6-week to 14-month olds at Temple Cowley Pools and Ferry Sports Centre. Each class has a maximum of nine babies and parents.
☎ 771937
www.babyswimming.co.uk
Cost: 10-week course £94.00

Outdoor swimming

Try the outdoor pools at **Abingdon, Banbury**,(See: Chapter 12 -Days Out) **Chipping Norton, Shillingford Bridge, Wallingford** and **Woodstock** which are all very pleasant.

*Wallingford
☎ 01491 835232
Free paddling pool next to main pool. Deep and large enough for inflatable boats with sizeable grass picnic area and helpful kiosk.

185

Activities for kids

*Hinksey Pool
Abingdon Road
☎ 467079
One of the largest outdoor swimming facilities in Europe with heated leisure pool, activity and relaxation areas and a gently sloping 'beach'. Very popular day out. NB No large lockers: only tiny lockers for purse, jewellery etc, don't bring large handbags,valuables.Pool is often closed on hot days due to over-excited children pooing in the water. Please help by using aquanappies for young children. Phone the pool to check before leaving home to avoid disappointment.
Open May–September
£3.80 adults, £2.40 3-17s
Free or reduced with a Slice card.

Gyms

Do you have a pre-school child climbing the walls because he or she needs some exercise? Surviving the British winter with an energetic toddler can be difficult! Gym classes can be a good way to use up energy! They offer an introduction to basic gymnastics and co-ordination. Different classes will use different equipment and all should be led by a qualified teacher. You usually need to stay with your child if under 5.

Kidlington

*Crazy Colosseum
Kidlington and Gosford Sports Centre
Gosford Hill School
☎ 376368
Soft play sessions for 0-4s and 4-8s.
See Ch. 12 – Days Out.

Marston

*Oxsrad Sports and Leisure Centre
Marsh Lane
☎ 741336
www.oxsrad.org.uk
Trampolining, movement and play for any child aged 2-5 with carer. Also offers sensory room and rebound therapy (trampoline) for disabled children. Tue and Fri 10.00-11.00. Cost: £2.00

Headington/Risinghurst

*Energizers
Brookes University
Cheney Lane
☎ 773021/873441
Cost: £3.00
Pre-school gym with qualified gymnastics coaches/PE teachers in a safe, clean, fun, learning environment. Climbing, balancing, bouncy castle, trampoline, ball play, soft play and group activities. No need to book.
Thur 9.30-10.00
Fri 10.00-10.50
Also at Radley College, see below. Plus 'Camp Energy' activity days during Easter and Summer holidays.

*Tumble Tots
United Reformed Church
☎ Donna Dallaway 01235 832305
Thur 9.30 onwards.

Activities for kids

Membership £15.00.
£3.50/session

Blackbird Leys

*Blackbird Leys Leisure Centre
Pegasus Road
☎ 467020
No organised classes but offers table tennis, football and badminton.

Littlemore

*Peers Sports Centre
Sandy Lane West
☎ 467095
Junior gymnastics: 5+
Trampolining: 7+

Radley

*Energizers
Radley School Sports Hall
☎ 773021/873441
18 months–5 years.
Pre-school gym: Tue and Fri 10.00
Cost: £3.00

Botley

*Tumble Tots
St Peter's Church Hall
Elms Parade
☎ Donna Dallaway 01235 832305
Weds from 9.30am
Membership £15.00, £3.50/session.

*Westminster Leisure Centre
Westminster College

Harcourt Hill
☎ 253575
Mum and tots gym: Mon and Fri
No need to book.
Cost: £3.00

Kidlington

*Ministagers
Aviators Health and Fitness Club
☎ 376600
Tues: 9.30–10.30 18 months–2 years.
Toddler gym and games.

Other Sports

We hope to build up this section so please contact us if you know of other courses or groups. If your child is interested in a sport we have not listed, phone **Sports Development** ☎ 0800 052 1455 or the individual Sports Centres (listed under **Leisure Centres** in the phone book) and they may be able to help. Also try Oxfordshire Children's Information Service
☎ 01993 886933 www.oxoncis.org.uk

Football

If your over-5 is football mad, ask around for details of your local children's Football Club; they are often based at recreation grounds. **Oxford United Football Club** runs after school and holiday courses for boys and girls aged 4–11 of all abilities (usually at Temple Cowley Middle School).
Cost: Fees for the 5-session after-

Activities for kids

school courses are about £2.50/session. The four day holiday courses are £8.00/day. Contact the **soccer course directors** for more details ☎ 337525

*Summertown Stars
☎ Martin Castle 368116
Football coaching for beginners age 5+

Tennis

*Community Play Tennis Programme
☎ Sports Development 467269 or 0800 0521455
kraval@oxford.gov.uk
Courses for 5-7s and 8-12s after school in various parks June-Sept. Cost: £1.50. Rackets and balls provided.

*Oxfordshire Active Sports
☎ 252345
Minitennis courses (7+) March to Oct.

*White Horse Leisure and Tennis Centre
Audlett Drive
☎ 01235 540700
www.whitehorse.gov.uk
Minitennis sessions (4-6 years)
Cost: Pay and play £3.00/session.
12-week course £48.00.

Horse Riding

*Oxford Riding School
Watlington Road
Garsington
☎ 361383

Introductory individual lesson, 30 mins. Cost: £24.00.
Group lessons for 5+ years
30 mins £13.00
45 mins £17.00
60 mins £19.00

Horses by Eloise Huxley aged 4

*Old Manor House Riding School
North Hinksey Lane
North Hinksey
☎ 242274
Begin with individual lessons; 30 minutes for £12.00. Progress to group lessons, One hour for £15.00. Includes hat. 6+.

Ice-Skating

*Oxford Ice Rink
Oxpens Road
☎ 467000 (times) 467002 (bookings)
Lessons: £41.00 for 10 weeks (plus entrance fee and skate hire). 3-16

Activities for kids

years. Book in advance, ring for more details. Parents do not accompany children on the ice. No more than 14 children per class with one instructor. Ring the rink for opening times of the various public sessions.
Cost: Adults £4.80 Children £3.20
Skate hire £1/person. (Child size 5 up)

*Oxford Ice Skating Club
☎ Pam Turnbridge 01993 702581
Friendly and civilized club session suitable for all ages including beginners.
Sun 12.15-2.45
Annual membership £85.00 per adult, £56.00 per child, £185.00 per family.

*Oxford City Ice Hockey Club
☎ Keith Tyler 391764
www.oxfordstars.com
Open to children from 6 up. Beginners session Sun 4.30.

Karate

*West Oxford Community Centre
Botley Road
☎ 245761
Mon 8.00-10.00

*Oxford School of Martial Arts
☎ 370339
Classes in many locations. Very popular.

Basketball

*West Oxford Community Centre
☎ 245761
Mon 4.00-6.00

Yoga

*Yoga
☎ Annabel Dunstan 248732 or mobile 07790 216441
annabeldunstan@hotmail.com
Parent and child classes, including fun workout, basic yoga, breathing and relaxation. Call for details.

ARTS AND LANGUAGES

Dance

There is a dance co-ordinator for Oxford who keeps up-to-date lists of all classes. ☎ Clare Thompson 252802. email dance@oxford.gov.uk

Botley

*Celia Benson School of Dance
Botley County Primary School
Elms Road
Wed: 3.30-5.30 (age 3+ ballet)
Fri: 3.30-6.00 (ballet grades 2-5)
and
West Oxford Community Centre
Botley Road
also ☎ Amanda Adler 01235 522270
Fri: 4.00-5.00 (6-8 tap and modern)
See Headington entry for details.

*Under 5s Dance
St Andrew's Church Hall
Orchard Road
☎ Wendy Sharp 436470
Sat 1.30 (4-5s)
Cost £1.00/session

Activities for kids

North Oxford

*Tac au Tac Dance Theatre
SS Philip and James
Leckford Road
☎ Joelle Pappas 251643
Sat 9.30-10.30 (3-5yrs), 10.30-11.30 (5-7yrs), 11.30-1.00 (8+).
Aims to encourage and develop movement and musicality.

*Mary Colegrove Ballet School
322 Woodstock Road
(hall behind Catholic Church)
☎ 511097
Mon 3.00-3.45 (from 3 years)
Sat 9.00-9.45 (4-5yrs); 9.45-10.30 (5-6yrs); 10.30-11.15 (6-7yrs).
Pre-school: basic ballet exercises and imaginative musical exercise with emphasis on movement (skipping, galloping, etc).
School age: Royal Academy dancing syllabus

*Oxford Academy of Dance
☎ Paula 01235 555496
Ballet: Mon, Tue, Thur, Fri after 3.30 Sat mornings.
From 3 and a half years. £17.00 for 6 classes.
Music and movement for under-5s
Classical ballet for over-5s.
Beginner's tap and modern: Wed 3.30

Marston

*Celia Benson School of Dance
Saxon Way Youth Centre
Marston
Mon: 4.30-5.30 (6-8 tap and modern)
See Headington entry for contact details.

*Integrated Dance
Tower Playbase
Maltfield Road
☎ Parasol 742816
Open to all children, with or without disabilities.
Sat 9.15-10.15 Tween Angels (8-12 yrs), 10.15-11.15 Making Traxx Kids (5-12yrs)

*Oxford Dance Centre
Bizzkids Dance Company
Mortimer Hall
Oxford Road
Old Marston
☎ 556382
Various days of the week.
Cost: £3.50 per session. From 5 years. Contemporary free style.

My ballet lesson
by Eloise Huxley
Aged 4

190

Activities for kids

*Vera Legge School of Dancing
Mortimer Hall
Oxford Road
Old Marston
☎ Diana Brown 881173
Drama, singing and dance groups. Occasional productions.
Sat 11.00-1.00 (6-16)
Cost: £8.00 per session

Headington

*Celia Benson School of Dance
69 Staunton Road
☎ 762592
celia.benson@ntlworld.com
Classical ballet taught to the ISTD syllabus for age 3 upwards. Also tap and modern dance.
Classes at:
St Andrews Parish Hall
Dunstan Road
Thurs: 3.30-7.15 (3+ ballet to grade 4)
Risinghurst Community Centre
Kiln Lane
Mon 4.45-5.45 Tap and modern, 6-8yrs.

East Oxford

*Contemporary Creative Dance
Oxford Karate Academy
Glanville Road
☎ Ms K Chandler 776394
Tues 4.00-4.45 (3-8 yrs)
5.00-6.00 (8+yrs)

*East Oxford School of Ballet
St Alban's Church Hall
Charles Street

☎ Penny Cullerne Brown 351752
Several classes for age 3 upwards.

*Fusion
Oxford Community Arts Agency
Behind East Oxford Community Centre
Princes Street
☎245735
Weds: 4.30-5.10 Kids' Dance (3-5)
☎ Monica Crowe 722069

*Jazz Dancing
Pegasus Theatre
Madgalen Road
☎ Beverley Harry 786553 or
Pegasus 792209
Jazzmates Fri 4.00-5.30 (5-11yrs)

*Tac au Tac Dance Theatre
Iffley Church Hall
Church Way
☎ Joelle Pappas 251643
Fri 3.30-4.15 (3-5yrs), 4.15-5.15 (5-7yrs) Aims to encourage and develop movement and musicality.

Cowley

*Celia Benson School of Dance
St Francis' C of E Primary School
Horspath Way
Cowley
Sat: 9.30-12.45 (3+ ballet)
See Headington entry for contact details.

*Oxford Youth Dance
Ark T Centre
Crowell Road

Activities for kids

Temple Cowley
☎ Cecilia Macfarlane 515576
Tues: 3.30–4.15 (under 3s and carers)
Saturday mornings: Various groups (3–9 yrs).
Contemporary and creative dance.

*Irish Dancing
John Bunyon Baptist Church Hall
Crowell Road
☎ Anne Flood-Brennan 776184
Weds: 6.00–10.00 (children and adults)

*Vera Legge School of Dancing
Cowley Community Centre
Barns Road
☎ Diana Brown 881173
Wed 5.00–6.30, Sat 9.45–10.45
General ballet, tap and nursery rhymes.
Cost: £2.50 per session. 3–5s

Rose Hill and Littlemore

*Contemporary/Creative Dance
Kipper Foot Dance Co.
Peers Sports Centre
Sandy Lane West
☎ Angela Stribling 07973 615239
Wed 4.30–5.30 (7+yrs)

*Irish Dancing
Rose Hill Community Centre
The Oval
☎ Anne-Marie Doyle 873719
Wed 5.00–6.00 Beginners

*Jacquie Bebbington's School of Dance
Rose Hill Community Centre
The Oval
☎ Jacquie 772967
Mondays and Thursdays.
From 3 years. £10.00 for 10 lessons. The class starts with nursery rhymes, tap and runs local annual panto performances. Jacquie has cheap clothes, shoes and second-hand kit available once the child is settled in.

South Oxford

*Ballet and European Folk dancing
St Matthew's Church Hall
Marlborough Road
☎ Karen Sellick 248497
From 3+ Pre-school classes Tues, Fri, Sat.
Mon 4.00 dancing games for 3–4s, boys and girls. Leading to ballet starting at 5 years. Call for details.

*Tac au Tac Dance Theatre
South Oxford Community Centre
Lake Street
☎ Joelle Pappas 251643
Thurs 3.15–4.00 (3–5yrs), 4.00–5.00 (5–7yrs), 5.00–6.30 (8+yrs)
Encourages and develops movement and musicality.

Kidlington

*Kidlington and Gosford Sports Centre
☎ 376368
Ballet and tap classes for 2–5 years.
Mon 1.30–2.30 5+ years. Various classes and disciplines, ballet, tap, acrobatic dance, modern tap, drama.

Activities for kids

*Upstage Dance
Edward Field School
Bicester Road
☎ Suzette Watson 07762 058620
Tues 3.00–3.35 (3–5yrs), 3.40–4.10 (5–7yrs)

Chalgrove

*Methodist Church Hall
Chapel Lane
Chalgrove
☎ Jill Saint 01869 350535
Tues: ballet for 3+
Royal Academy of Dance syllabus. Qualified RAD teacher.

Witney

*Debbie's School of Dance and Fitness
☎ 01993 779125
Mon: 5.15–5.45 (Jazz at Eynsham for 3–6yrs)
Tue: 4.00–6.00 (Ballet and tap at Witney for 3–7yrs)

Drama

Oxford

*Kidsplay
Pegasus Youth Theatre
Magdalen Road
☎ Caroline Cooper 792224
Classes: Wed 3.30–4.30 6–9s (term-time only).
Call for details.
Cost: £4.00 per session.

*Pegasus Theatre
☎ 792209
Saturday drama clubs: 2.00 for 5–6s
3.00 for 7–9s

*Sparkle Stage Set
Risinghurst Community Centre
Kiln Lane
☎ 765732
Stage school for children ages 3-18. Sundays. Acting, modern/tap dancing, singing. Students entered for TV, theatre, etc. through own agency.
Cost: £6.00–7.00/session

*Spotlight Stage School
Neighbourhood Centre
Cuddesdon Way
Blackbird Leys
☎ Mrs P. Dickson 717358
Sat, Sun, Wed (Age 4+)

*Stagecoach Theatre Arts School
1. Cherwell School
Marston Ferry Road
2. Headington Junior School
Headington Road
☎ Maya Sprig 01869 278600
Part-time drama school offering classes in singing, dance and drama for 4-16s. No audition necessary. Sessions on Fri, Sat and Sun. Holiday workshops.

*Vera Legge School of Performing Arts
Mortimer Hall
Oxford Road
Old Marston
☎ Diana Brown 881173

Activities for kids

Drama, singing and dance groups. Occasional productions.
Sat 11.00–1.00 (6-16)
Cost: £8.00 per session

Abingdon, Banbury and Burford

*Theatre Express
☎ 01253 868757
perform@theatre-express.com
www.theatre-express.com
Acting singing and dancing. Free prospectus for 5-16 classes. Variety of activities in acting, singing and dance which help to develop self-confidence, self-esteem, articulation, imagination, co-ordination and expression

Music

You do not have to have any musical knowledge to be able to help your child to enjoy music. From the early weeks babies enjoy music, and being sung to helps the development of their social and language skills. If you lack confidence you might find it easier if you join one of the groups listed below. They are fun, you will learn new songs and meet new people. Or why not get together regularly with a group of friends or start up a singing session in your local baby and toddler group? There are now available lots of music cassettes for young children, for example the range of cassettes from the **Early Learning Centre** or the tapes and songbooks from the Oxford University Press bookshop in High Street. Once your child is at school, they should get plenty of music opportunities. As well as music lessons, many first schools have choirs, bands and instrument tuition.

Learning an instrument

Teachers from the **Oxfordshire Music Service** ☎ Liz Stock 798855, also go into first schools and teach various instruments to under-8s. If your child would like to learn an instrument, ask your child's teacher. There may be a waiting list and you do have to pay. The Service also runs after-school and Saturday Music Schools.

If your child wants to learn outside school you have to find a teacher yourself. Ask your child's teacher to recommend someone or look in the Yellow Pages. Some teachers advertise locally in the papers and shop windows.

Choirs

*The Hildegard Junior Choir
St Margaret's Institute
Polstead Road
☎ Lucy Haigh 07958 669396
lvc.haigh@virgin.net
Thu 4.30–6.00; girls aged 6-11. Music includes folk songs and church music. Call for more information and to arrange an audition.

*Palestrina Boys Choir
☎ Lucy Haigh 07958 669396
Weds: 4.00–5.00; boys aged 5+. General music e.g. folk songs and sea shanties.

Activities for kids

*Oxford Youth Choir
Oxford High School
Belbroughton Road
☎ Jane Brown 01993 881061
☎ Camilla Stephenson 01993 883730
www.oxfordgirlschoir.org
Sat: 9.15-10.45 boys and girls 4-8.
From 8 years: Training Choir and Boys' Choir.

*South Oxfordshire Starter Choir
Thomas Reade School
Radley Road
Abingdon
Wed 4.45-5.45 (8-9s)
Variety of material from different cultures and styles. No audition.
☎ Sarah Gunn 01869 248680
Cost: £31.00/term. Free if children are having lessons with the Oxford Music Service.

Under-fives music groups

Headington

*Busy Bees Music Group
Headington Community Centre
Gladstone Road
☎ Rachel Shearer 01235 521039
rachel.shearer@tesco.net
Action songs, rhymes, rhythms, puppets and percussion instruments.
Refreshments before each session.
Tue 11.45-12.15 Under 5s. 11.40 Babies (2 months-walking)
Fri mornings mixed ages. Baby session 10.30.
Cost: £2.00/session. Term-time only.

*Monkey Music
United Reformed Church
Collinwood Road
Risinghurst
☎ Lisa Astley-Sparke 424612
www.monkeymusic.co.uk
For children 6 months-4 years. Also at Thame and Witney. Call for details.

East Oxford

*Fusion
Behind East Oxford Community Centre
Princes Street
☎ Melissa 245859
Thurs 4.00 Kids singing class.

*Humpty Dumpty Music Group
Donnington Community Centre
Townsend Square
☎ Emily Marshall 725516
Fri 10.30 (0-5s).Term-time.
Music and fun for babies, toddlers and pre-school children accompanied by carer.
Cost: £1.50 per session for first child. £2.00 for families with more than one child.
Register early for term.

*St Clements Family Centre
Cross Street
Mon 10.00-10.30
☎ Henrietta 726818

*East Oxford Community Association
Princes Street
☎ 424612
Mon: 10.00-12.15

Activities for kids

North Oxford

*Monkey Music
St Margaret's Institute
Polstead Road
☎ Lisa Astley-Sparke 424612
www.monkeymusic.co.uk
For children 6 months–4 years. Also at Thame and Witney

*Music and Fun for 0–4s
North Oxford Association
North Oxford Community Centre
Diamond Place
☎ 511757

Botley

*Monkey Music
West Oxford Community Centre
Botley Road
☎ 424612
Mon: 1.30–3.45

Kidlington

*Musical Tots
Kidlington Community Centre
☎ 372165
Fri: 9.30 (0–5 years)

*Sing-along Music Group
Kidlington Baptist Church
☎ Helen Temple 371681
Weds 9.45–11.00 (0–5 years)
Sing along music group, all preschool children welcome with carers.
Cost: £2.00 per family.
Refreshments.

*Sing-along Music Group
Yarnton Village Hall
☎ Helen Temple 371681
Thurs 9.45–11.00 (0–5 years)

Cumnor and Kennington

*Busy Bees Music Group
Old School Community Centre
Cumnor Village
☎ Rachel Shearer 01235 521039
rachel.shearer@tesco.net
Action songs, rhymes, rhythms, puppets and percussion instruments.
Refreshments before each session.
Weds: mornings under 5s. Babies (2 months-walking), 11.40, term-time only.

*Jack and Jill Club
1. United Reform Church Hall
Leys Road Cumnor and
2. Community Room
Old School Buildings
The Avenue
Kennington
☎ Isabel Birse 736170
Singing for babies and toddlers
Mon afternoons at Cumnor, Friday mornings at Kennington.

Abingdon

*Abingdon Music Centre
Old Magistrates Court
Abbey Close
☎ 01235 533633 (a.m. only)
www.abingdonmusic.co.uk
Provides a huge range of classes for pre-school and primary children.

Activities for kids

Harwell

*Busy Bees Music Group
Harwell Village Hall
☎ Rachel Shearer 01235 521039
rachel.shearer@tesco.net
Call for details.

Wheatley

*Smiley-Miley Music
Mary Bell's Village Hall
☎ Corinne Miley-Smith 873509
Weds 2.00 (toddler/pre-school)
       3.00 (6 weeks to too wriggly!)
Cost: £2.00/family including tea and coffee.

Henley on Thames

*Little Music Group
The Old Smithey
Northend
☎ Annabel Walsh 01491 638982
Weds and Fri 9.30 for coffee. 10.00 for singing.

Suzuki teachers in Oxford

The **Suzuki** or **Talent Education** method was developed by the Japanese violinist Sinichi Suzuki, who believes that any child can be taught to play a musical instrument well.

Children start very young, from two on the violin and three on the cello, and come for individual and group lessons each week, accompanied by their parents who are expected to practise with them. In the early stages they are taught by listening and imitation. Reading music is taught later. Tuition costs from about £20 an hour (but a lesson for a 3 year old may be only 15 minutes long). Parents who would like to watch a lesson or group are invited to contact any of the teachers listed below. Additionally, Suzuki also covers flute, piano, viola and recorder. Details of teachers can be obtained from the British Suzuki Institute.
☎ Landa Melrose 01582 832424.

*David Ormerod (violin)
146 Kingston Road
Walton Manor
☎ 553503

*Virginia Bennet-Clarke (violin)
3 Beauleigh Court
Sunningwell
☎ 730749

*Annette Costanzi (cello)
☎ 020 7286 8862

*Janet Tinbergen (cello)
26 Fane Road
Old Marston
☎ 725644

Languages

If you are keen for child to learn a second language, there are some nurseries that offer French from 2 or 3 years. You could also try a holiday playscheme (See: *Ch. 13 Holidays*).

Activities for kids

Arabic

***Arabic classes**
☎ Rayhana Khan 240808
Sat 1.30–3.30
For children up to age 8 and their parents.

French

Several games and books of first French for children are available. Try the **Early Learning Centre**.

***Alliance Française d'Oxford**
16 Polstead Road
☎ Caroline Lecointe 310946
French groups for children aged 5-19.

***Le Club Français**
Various groups in Oxfordshire.
☎ Aline Shand 01295 266093
www.leclubfrancais.com
Ages 3–11
French and Spanish instruction for children.

Spanish

***Ruth Garcia**
10 Grangers Place
Witney
☎ 01993 704535
Private tutor offering home lessons to children from 5 years. References available on request.

Alexandra drawing herself
by Alexandra Waring Paynter
aged 5

Art and crafts

See also: Ch. 13 - Holidays for art and craft holiday courses.

***Art Classes for Children**
☎ 204412
For children 6–13 years
Professional artist and teacher. Various creative art media and materials. For creativity and fun. Also half term and holiday activities. Call for details.

***Art Works School of Art and Design**
225 Iffley Road
☎ Joanne Acty 250400 (home) or 794368 (work)
Weekly after-school and Saturday art classes for over-7s. Day classes (10.00-3.00) during school holidays. Wood carving to linoprinting, glass painting to pastels, calligraphy to batik.

***Kangaroo Craft Club**
3-5s playgroup
Oxford School
Glanville Road
Tue and Thu 1.15–2.45. Crafts, music and cooking for children aged 4-5. Cost: £10 for 4 week course.

***Kids' Art**
West Oxford Community Centre
Botley Road
☎ 245761
Tues: 3.30–5.30 (7-15)

Activities for kids

*Modern Art Oxford (formerly Museum of Modern Art)
30 Pembroke Street
☎ 722733
www.odernartoxford.org.uk
Modern art trolley – art activities for children. Drop-in sessions. Children must be accompanied by an adult.
Making Art family days – drop-in activities. All ages welcome. Children must be accompanied by an adult.
Activities change during the year.

*Orinoco Scrap Store
Bullingdon Community Centre
Peat Moors
☎ 761113
orinoco.scrapstore@lineone.net
Wed and Thur 11.00–3.00
First Saturday of the month from 11.00. (except bank holidays).
Recycles scrap waste from industry for use in creative play. Membership is for charities, voluntary organisations, community and non-profit groups who pay an annual subscription, and then a low price for the materials.
    Free training workshops are held for play workers.

*Sunningwell School of Art
The Old School
Sunningwell
☎ 730442
sunningwell@artschool.org.uk
www.artschool.org.uk
Runs a range of term-time early evening classes, including Creative Fun and Pottery from 5 years up.

Pottery

*Milham Ford School
Marston Road
☎ Janet Crombie 722429
After-school pottery classes run on Mondays 6-9 years. Cost: £8.00/session.

*Sunningwell School of Art
See previous section for details.

Play Projects

This is a selection of the drop-in activity clubs and after-school clubs in Oxford. They are open to all and cost between 30p and £5.00 per session. For more information, or to check if there is a club near you, contact the City Council's **Play Development Team**
☎ 252812
or write
c/o The City Council
St Aldates Chambers
Oxford OX1 1DS

Up-to-date information is also available promptly from the:
Oxfordshire Children's Information Service.
☎ 01993 886933
www.oxoncis.org.uk

*Barton Open Door Saturday Club
Waynflete Road
☎ Trudy Hewitt-Taylor 764952
July –August 9.30-12.30 (3-7s)
Alternate Saturdays 10.00-11.45; 5-12s

Activities for kids

*Baynard's Hill Primary
Barton
☎ 761536
Mon and Wed 2.45-4.15 5-9s

*Chinese Community Centre Saturday Club
Upstairs Hall, 44b Princes Street
☎ 204188 Estella Packwood
First Sat of month, 1.30-3.30; 4-14s

*Cutteslowe Community Centre
Wren Road
☎ 558944
Tues, Thurs 3.00-6.00; 5-9s

*Dovecote After School Club
The Dovecote Centre
Windale Avenue
☎ 712299
Mon-Thu 3.15-4.45; 5-12s

*Headington After School Club
Headington Community Centre
Gladstone Road
☎ 252812
Mon 3.45-5.15; 5-9s

*Hinksey Kids' Club
New Hinksey Primary School
(special needs provision)
Vicarage Road
☎ 453173
Mon-Fri 3.00-5.30; 4-12s

*Larkrise Primary School After School Club
Boundary Brook Road
☎ 721476
Mon-Fri 3.00-5.30 (5-9s)

*Oxkids After School Club
Oxford College of Further Education
Oxpens Road
☎ Tina Jardine 269380
Mon-Fri 3.00-6.00 (5-8s)

*Pegasus Primary School After School Club
Pegasus Road
☎ Cathy Barratt 777175
Tues and Weds 3.15-5.15 (5-9s)

*Rose Hill After School Club
Sure-Start Family Centre
The Oval
☎ 716739
Mon-Fri (term-time) 3.00-6.00. (5-11s)
Cost: £1.50/hour for the first child attending, and, if you live in Rose Hill or Littlemore, 50p/hour for siblings.

*SS Mary and John Primary School After School Club
Hertford Street
☎ Alston Quammie 248865
Mon-Fri 3.15-5.30 (5-9s)

*Tower Playbase After School Club
Maltfield Road
☎ Angela Taylor 742816
Mon and Tue 3.30-5.00 (4-12s)

*Tip: See the **Play for All** leaflet produced each year by the City Council for up-to-date details of after school clubs and summer holiday activities.*

Activities for kids

*St Andrews Morning/After School Club
St Andrews First School
London Road
☎ Teresa Furze 742634
Mon-Fri 8.30-9.00 and 3.30-5.50 (5-9s)

*St Barnabas After School Club
Hart Street
☎ 252812
Tue 3.00-4.40; 5-9s

*St Francis Primary School
Horspath Road
☎ 468190
Thur 3.15-4.45 (5-9s). School pupils only.

*SS Philip and James After School Club
St Phillip and St James First School
Leckford Place
☎ 556240 pm only
Mon-Fri 3.00-5.30 (5-9s).Pupils only.

*Oxfordshire Playbus Association
☎ 767700
The Association owns a converted double-decker bus which is equipped with arts and crafts activities, toys, games and sports. It runs regular early-years and after-school sessions, in and around the city and has a fully accessible minibus for outings. Call for details of the current timetable of activities.

Youth organisations

*Girl Guides Association
☎ Mrs McHugh 873571 for Cowley, Headington, East Oxford, Blackbird Leys, Iffley and Littlemore groups.
☎ Ms Sam Blood 396480 for Marston, North and West Oxford groups.
☎ Mrs C. Beer 861689 for Botley, Osney and Central Oxford groups.
An organisation for girls (Rainbows 5-7, Brownies 7-10) offering a variety of activities including crafts, cooking, camping and having fun.

*Scout Association
☎ Margaret Jarvis
150a Poplar Grove, Kennington
www.oxfordspirescouts.oxfree.com
There are 25 groups: Beavers (6-8s) Cubs (8-10s) and Sea Scouts in Oxford for both boys and girls.
Various activities are offered including games, crafts and camping.

*St John Ambulance, Badgers and Cadets
☎ 378228
Badgers 6-10s
Meet weekday evenings depending on group. Children play games and do a variety of activities. Includes a preliminary introduction to first aid issues and to begin developing children's awareness.
Cadets 10-18s
Children participate in a variety of activities including crafts, outdoor pursuits, map-reading, camping and sports.

*Woodcraft Folk
☎ Sid Phelps 727723
An organisation for girls and boys aged 6-20 based on the principles of co-operation, equality, democracy and

Activities for kids

peace. Activities include games, crafts, drama, camping, hiking, etc.

There are groups in East Oxford, South Oxford, West Oxford, Wolvercote and Cumnor, some of which have waiting lists.

Environmental groups

*RSPB Wildlife Explorers Club
South Oxfordshire
☎ Nigel 327854
North Oxfordshire
☎ Tabby Lucas 01608 737083
www.rspb.org.uk/england
Outdoor activities exploring wildlife in the local area. To start a group contact Rachel Sharp, RSPB Youth and Education Officer ☎ 01295 676449

*The Oxford City Council Countryside Service
☎ Oliver de Souisson 715830
Regular environmental activities run throughout the year, some of which are specifically aimed at children, e.g. bird-watching, minibeast safaris, orienteering, fossil hunting.

*Watch
☎ Emma Sirth, Wildlife Watch Co-ordinator 775476
An environmental and wildlife club for children. Local groups meet monthly for pond dipping, nature safaris, etc.

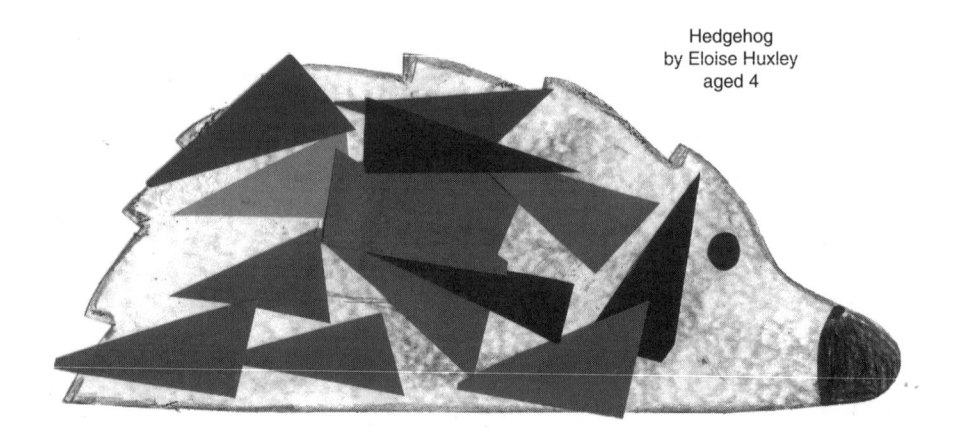

Hedgehog
by Eloise Huxley
aged 4

Chapter 16 – Childcare

Nowadays there is some very good quality childcare available from birth to age five and after school childcare for school age children. If you can find an option that you are happy with it makes going back to work far less stressful. But this can be a big 'if' and it can take some time and effort to find something right for you and your child. If you're not happy with your initial choice, don't be afraid to change it.

There are five main commercial options open to you; childminders, nannies, au pairs, workplace nurseries or private daycare nurseries. Playgroups and school nurseries take children from around age two-and-a-half to five and have much shorter hours. These are dealt with in the next chapter. Here we look at childcare options from birth, having hours more suited to a normal working day, and try to guide you through the pros and cons of each.

Help with childcare costs is available through the Child Tax Credit system, on a sliding scale corresponding to income. To qualify, you, and your partner if you have one, must work at least 16 hours a week. You will also need to use an approved childcare provider (one who is registered with a local authority or OFSTED). For Inland Revenue contact details, see *Chapter 3 – Parental Support.*.

Childcare

Childminders

This is probably, but not necessarily your cheapest option. Childminders look after your children in their own homes as part of their families. They are usually well-established in the community and tend to be experienced parents. Many belong to the **National Childminding Association**, which you can contact for information ☎ 020 8464 6164. www.ncma.org.uk

Childminders have to be registered with, and vetted by, **OFSTED**. Assessment includes showing that they have the skills to care for children, a check for criminal records and that their homes and gardens are safe and secure. You should ask to see this report when you visit prospective childminders. They are also inspected annually and again, should have this report available for inspection.

Looking after baby

The most important thing in a childminder/parent relationship is trust. It is not possible to find someone identical to you but try and find someone who parents like you. The balance between careful and carefree styles is the main issue here. Visit as many childminders as possible so that you feel happy with your choice.

It is essential that all money arrangements are discussed at the beginning so that everyone knows where they stand. Rates in Oxford range between £3.00 and £4.50 per hour. Childminders usually expect to be paid over holiday periods but establish conditions with them at the outset. If you intend to use the childminder for several years, try and ensure that they will take your child to a playgroup/nursery at the appropriate age. See: Ch. 17 - *Playgroups and Nursery Schools*.

If your child gets on well with their childminder and family, this can be a very happy and satisfactory childcare solution. To find a childminder, contact the Oxfordshire Children's Information Service on ☎ 01993 886933 www.oxoncis.org.uk for a list of those in the Oxford area, and for a guide containing useful points to consider when choosing a childminder.

Nannies

Nannies are a more expensive option but also more convenient as they come to you and you don't have to worry about getting the children ready before you leave for work. You can employ a live-in or live-out nanny or share one with another family (in which case you might have to take the children to your sharer's house). They also offer flexibility in that they are usually prepared to work longer hours than childminders.

Nannies range from the untrained and inexperienced to being NNEB trained, experienced and professional.

Childcare

Their rates vary but the average in Oxford is around £6.50 per hour.

In an emergency you can arrange via a nanny agency for a temporary nanny to look after your children for just a day or two. This is particularly useful if your child is ill and unable to attend their normal nursery or childminder.

The grapevine is often the best way to find a nanny, but you can advertise in *The Oxford Times*, *Nursery World Magazine* or *The Lady* (ask at your newsagent). You could also advertise at Oxford College, for newly qualified NNEB students. Alternatively, you could contact an agency such as:

*All Counties Nannies
Abingdon Road, Drayton
☎ 01235 524462
www.allcountiesnannies.co.uk

*Lauvic Babysitters and Nanny Service
Littlegate Street, Oxford
☎ 241542
www.lauvic.com

*Mum's the Word
4 Hill View, Sandhills
☎ 751825

*Select Nanny & Babysitting Service
☎ 01869 249753
selectnannyservices@btinternet.com

*Tinies Oxford
Alec Issigonis Way
☎ 487166
oxon@tinieschildcare.co.uk

• •

Tip: For nanny shares, try advertising (free of charge) in the New Parent Network Magazine tel: 775832, or use the NPN e-group.

• •

Au pairs

Au pairs are generally here to learn English or to study. They are young and inexperienced and are only supposed to work for part of the day. They should not be given sole responsibility of children for any extended time. However, they can provide welcome help with various household tasks for busy mothers.

Look out for ads in local shops or schools, or contact the local agency listed below which provides references and all necessary paperwork!

*ML Au Pairs
22a Davenant Road
☎ 556368
michael@minnsox.freeserve.co.uk

• •

Tip: See lots of nannies/minders so you can have a comparison and make a real choice. Trust your instinct; it has to feel right for you.

• •

Day nurseries

Day nurseries not only offer childcare, but also provide excellent pre-school education. They are inspected by

Childcare

OFSTED. Most nurseries are also eligible for government grant funding. See: *Chapter 17 – Playgroups and Nursery Schools*. Ask to see their OFSTED report, or look it up at *www.ofsted.gov.uk*. NB not all reports are on the website.

Oxfordshire Children's Information Service ☎ 01993 886933 can provide information on local day nurseries.

Workplace day nurseries

Some colleges and workplaces offer convenient full or part-time care for the children of their staff or students. Sometimes, when they are not full, they can offer places to people not working or studying at the organisation. Places can be expensive when unsubsidised.

• • • • • • • • • • • • • • • • • • • •

Tip: Get your child's name down as soon as possible – at birth, or before!

• • • • • • • • • • • • • • • • • • • •

All nurseries listed in these sections are open Mon-Fri, hours as specified.

⚀ = wheelchair access
() = special needs provision

Central Oxford

*St Thomas Day Nursery ()
40 St Thomas Street
☎ Philippa Clitherow 249800
Preference to County Council and Oxford University Press employees.
35 children 4 months-5 years.
8.15-5.30 Mon-Thurs; 8.15-5.00 Fri.

*Little Scholars (Oxford College Day Nursery) ()
Oxpens Road
☎ Sarah Shepherd 269443
Students, staff and external users.
58 children, 4 months-5 years.
8.00-5.30

North Oxford

*RI Nursery () &
Radcliffe Infirmary
Woodstock Road
☎ Janet Clarke 224083
NHS Trust staff only.
30 children, 0-5 years.
7.30-6.00

*St Anne's Nursery
48 Woodstock Road
☎ Louise King 274868
Preference St Anne's students/staff.
12 children.
8.45-5.15

*Balliol Day Nursery ()
2a Rawlinson Road
☎ Syan Lavery/Jane Carter 515654
Priority given to those with a Balliol connection.
16 children, 3 months-5 years.
9.00-5.00

*Kids Unlimited: Bradmore Road ()
4c Bradmore Road
email: childcare@admin.ox.ac.uk
Oxford University staff/students only.
52 children, 4 months-5 years.
8.00-6.00

Childcare

*Wolfson College Day Nursery ♿ ()
Linton Road
☎ Angela Jones/Secretary 274071
Preference to Wolfson students and staff, but other places available.
29 children, 0-5 years.
8.45-5.15

*Oxfam Workplace Nursery ♿ ()
274 Banbury Road
☎ Hilary Smout 312264
Preference to Oxfam staff but other places available.
26 children, 6 months-5 years.
8.45-5.15 (Fridays 5.00)

*Kids Unlimited: Mansion House
Apsley Road
email childcare@admin.ox.ac.uk
Oxford University staff/students only.
40 children, 4 months-5 years.
8.00-6.00

*Somerville College Nursery ♿ ()
119a Walton Street
☎ 270686
Preference to Somerville staff/students.
6 months-5 years.
9.00-5.00

Headington

*Oxford Brookes Uni. Nursery ♿ ()
Morrell Hall Campus
☎ Jean McPhee 485050
Students and staff only.
60 children, 4 months-5 years.
8.45-5.10

My nursery by Eloise Huxley aged 4

*Rookery Nursery ♿ ()
Ruskin Hall, Dunstan Road
☎ Tracy Heath 760539
A few places for Ruskin students and staff, the rest for anyone.
26 children, 3 months-5 years.
8.30-5.30

*Sandfield Day Nursery ♿ ()
John Radcliffe Hospital
☎ Bernadette Hayes 744200
Priority to Oxford Radcliffe NHS Trust staff.
52 children, 6 weeks-5 years.
7.30-6.30

*Julia Durbin Day Nursery ()
Churchill site
Old Road
☎ Gaynor Mangan 744448
Priority to Oxford Radcliffe NHS Trust staff.
93 children, 6 weeks-5 years.
7.30-6.30

Childcare

*Kids Unlimited: Jack Straws Lane
Jack Straws Lane
email: childcare@admin.ox.ac.uk
Opened January 04.
Oxford University students and staff only.

East Oxford

*Rover Rompers Nursery ♿ ()
Roman Way
Cowley
☎ Samantha Flanagan 825900
Priority to BMW employees.
28 children, 3months-5 years.
7.30-5.15 Mon-Thur; 7.30-1.00 Fri.

• •

Tip: It is always worth enquiring if a workplace nursery has any places for 'outsiders'. Several workplace nurseries say they have places for external children that are not filled.

• •

Private day nurseries

These also offer full- and part-time day care but are privately owned and managed. Costs, staffing and premises will vary, but all have to be registered with OFSTED.

If your child is over two, you may find a private nursery school could also meet your childcare needs.

See also *Ch. 17 – Playgroups and Nursery Schools*.

Central Oxford

*Buffer Bear Turbo Ted's Nursery ♿ ()
1 Roger Dudman Way
☎ Kate Launder 200967
56 children, 3 months-5 years.
7.30-6.30

North Oxford

*Barnett House Crèche
1 Warnborough Road
☎ Jenny Ferguson 552366
6 children, 6 months-5 years.
8.45-12.45 and 1.15-5.15 or all day.
A small home group.

*The Nursery ()
17 Lathbury Road
☎ Sarah Green 516636
24 children, 2-5 years.
8.30-5.00

*St Paul's Day Nursery
119a Walton Street
☎ Louisa Davis 270686
16 children 0-5 years
9.00-5.00

Headington

*Kiddies Korner
Quarry Village Hall
☎ Trish Medlicott 766762
12 children 2-3 years
16 children 3-5 years.
8.00-5.30

Childcare

East Oxford

*Blue House Nursery ()
34 Union Street
☎ Kimberley Wilder 247877
8 children, 2-5 years.
8.30-5.30

*Dinky Doo Nursery
13 Stanley Road
☎ Sara Mander 727281
20 children, 18m-5 years.
8.30-5.30

*Jigsaw Day Nursery ♿ ()
2 Armstrong Road
Littlemore
☎ Susan Long 748607
126 children 3m-5 years.
8.00-6.00

*Kids Unlimited ()
Oxford Business Park
(by Longwall Travel Inn)
Garsington Road
☎ Paul Evans 711422
120 children 3m-5 years
7.30-6.00

*Little Scholars (Blackbird Leys) ♿ ()
College of Further Education
Cuddesdon Way
☎ Sharon Griffiths 269917
53 children 3m-5 years
8.00-5.30

*The Oxford Nursery ♿ ()
Glanville Road
☎ Natasha Hurry 396767
49 children 2 months-5 years.
8.00-6.00

*The Oxford Nursery ♿ ()
Oxford Science Park
☎ Clare Spears 396792
72 children 2m-5 years.
8.00-6.00

*Stepping Stones Day Nursery
55 Glanville Road
☎ Mrs Hamilton/Lorraine 717139
24 children, 2-5 years.
8.30-5.30

Kennington

*Small World Montessori
89 Bagley Wood Road
☎ L. Couper 326660
3m-5 years
8.00-6.00

Kidlington

*Cygnet Nursery
44-45 Evenlode Crescent
☎ David Smith 842006
60 children 3m-5 years
7.30-6.00

Chapter 17 – Playgroups & Nursery Schools

At around the age of two, children can attend pre-school nursery classes and playgroups. The distinction between these and some daycare nurseries is somewhat blurred with both offering early years education to the 2-5s. The main differences are that pre-schools take children from two, or older – while daycare nurseries can cater from birth. Pre-schools follow school terms and the hours tend to be shorter than daycare nurseries. There is both state and community provision for pre-schools whereas daycare is almost entirely private.

Many pre-school nurseries and playgroups are affiliated to schools, both state and private. Please note that some private schools with nursery provision might not be included here. It is difficult to keep this information up-to-date so please check details with the pre-school of your choice. Additional information can also be found from the **Oxfordshire Children's Information Service** ☎ 01993 886933. See also: *Chapter 16 – Childcare*.

GOVERNMENT FUNDED PLACES

There is a government-funded early years education grant scheme. Children in Oxfordshire are eligible for five, two and a half hour sessions. This now includes all children from three to five years (from the term after their third birthday). From a practical point of view, all you have to do is find a place for your child at

Playgroups & nursery schools

an institution (it can be statutory, voluntary or private) which is registered to receive this funding. They will organise all the paperwork and claim the funding on your behalf. At some private nurseries you will have to pay a 'top up' fee to cover any extra hours. For further information please contact the **Early Years Information Line** ☎ 815630. **Oxfordshire Children's Information Service** ☎ 01993 886933 can also give information about childcare providers where parents can access funded places for 3 and 4-year-olds.

Pre-school Learning Alliance (PLA)

The PLA represents playgroups (and other pre-school groups which are members) at both national and local levels. The Oxford branch provides help, advice and support to member groups.
Contact points for the **Pre-School Learning Alliance** are:
National Pre-School Learning Alliance ☎ 020 7833 0991
Oxfordshire Pre-School Learning Alliance ☎ 744470

PLAYGROUPS/PRE-SCHOOLS

A playgroup is often the place where a child has his or her first taste of independence! Traditionally, children started playgroups at three but many now take children from two. Playgroups usually run in the morning or afternoon and children attend for three or more sessions per week.

Playgroups offer children space to play, different equipment and play ideas and a chance to make friends before going on to nursery or school. Playgroups may receive grants but some rely on fundraising and fees. An average session costs about £3 but if you can't afford it ask the supervisor or your health visitor about assisted places,

Playgroups are community groups and depend on the support of their parents. Most are run by a parents' committee which employs the staff. Playgroups are registered with OFSTED and the staff/child ratio should be one to eight. If you want your child to go to a playgroup, get his or her name down on the waiting list early. Playgroups welcome visitors, so go to several, see how they differ and decide which you like best.

In this section we list playgroups and both state and private nursery school classes which are registered as early years providers in Oxfordshire's **early years development plan**. Inclusion in this scheme involves regular inspections and OFSTED reports. Many parents use playgroups which are not included in this plan and are quite happy with them. You will see them advertised locally.

Playgroups & nursery schools

() = special needs provision available.
♿ = wheelchair access.

North Oxford

*Polstead Playgroup
St Margaret's Institute
30 Polstead Road OX2 6TN
☎ 428586
2.5-5 yrs, Mon-Fri 9.00-12.00

*St Peters Under 5s Group () ♿
Church Rooms
First Turn, Wolvercote OX2 8AQ
☎ Liz Halsey 511817
2.5-5 years; 20 children
Mon-Fri 9.00-12.00

Marston

*New Marston Pre-School
St Michael's School
Marston Road OX3 0EJ
☎ 798320
Rising 3 to rising 5; 24 children
Mon-Fri 9.05-11.45, Mon/Tues 12.40-3.10

*Mortimer Hall Playgroup ()
Oxford Road
Old Marston OX3 0PH
☎ 724188
2.5-5 years; 24 children
Mon-Fri 9.15-12.00 Mon/Thu 12.45-3.00

Kidlington

*Kidlington Pre-School
West Kidlington School
☎ 373369

2 years to school entry
Mon-Fri 9.15-11.45, Mon-Thu 1.15-3.45
£3.00/session

South Oxford

*Lake Street Playgroup
Lake Street Community Centre
☎ Secretary 242666
2.25-4 years
Mon-Fri 9.30-12.00 term-time.

East Oxford

*East Oxford Playgroup
East Oxford Community Centre
44 Princes Street
☎ Vanessa Lamb 249449
2-5 years

*Donnington Playgroup
Townsend Square
Freelands Road OX4 4BB
☎ 791200
3-5 years; 34 children
Mon-Wed 9.15-1.15
Thu-Fri 9.15-11.45

*Our Lady's School Playgroup () ♿
Oxford Road
Cowley OX4 2LF
☎ 749629
3-5 years; 24 children
Mon-Fri 8.45-11.15 (4-year-olds)
Mon-Fri 1.00-3.00 (3-year-olds)

*St Clements Church Pre-School () ♿
St Clements Family Centre
Cross Street OX4 1DA

Playgroups & nursery schools

☎ 202512
24 children; 3-5 years
Mon-Fri 9.15-11.45
Tues, Thu until 2.45 for 3.5-5s

Blackbird Leys

*Shepherds Hill Playgroup () &
The Dovecote
Nightingale Avenue
☎ 779504
3-5 years
Mon-Fri 9.15-11.45 and 12.30-2.45

*Blackbird Leys Pre-School () &
Moorbank
Blackbird Leys OX4 5HW
☎ 747166
3-5 years; 20 children
Mon-Fri 9.15-11.45 and 12.30-2.45

Headington

*Cherry Tree Pre-School
Headington Community Centre
Gladstone Road
Headington
OX3 8LL

Rowan and me at nursery
Eloise Huxley
aged 4

☎ 769794
2.5-5 years; 24 children
Mon-Fri 9.15-11.45 and 12.30-2.45

*Sandhills Pre-School Playgroup () &
Sandhills County Primary School
☎ 07974 990627
Mon-Thu 9.00-2.55, Fri 9.00-11.45
3-5 years.

STATE NURSERIES AND CLASSES

State nursery schools and classes differ from playgroups in that they are free, well-resourced, are usually bigger and purpose-built, and offer more activities. You may decide that your child would be happier staying on at a playgroup until he or she is 5 or you may feel that a change would be beneficial.

Oxford City has, in comparison with other parts of Oxfordshire, a high level of nursery provision but even so, most children are only offered three or four terms, and generally only if they live within one of the catchment areas.

However, if you feel your child has special needs (e.g. hearing/speech problems) and would benefit from a longer nursery place, discuss it with your health visitor who may be able to help organise this. This also applies if you have been late in getting your child's name onto a nursery's waiting list.

Although full-time places may be offered, children usually attend

Playgroups & nursery schools

either in the morning or afternoon. Lunch may be available. Nursery schools and classes often have long waiting lists, so ring local nurseries to find out when you need to put your child's name down and to organise a visit.

State nursery schools

Nursery schools are self-contained units with their own head teacher and governing body with staff being either trained teachers or nursery nurses. About forty children attend each session but they may be divided into groups.

All five of these nurseries listed below have family rooms with a range of toddler groups, music groups and toy libraries.

Headington

*Headington Nursery School ()
William Kimber Crescent
Headington OX3 8LW
☎ 762345

*Slade Nursery School ()
Titup Hall Drive
Headington OX3 8QQ
☎ 750670

East Oxford

*Bartlemas Nursery School () &
269 Cowley Road OX4 2AJ
☎ 245768

South Oxford

*Grandpont Nursery School
Whitehouse Road OX1 4QH
☎ 242900

Botley

*Elms Road Nursery School
Elms Road
☎ 243955

State nursery classes

State nursery classes are attached to primary schools in Oxford. They are part of the school's management and are answerable to the Head and Governors of the host school. They generally have one nursery teacher and one nursery nurse and offer at least 26 morning and 26 afternoon places. Many now have 39 or more places

North Oxford

*St Barnabas School () &
Hart Street OX2 6BN
☎ 557178

*Wolvercote School
FirstTurn,
Wolvercote OX2 8AQ
☎ 558301

*Cutteslowe School
Wren Road OX2 7SK
☎ 558944

Playgroups & nursery schools

Marston

*St Nicholas School
Raymund Road , Old Marston OX3 0PJ
☎ 242838

*New Marston Primary School
Copse Lane OX3 0AY
☎ 761560

Barton

*Bayard's Hill Primary School
Waynflete Road, Headington OX3 9NU
☎ 761656

East Oxford

*East Oxford School
Union Street OX4 1JP
☎ 240219

*Larkrise School
Boundary Brook Road OX4 4AN
☎ 721476

Cowley

*Our Lady's (RC) School
Oxford Road, Cowley OX4 2LF
☎ 779176

*St Francis School
Horspath Road OX4 2QT
☎ 777408

*Church Cowley St James School
Bartholomew Road OX4 3QH
☎ 778484

Blackbird Leys

*Orchard Meadow School
Wesley Close OX4 5BG
☎ 778609

*Pegasus School
Field Avenue OX4 5RG
☎ 777175

*Windale School
Windale Avenue
Blackbird Leys OX4 5JD
☎ 777796

Rose Hill and Littlemore

*Rose Hill Primary School
The Oval OX4 4SF
☎ 777937

*Littlemore Primary School
Sandford Lane OX4 4PU
☎ 815757

*St John Fisher (RC) School () &
Sandy Lane West OX4 5LD
☎ 779676
Integrated nursery which caters for both disabled and non-disabled children.

South Oxford

*New Hinksey School
Vicarage Road OX1 4RQ
☎ 242169

Playgroups & nursery schools

Kennington

*St Swithun's Primary School
☎ 438933
Integrated nursery which caters for both disabled and non-disabled children.

West Oxford

*West Oxford Primary School () &
Ferry Hinksey Road
☎ 248862

PRIVATE NURSERY SCHOOLS

These are similar to state nursery schools and classes but they may be more structured. The fees can be high but they take children at an earlier age. The staff are usually qualified teachers or NNEB (or equivalent) trained.

The following nursery schools are listed in this section because they offer either sessional or term-time care only. There are others which offer longer hours and can therefore be used as day care and they are listed in *Chapter 16 - Childcare*.

North Oxford

*The Oxford Montessori Nursery
Wolvercote Village Hall
Wolvercote OX2 8BD
☎ Daniel Ardizzone 358210
2-5 years, 26 children Mon-Fri
Full day and half day sessions available.

*Field House Montessori Nursery ()
St Gregory's & St Augustine's Church Hall
322 Woodstock Road
Summertown OX2 7NS
☎ Rose Magaka-Smith 316641
2-6 years, 20 children
Mon-Fri 8.00-3.00

*The Oxford Montessori Nursery
Forest Farm
Elsfield OX3 9UW
☎ Daniel Ardizzone 358210
2-5 years; 20 children Mon-Fri
Full- and half-day sessions available.

Headington

*The Phoenix Day Nursery
Headington Parish Hall
Dunstan Road OX3 9BY
☎ 767836
After school care available.

*Hunsdon House Nursery School
12 Osler Road
Headington OX3 9BJ
☎ 762704 2.5-5 years,
40 children Mon-Fri 9.00-12.00
Tue & Thu till 2.30 for over 4s

*Beech Tree Nursery School ()
Rye St Antony School
Pullen's Lane
Headington Hill OX3 0BY
☎ 229215/762802
3-5 years
Mon-Fri 8.45-3.00
Limited after school care available.

Playgroups & nursery schools

Cowley, Littlemore & Iffley

*The Oxford Montessori Nursery
Church Way
Iffley OX4 4EG
☎ Daniel Ardizzone 358210
2-5 years; 20 children; Mon-Fri
Full and half-days available.

*Emmanuel Christian School
Sandford Road
Littlemore OX4 4PU
☎ 395236
3-5 years; 18 children 8.40-12.00
Christian emphasis, realistic fees.

Bicester

*The Oxford Montessori Nursery
St Edburgh's Church
Old Place Yard
Bicester
☎ Daniel Ardizzone 358210

Kidlington

*The Children's House Montessori Nursery School
Benmead Road, Kidlington OX5 2DA
☎ Henrietta Ussher 724826
2-5 years, Full and half-days available, term-time only.

Cumnor

*Cumnor Montessori Nursery
United Reform Church Hall
Leys Road
Cumnor
☎ Sarah Wimborne 865035
2-5 years; 20 children
Mon-Fri 9.00-12.30 term-time only.

Up to date information on playgroups and nursery schools can be obtained at any time from **Oxfordshire Children's Information Service**, ☎ 01993 886933. Email enquires@oxoncis.org.uk.

Chapter 18 - Off to School

Choosing the right school for your child can be a daunting prospect and the whole process can seem very complex. In this chapter we look at the school system in Oxford and guide you through the choices available. We also look at preparing your child for school.

THE SCHOOL SYSTEM IN OXFORD

When to start

Children are expected to start school by the term after their fifth birthday. The current policy in Oxfordshire is to offer children a part-time place a term earlier, i.e. for the term in which they turn five. The place will be in a reception class, a nursery class or an early years unit, depending on the provision at the school. Some schools make the place up to a full-time one. You are free to choose whether or not to accept the place.

However, from September 2004, a new entry system will be in place. All children in Oxfordshire will be entitled to a half-time place in a nursery class or primary school starting the September after their fourth birthday. In other words, children will be able to start school at the beginning of the academic year in which they are five. The academic year runs from September to August. There will be a yearly entry into school, as opposed to the current termly entry. As now, some schools may choose to make the place up to a full-time one. You will still be able to refuse the place and wait for your child to be five before he or she starts school.

Changes to the system in Oxford

From September 2003 a two-tier system will operate in Oxford, replacing the three-tier system that existed previously. Children attend primary school from five to 11 and secondary school from 11 to 16 or 18.

Each primary school has a defined catchment area from which it draws its pupils. This ensures that every child has a guaranteed place at one school. Don't assume, however, that you live in the catchment area of the school nearest to you – some catchment areas are very oddly shaped! You can find out in which catchment

Off to school

area you live by asking at a local school or contacting the **Oxfordshire Education Department**, Macclesfield House, New Road, OX1 1NA ☎ 815449 and asking for the free booklet: *Admissions and Transfers: Information for Parents*. You can choose to send your child to a school in a different catchment area from the one in which you live, provided, of course, that the school has a place available. You have a right to appeal should your child not be offered a place.

Each school has its own distinctive atmosphere and so it is useful to visit as many as you can to make the choice that will best suit your child. Schools are listed under 'Schools' in the phone book. Some schools organise open days for groups of prospective parents. Alternatively, you can arrange to make an individual visit. You can usually take your child with you but if you are visiting a lot of schools this may confuse or worry them. Each school should give you a prospectus with further information.

Once you have made your choice, you need to complete a preference card, found at the back of the *Admissions and Transfers* booklet and return it to your school of first choice. This needs to be done by the March of the year prior to the academic year in which your child is five.

If you decide to send your child to a school 'out of catchment' and a place is available, do remember that this does not mean that he or she will automatically gain a place at the secondary school fed by the first school. Again, it depends on where you live. You may end up with the unfortunate situation where your child, at age 11, has to go to a different school from most of his or her friends.

Other Options

*Independent schools
If you would like more information on educating your child privately, contact:
The Independent Schools Council information service (ISCis)
☎ 01572 722726
for a free handbook listing junior and senior day/boarding schools in the Oxford area for 3-19s.

*The European School
Culham, near Abingdon
☎ 01235 522621

Children may be able to attend this kindergarten and school (from 4) if one of their parents is of another European nationality, if a parent is employed by an EC institution or if they have been taught in a European school abroad.
The European education system is followed in a variety of languages and fees are usually charged.

*Steiner-Waldorf Schools
Steiner schools take a holistic approach to education and are keen not to force formal learning on to children too early. If you are interested in a 'Steiner' edu-

Off to school

cation for your child, or would like to find out more, contact:
The Steiner Waldorf Schools Fellowship
☎ 01342 822115
email: info@swsf.org.uk
Website: www.steinerwaldorf.org.uk
The nearest kindergarten (for 3–6s) and school (for 8–14s) to Oxford is:
Alder Bridge School, Mill Lane, Padworth, Nr Reading, Berks, RG7 4JU.
☎ 0118 971 4471
They also run parent and toddler sessions. Fees are charged.

*Home Education

The law requires all children from the age of 5 to receive a suitable education. Most parents choose school to provide this. However, if you feel that a home education would suit your child better, contact **Education Otherwise**. This well-established, national self-help organisation provides support and advice for families practising or contemplating home-based education for their children. There is a large, active local group that runs regular classes, workshops, events and field trips.
☎ Wendy Plested 514973. (local contact). For further information and a range of useful publications contact:
Education Otherwise
PO Box 7420
London N9 9SG
www.education-otherwise.org

PREPARING FOR SCHOOL

Once your child has been formally accepted by a school it is a good idea to find out if you can visit frequently, so that they can get used to the building and what goes on there, and to meet the staff. Most schools ask new children to come in and meet their new teacher and future class on a regular basis in the term before they start school. Teachers in reception and nursery classes follow the government's curriculum guidance for the Foundation Stage. This covers the ages of 3–6. There is an emphasis on learning through play and exploration. Also they encourage making firm partnerships with parents and pre-schools. In this way, the teacher should aim to make your child's transition to school as easy and happy as possible.

*PEEP
(Peers Early Education Partnership)
The PEEP Centre
Peers School, Sandy Lane West
Littlemore
☎ 395145
See also *Ch 3 Support for Parents*
PEEP is a voluntary organisation that aims to give children a flying educational start working with parents/carers. It provides folders, song-books, tapes and videos for each year of a child's life up to five. These are full of practical ideas for making the most of everyday life with babies and young children, thereby supporting their learning.

Off to school

If you live in Rose Hill, Littlemore, Blackbird Leys or Greater Leys, you are eligible to receive these materials for free. You will be contacted by PEEP soon after the birth of your baby and offered a home visit. You can then opt to carry on with home visits or join a weekly group. The groups are for adults and children together and the focus is on playing, talking, singing and sharing stories with babies and children.

If your child attends a local pre-school or nursery when they are 3 or 4 you will find PEEP there too. If you have recently moved into the PEEP area or think you have missed out, do give them a ring.

If you live outside the PEEP area, there may still be the opportunity to go along to a PEEP group. New Parent Network has recently run some groups, so give us a ring, or phone the **Oxfordshire Parent Education Development Team** on 428085 to see if there are any possibilities elsewhere.

CHILDREN WITH ADDITIONAL NEEDS

If your child is significantly delayed in their development or if he or she has a medical or behavioural condition likely to cause a delay, you are eligible for free support from a **pre-school teacher-counsellor** who will visit you both at home and discuss how you can best support your child. If your child is at pre-school or in daycare, they will visit there and advise the staff on how best to cater for your child's needs. They can also advise you on the most appropriate nursery and school provision for your child and will help you prepare your child for the move. You can contact the service at:

Pupil Services
Macclesfield House
New Road, Oxford OX1 1NA
☎ 810513

A pre-school teacher-counsellor with a particular interest in supporting disabled children with starting school is Netta Buckett ☎ 428013 (or via Rosie Cassar ☎ 428013).

ONCE YOUR CHILD IS AT SCHOOL

These days schools see themselves as being in partnership with parents and will encourage your involvement with your child's education. There is usually an expectation on parents to share books with their children at home as well as supporting other 'home work'. Generally, schools also welcome help from parents in the classroom, such as listening to children read or helping with group or sports activities. Have a chat with your child's teacher about possibilities. Be aware, though, that your child might be embarrassed or inhibited by your presence in the class, so in some instances it might be a good idea to help out in a different class.

You could also consider getting involved with the **Parent Teacher Association** (PTA), especially if you

Off to school

work during the day so cannot help out in school hours. PTAs help their schools by fundraising, putting on social events and discussing school issues. Look out for their notices or ask at the school office. It's also a good way of getting know other parents.

*Volunteer Reading Help
36 Windmill Road, Headington
☎ 0845 450 0329
If you want to volunteer to help children read on a more formal basis at a local school, contact this organisation for training, information and support.

*Family Links
New Marston Centre
Jack Straws Lane
☎ 454004
Ask your school if they run the **Family Links Programme for** children and their parents which helps boost self-esteem and improve children's behaviour.

My new school by Coral Flitney, aged 4

Index

A Piece of Cake: 175
Abacus Swim School: 184
Abbey: 114
Abbey Meadow: 146
ABC Cinemas: 180
Abingdon: 109, 146, 152, 194
Abingdon College: 48
Abingdon Music Centre: 196
Abingdon Twins Club: 52
Abingdon, swimming pool: 185
ABLE Open Learning Centre: 111
accident prevention: 24
accidents: 21, 24
acrobatic dance: 192
acting: 193–194
Active Birth: 8
Active Toy Company: 87
activity clubs: 199–201
activity holidays: 168
Activity World: 151
acupuncture: 30, 31, 35
Adams: 81, 86
ADHD: 34
adoption: 2
Adult Basic Skills Unit: 112
adult education: 25
adult literacy: 55, 111–112
adventure games: 177
adventure playgrounds: 154, 164–165
advice centres: 40–42
Advisory Service for the Education of Travellers: 106
aerobics: 109–110
African Caribbean Women's Support Group: 54
after school care: 216
after school clubs: 183, 199–201
afternoon teas (see tea in the country):
Agnes Smith Advice Centre: 40
agricultural shows: 153
AIMS (improvements in maternity services): 9

air–bags: 76
aircraft: 159
Alder Bridge School: 220
Alexander technique: 30, 31–32
Alice in Wonderland: 138
All Counties Nannies: 205
All Saints Church: 66
All Saints Church Hall: 60
Allders: 81, 123
allergies: 26, 34
allergy centre, Oxford: 26
Allergy UK: 26
Alliance Francaise d'Oxford: 198
allotments: 143
alternative medicines and therapies: 30–35
Amazon: 93
Angel & Greyhound: 126, 131, 133
animals: 153–157
animals, rare breeds: 156
animatronics: 162
annual events: 141–144
antenatal care, choices of: 3
antenatal classes: 6, 52
antenatal exercise: 8, 9
Apollo Theatre, Oxford: 181
Appleton: 155
Aqua Vale: 149
Aqua Vitae: 119
Aquababies: 183
aquanappies: 183–184
aquanatal waterbased exercise: 8, 9
aquarium: 118, 140, 157, 162
Arabic: 198
Arena Fitness: 109
Aristotle Lane Recreation Ground: 165
Ark T Centre: 110, 191
aromatherapy: 30, 32
art: 142, 198–199
art classes: 198
art courses, summer and after–school: 167
art groups: 110–111
art materials: 83, 91, 199

Art Works School of Art & Design: 198
arts activities: 166–167
Artweeks: 142
Asda: 92
ASET: 106
Ashmolean Museum: 117, 137
Asian Baptist Fellowship: 68
Asian Cultural Centre: 53, 112
Asian families: 45
Asian women's activities: 112
Asian Women's Helpline: 46
assertiveness courses, with crèches: 111
asthma: 26
asylum seekers: 21, 46, 54, 112–113
Asylum Welcome: 46, 54
au pairs: 205
Aunt Sally: 129
autism: 33, 34
aviation: 159
Aviators: 109
Aviators Health & Fitness Club: 187
Aylesbury: 156, 162, 177
Aylesbury Civic Centre: 180
Aziz: 119
B
Babies R Us: 37, 72
Baby Bjorn: 70
baby blues: 15
Baby Borrows: 72, 96, 175
baby carriers: 70–71, 83
baby changing: 83–84, 86, 90
baby equipment hire: 72–73, 96
baby groups: 51
baby massage: 17
baby swimming: 185
Babylab: 29–30
babysitters: 205
Babyworld: 97
back packs: 70, 93, 96
back pain: 14, 30, 34
Badgers: 201
badminton: 109–110, 187
bakeries: 78, 80, 155
ball play: 186

223

ballet lessons: 189–193
   preschool preparation for: 190
ballets: 181
Balliol Day Nursery: 206
Balloon Festival: 166
balloons, hot air: 143
ballpits: 150–153, 176, 177
ballpool hire: 96, 175
Banbury: 151, 157, 185, 194
Banbury Museum: 157
Bangladeshi community: 21, 69
Bangladeshi Islamic Education Centre: 69
Baptist Church Hall, Woodstock Road: 61
Bar Meze: 119
barbecue equipment, public: 131, 137
Barefoot Books: 93
Barnett House Creche: 208
Bartlemas Nursery School: 58, 104, 214
Barton Early Years playscheme: 168
Barton Information Centre: 40
Barton Neighbourhood Centre: 176
Barton Open Door Saturday Club: 199
Barton's Open Door: 54, 60, 104, 116
basic education (see basic skills):
basic skills: 111–112
Basildon House: 129
basketball: 176, 178, 189
Bat & Ball Inn: 128
batik: 198
Bayard's Hill Primary: 200, 215
BBC education: 94
beaches: 161
Beaconsfield: 160
Beale Park: 129, 153
Beanoland: 160
Beat Café: 84
Beavers: 201
Bedruthan Steps Hotel: 172

beds, children's: 94
bedwetting: 26
Beech Tree Nursery School: 216
behavioural problems: 26, 221, 222
Bekonscott Model Village: 160
Bell Trees Clinic: 31, 34
Ben Molyneux Photography: 94
benefits, welfare: 40–41, 183
bereavement: 12, 27, 46
Berinsfield: 109
Berrick Salome: 151, 177
BHS: 81, 123
Bible study: 65
Bicester: 217
Bicester Village: 86
Bickiepegs: 94
bicycle hire: 147
bicycle seats: 74–75
bicycles: 73–75, 86, 93
Birdland Park: 153
birds: 133, 134, 146, 147, 153–157
birth afterthoughts: 14
birth, registering: 12
birthday cakes: 175
birthday parties & treats: 174–181
Birthdays: 175
births, home: 5
births, hospital: 5
births, marriages and deaths: 12
Bishop Blaize Inn: 128
Bishopston Trading Company: 90
Bizzkids Dance Company: 190
Black Child Mixed Parentage Group: 43, 54
Blackbird Leys: 102
Blackbird Leys Adventure Playground: 164
Blackbird Leys Leisure Centre: 110, 167, 176
Blackbird Leys Pool: 177, 184
Blackbird Leys Pre–school: 213
Blackfriars: 64
Blackwells: 80, 83

blankets: 86, 90
Blenheim Palace: 75, 146
Blooming Marvellous: 89
Blooms: 124
Bloomsbury: 93
Blue House Nursery: 209
Blue Palms: 119
bluebells: 147
BMW workers, childcare: 208
Boar's Hill: 147
boat hire: 141, 147
Boat Inn: 128
boat museum: 154
boat races: 142
boat trips: 141
boating lake: 134
boats: 157
boatyard: 157
Boden, mini: 90
Bonfire Night: 144
book clubs: 93
book groups, children's: 106
Book People: 93
book shops: 83
Bookhouse: 83
books, parenting: 93
Books for Children: 93
books, children's: 100–101, 114
books, discount: 93–94
books, multicultural: 93
books, non–sexist: 93
Boots: 86, 90
Borders: 83, 117
Boswells: 82
Botanical Gardens: 131, 135
Botley: 103, 187
Botley County Primary School: 189
Botley Road Recreation Ground: 133, 166
Botley Road, shops on: 85
bottlewarming: 117
bouncy castles: 151, 156, 166, 176, 177, 178, 179, 186
Bourton on the Water: 151, 153
bowling alleys, 10–pin: 87, 177
bowls: 166

Boy Scouts: 201
bra, breastfeeding: 89
bra, fitting services: 89
bra, maternity: 89
Bracknell: 149, 161
Bradmore Road nursery: 206
Brambles: 81
Branca: 119
breast pump hire: 96
breastfeeding: 14, 22, 26, 84
breastfeeding clinic: 12, 14, 15, 22
breastfeeding counsellors: 14
breastfeeding, in libraries: 101
breastfeeding, out and about: 116, 117, 118
Bricklayers Arms: 126
Brill: 146
Bristol: 161
British Holidays: 173
British Humanist Association: 13
British Suzuki Institute: 197
Brookes Restaurant: 119
Brookes Sport: 110
Brookes Sports Centre: 177
Broughton castle: 146
Brownies: 201
Browns: 119
Bryan Down Oldtime Entertainment: 176
Buckinghamshire County Museum: 162
Buckinghamshire Railway Centre: 157–158
Bucks Goat Centre: 153
Buddhist Centre: 69
Budgen: 78
budgeting: 41
Buffer Bear Turbo Ted's Nursery: 208
buggies: 71–72, 93
buggies, double: 72
buggies, on buses: 75
buggy boards: 72, 86, 90
buggy hire: 72, 96
buggy repairs: 73, 96
Bullingdon Community Centre: 61, 199
Bumblebaby: 90

Bumps & Beyond: 63
bunkbeds: 94
Burford: 94, 194
Burford Garden Centre: 124
Burger King: 122
Bury Knowle: 133
Bury Knowle Health Centre: 51
bus tours: 140
buses: 75, 76, 154
buses, historic: 158
buses, open–top: 140
buses, to London: 75, 162
business, starting your own: 112
Busy Bee: 81
Busy Bees music group: 195, 196, 197
butchers: 78, 80, 95
butterfly house: 146
C
Café Club: 53
Café Coco: 119
Café Rouge: 119
cafes: 84, 117–118
Cake Expectations: 175
Cake Shop: 175
cakes: 125, 145
cakes, birthday: 175
cakes, decorating: 175
calligraphy: 198
Camp Energy: 186
camping: 170, 201–202
canal: 136, 157
Canal Festival: 143, 165
car roof box: 76, 170
car seat fitting: 76, 97
car seat hire: 72
car seats: 76, 86, 96
caravan holidays: 173
cards: 92
Carfax tower: 139
Carmelite Priory: 114
carols by candlelight: 144
carols in the woods: 148
cars: 76, 158
cars, electric: 158
cars, historic: 158
carving wood: 198
Cash's name tapes: 94

castle: 146, 148
catalogues: 89–94, 95
catchment areas: 218–219
catering, for parties: 175, 176–179, 180–181
caves: 147
CBeebies: 98
Celebrations: 175
Celia Benson School of Dance: 189, 190, 191
cello teachers: 197
Center Parcs: 172–173
Central Library: 101
cerebral palsy: 33
ceremonies, naming: 13
Chalgrove: 193
changing facilities: 84, 86, 101
charity shops: 86
Charlie & the Chocolate Factory: 162
Charney Manor: 114
check up, postnatal: 13
Cheeky Rascals: 90
cheese: 78
Chequers (High Street): 125
Chequers Inn (Headington Quarry): 144
Cherry Tree Pre–school: 213
Cherwell Vineyard: 64
Chessington World of Adventures: 160
Chiang Mai: 120
Child Benefit: 41
Child Credit helpline: 42
child development studies: 29–30
child health & development classes: 25
child health clinics: 18, 22
child health, promoting: 22–23
Child Maintenance: 41
Child Support Agency: 42
Child Tax Credit: 41, 203
childcare: 44
childcare costs, help with: 203
Childcare Development Officer (Disabilities): 29
Childcare Develop't Team: 107

225

Childcare Grant: 40
childcare, choosing: 97, 107
childcare, cost of: 204, 205
childhood problems: 25
Childline: 27
childminders: 204
children with special needs (see also special needs): 28–29
children's authors: 141, 142
children's certificate: 125
children's clothes: 90
children's clothes shops: 81
children's clothes, labelling: 94, 95
children's guides: 145
Children's hospital: 20
Children's House Montessori Nursery School: 217
children's libraries: 100–101
children's parties: 174–181
Children's Podiatry Clinic: 28
Children's Services Librarian: 101
Chiltern Sculpture Trail: 147
Chinese Christian Church: 68
Chinese community: 21
Chinese Community & Advice Centre: 41, 54
Chinese Community Centre Saturday Club: 200
Chinese herbal medicine: 30,35
Chinese playscheme: 168
Chinese restaurant: 120
Chinese supermarket: 78, 140
Chinnor & Princes Risborough Railway: 159
Chipping Norton: 180
chiropractors: 30
choirs: 194–195
Cholsey & Wallingford Railway: 159
Christ Church Meadow: 131, 135
Christmas Common: 147
Christmas, Father: 144, 157, 158
Chunky Monkeys: 151, 177
Church Cowley St James School: 58, 215
churches: 64–67

Churchill hospital: 20
cinemas: 180–181
Citizen's Advice Bureau: 40
City Council Events Team: 165
City Council, website: 182–183
Civic Centre, Aylesbury: 180
Clarks: 82, 86, 87
classes, antenatal: 6
classes, parenthood: 6
classes, postnatal: 17
clay: 167
Clifden Arms: 129
climbing frames: 87
climbing wall parties: 179
Clockhouse: 41
clothes agency: 85
clothes shops: 81
clothes, breastfeeding: 89
clothes, children's: 90
clothes, dressing up: 92
clothes, secondhand: 84–85
clothes, waterproof: 91
clowns: 176
Club Francais, le: 198
clumps: 148
Co–op: 78, 79
Coach House, Headington Quarry: 60
coffee groups: 50
Cogges Manor Farm Museum: 141, 154
colleges: 135
Colonel Custard: 176
community–based antenatal care: 4
community church: 64, 65
community education: 25, 113
Community English School: 113
Community Health Council: 22
Community Midwives: 4
Community Play Tennis Programme: 188
Compassionate Friends: 27
complaints about births: 14
complementary medicines: 10, 30–35
computer games for children: 98–99

computing classes with crèche: 111
concerts: 180–181
Contemporary Creative Dance: 191
continuing education: 113
continuous payment authorities: 89
contraception, emergency: 2
contraception, postnatal: 13
Convocation Coffee House: 84, 117
Cookerburra: 97
cooking, for children: 198, 201–202
Coral Reef: 149
Corn Exchange, Newbury: 180
Corner Farm: 80
Cornwall: 172
Corpus Christi: 66
costumes: 163
Cot Death Helpline: 27
cots, travel: 96
Cotswold Farm Park: 154, 180
Cotswold Water Park: 147
Cotswold Wildlife Park: 154
cottage hospitals: 4
cottages, holiday: 169–170
Cotton–tails: 37, 90
cotton nappies: 36–38
Council Tax Benefit: 41
counselling: 44, 45, 46, 47, 55
counselling, for children: 27
country crafts, demonstrations: 154
Country Lanes: 147
countryside events: 167, 202
countryside sites: 136–137, 202
County Council employees, childcare for: 206
County Council, early years services: 39–40
Courses for Parents: 48
covered market: 78, 80, 117, 175
Cowley: 102, 103
Cowley Community Centre: 192
Cowley Road festival: 143

Cowley Road Methodist
  Church: 58, 65
cows: 135, 136
craft materials: 55, 91–92, 95,199
craft workshops: 166–167, 180
crafts: 198–199, 201–202
cranial osteopathy: 32–33
Crazy Colosseum: 151, 165, 186
crazy golf: 133, 166
crèche: 25
crèche workers: 107
crèche, mobile (for hire): 108
crèches: 51, 53
crèches: 65, 107, 152, 183
crèches at sports & leisure
  centres: 109
crèches, drop–in: 108
crib services: 144
cricket: 134
crisis loans: 41
crocodile, giant inflatable for
  parties: 177
croquet: 91
Crown: 129
CRUSE: 27, 46
Cry–sis: 15, 26
crying: 26
CS Lewis Nature Reserve: 136
Cub Scouts: 201
Cuddesdon Corner: 55, 111, 116
Culpeper herbalists: 32, 35
Cumnor: 63, 196
Cumnor & Kennington
  Community Education Centre:
  113
Cumnor Montessori Nursery:
  217
Curioxity: 137
curry houses: 119, 121
cushions, maternity: 90
Cutteslowe Community
  Centre: 61, 200
Cutteslowe for Under–8s: 40,
  43
Cutteslowe Park: 133
Cutteslowe Pavilion, hire of:
  178
Cutteslowe School: 214

Cutty Sark: 163
cycling: 73–75, 133, 134
cycling proficiency classes: 165
Cygnet Nursery: 209
D
Dairy Crest: 79
dance: 189–193
dance classes with crèche: 111
dance co–ordinator: 189
dance theatre: 190
dance, acrobatic: 192
dance, contemporary: 190, 191,
  192
dance, integrated: 190
dancing games: 192
dancing, European folk: 192
dancing, for under 5s: 189–193
dancing, Irish: 192
dancing, jazz: 191, 193
Dao Clinic: 31
Dawson & Son: 91
day care, day nurseries – see
  nurseries:
Days Lock: 149
Deaf & Hard of Hearing
  Centre: 43
deaf children (see also special
  needs): 43
death (see bereavement)
death of a baby: 12
Debbie's School of Dance &
  Fitness: 193
Debenhams: 123
decorative arts: 163
Deddington Arms: 129
deer park: 135
delivery (see home delivery)
Dennis the Menace: 160
dentists: 23
dental treatment, free: 41
depression, postnatal: 15, 44,
  45, 46, 47
Derek & Christie: 176
design, art &: 198
Designaway: 177
Devil's Backbone: 134
Didcot: 158
Didcot Railway Centre: 158

Didcot Wave: 150
dietary supplements: 1
dietitians: 27, 34
Dinky Doo Nursery: 209
Dinosaur School: 48
dinosaurs: 139, 160, 162
diphtheria: 23–24
disabilities, preventing: 1
disabled children: 28–29, 169,
  183, 186, 190, 206–209, 215,
  216, 221
disabled parents: 9, 43, 58
Disabled Parents Network: 43
disadvantaged areas,
  children in: 45
discount goods: 85
discounts on council sports
  facilities: 183
Disney shop: 81, 82
divorce: 44
Docklands: 163
doctor, registering with a: 1, 13
dodo: 139
dogs: 165
dolls' houses: 91–92, 160
domestic help: 96–97
domestic violence: 47
donkeys: 155
Donnington Doorstep: 50, 55,
  116, 166
Donnington Doorstep
  (crèche): 108
Donnington Doorstep
  (toy library): 104
Donnington Playgroup: 212
Dorothy Perkins: 86
doula: 5
dovecote: 148
Dovecote After School Club:
  200
Dovecote Centre: 59
Dovecote playscheme: 168
drama: 191, 192, 193–194
drama clubs: 193
drama schools: 193–194
dressing up clothes: 92
drop–in activity clubs: 199–201
drop–in centres (see also

227

family centres): 116
drop-in crèches: 108
DSS: 42
Ducklings, water confidence sessions: 184–185
ducks: 133, 134
dyslexia: 26–27
Dyslexia Research Trust: 26
Dyslexic Association, Oxfordshire: 27

E
Early Learning Centre: 82, 91
Early Years Development & Childcare Partnership: 39–40
Early Years Development Plan: 211
early years education grant: 210–211
Early Years Grant: 40
Early Years Information Line: 39, 211
Early Years playscheme: 168
earthquake: 162
EASOCEC: 25, 113
East Oxford Community Centre: 191, 195
East Oxford Health Centre: 23
East Oxford Playgroup: 212
East Oxford School: 215
East Oxford School of Ballet: 191
Easter Monday: 141
Eastern European restaurant: 121
eating, faddy: 27
eczema: 27, 34, 56, 90
Edamame: 120
Edgar's Café: 84, 117
educating your child at home: 220
Education Department: 219
Education Otherwise: 220
education, adult: 25
education, community: 25
education, for travellers: 106
education, parenting (see parenting):
egg collecting: 156, 171

eggs, Easter: 141
Eights: 142
Elder Stubbs Allotment Festival: 143
electric breast pump hire: 96
Elms Road Nursery: 105
Elms Road Nursery School: 214
EMBS: 112
emergencies: 21, 23
emergency contraception: 2
Emmanuel Christian School: 217
emotional support for parents: 43–46
emotional upsets, children: 27
Energisers: 186, 187
English Country Cottages: 170
English languages classes, free: 112–113
entertainers: 176
Enviro (UK) Ltd: 37
environmental groups: 202
equipment for babies and children: 90
equipment hire (see also specific item): 72–73, 96
equipment, secondhand: 84–85
Escor Toys: 91
Esporta Health & Racquets Club: 109, 168
ethical traders: 90
Ethnic Minority Business Service (EMBS): 112
ethnographic museum: 138
European folk dancing: 192
European School: 219
events, annual: 141–144
exercise, antenatal: 8, 9
exercise, postnatal: 12, 16
exhibitions: 166
experimental psychology, child development: 30
Explore @ Bristol: 161

F
fabrics: 82, 94
face painting: 180
facilities for children, local: having your say: 39–40

faddy eating: 27
fair: 143
fairtrade goods: 95
famers' markets: 117
family centres: 51, 54–56, 116–117, 165
Family Connections: 48
Family Links: 222
family mediation: 44
Family Nurturing Network: 26, 48
Family Science: 142
Far from the Madding Crowd: 125
farm animals: 153–157, 161
farm holidays: 170–171
farm parties: 179–180
farm shops: 95, 125, 155, 156
Farmer Gow's Activity Farm: 141, 155, 180
farmers' market: 78
Farmhouse: 41
Farmoor Reservoir: 147
farms: 141
Farmstay UK: 171
Father Christmas: 144, 157, 158
fathers' groups: 45, 48, 52, 53, 59
February events: 141–142
Federation of Children's Book Groups: 101
feeding babies & children: 22
feeding animals: 154, 155, 156, 171
feeding equipment: 94
feet: 28
Fellers: 80, 95
fencing: 165
ferry: 129
Ferry Centre, hire of: 178
Ferry Pool: 177, 184
Ferry Sports Centre: 110
Ferryman Inn: 129
fertility problems: 2
Festival of Sport: 166
festivals: 142, 143
Field House Montessori Nursery: 216
film club for children: 181

Film in the Parks: 141
films: 161
films, free: 141
Fire Station, Old: 181
fireworks displays: 144
First Aid: 24–25, 112
First Born: 37
First Church of Christ,
   Scientist: 68
fish: 157
fish restaurant: 120
Fishers: 120
Fishes Inn: 127
fishmongers: 78
fitness: 109–110
Flame: 120
fleeces: 89, 91
Florence Park Family Centre:
   51, 55–56, 116
Florence Park Open Day:
   165
flute teachers: 197
Flying Start: 61
Focus 4 Health: 32, 34
folic acid: 1
folk dancing: 192
food, organic: 79, 80, 83
football: 165, 166, 168, 176, 177,
   187–188
football coaching: 187–188
Footsteps: 76
foreign language books: 101,
   106
Foresight (pre-conceptual
   care): 34
Forest Farm nursery: 216
fossils: 136, 137, 139, 202
fostering: 2
Four Pillars Hotels Leisure
   Clubs: 110
French: 197, 198
French speaking families: 58
friends, making: 50, 221–222
frogs: 155
Fun in the Parks: 141 ff, 165–166
Fundays: 151
Funtasia: 151
Fusion: 111, 191, 195

G
Galt Education: 91
games: 91–92, 106, 201–202
games, toddler gym &: 187
Gap: 81
garden centres: 124, 157
Gardener's Arms: 127
gardening: 165
gardens: 125, 145, 146, 160
gardens, of colleges: 135
Garsington opera: 130
Gaydon: 158
General Elliot: 127, 134
general practitioners
   (see GPs):
George & Davis: 117
George & Kay Luck: 91
George clothes: 92
George Inn: 129
German measles: 1, 24
Gibbons: 80
gifts: 91
Gingerbread: 42
Gino's: 117
Girl Guides Association: 201
glass painting: 198
glasses, free: 41
GNC: 80
go karts: 153, 158, 179
Godstow Nunnery: 137
Godwin's Ice–Cream Farm: 124
Golden Cross: 129
Goldfish Bowl: 118, 140
golf, crazy: 133
golf, pitch & putt: 166
Good Bean Coffee Co: 118
gorillas: 160
Gourmet Pizza: 122
GP, changing: 22
GP, registering with a: 1, 13
GPs: 19
Grandpont Nursery School: 214
Great Little Trading Company: 90
Great Western Outlet Village: 87
Great Whipsnade Railway: 159
Greek Orthodox church: 68
Green Board Game Co: 91
Green Pack: 28–29

Green Pages: 31
greengrocers: 78
greenhouses: 125, 135, 155
Greenwich: 163
Greyfriars: 65
grottos: 144, 157
groups, email: 52
Gubbins Farm: 180
Guide Friday: 141
Guides, Girl: 201
guinea pigs, free range: 157
gymnastic clubs & classes:
   186–187
gyms: 109–110, 186–187
gypsy community: 21, 106
H
HACEC: 113
hair analysis: 34
halls for hire: 177–179
Happy Valley: 136
Harcourt Arboretum: 147
Harwell: 197
Haven Holidays: 173
Hawkins Bazaar: 91
Head of the River: 125
Headington: 85, 102
Headington After School
   Club: 200
Headington Baptist Church:
   60, 66, 68
Headington Hill Park: 134
Headington Nursery School:
   214
Headington United Reformed
   Church: 66
headlice: 28
health advice: 18–19
health advocacy: 21
health centres: 51
health information: 21
health problems: 25
health promotion: 24
health services, complaints: 22
health services, out of hours:
   21
health support services: 20–21
health visitor parent & baby
   groups: 51

229

health visitors: 18–19, 213
health, postnatal: 14
hearing problems (see also deaf children): 213
Hedgehog World: 156
hedgehogs: 156
Hell–Fire Caves: 129, 147
help, live–in: 204, 205
Henley on Thames: 197
herb garden: 146
herbal medicine: 30, 32, 33, 35
Heritage Motor Centre: 158
heritage railways: 159
Hexagon Theatre, Reading: 180
HIB: 24
hide and seek: 125
High Wycombe: 87, 92, 94, 151, 152, 156, 178, 180
Higher Nature: 34
hiking: 201–202
Hildegard Junior Choir: 194
Hill Farm: 141
Hill Toy Company: 91
Hinksey Kids' Club: 200
Hinksey Parks: 131
Hinksey Pool: 110, 186
hire services: 95
hire, bicycle: 147
hire, car roof box: 76, 170
hire, rooms for parties: 176–179
hiring baby equipment: 72
hockey, ice: 189
holiday activity clubs: 172–173
holiday camps: 168
Holiday Care Service: 169
holiday parks: 172–173
holiday playschemes: 165
holiday workshops: 166–167
holidays, cheap: 169, 171–172
holidays, for lone parents: 169
holidays, home exchange: 171–172
holidays, organic: 171
holidays, school: 143
holidays, summer: 143
Holland & Barrett: 35
Hollycombe Steam Collection: 159

Holton Village Hall: 105
Holy Trinity: 66
Home–Start: 20–21, 43–44
Home Base Holidays: 172
home births: 5
home delivery, food: 78, 80, 95
home delivery, meat: 95
home delivery, milk: 79
home delivery, vegetables: 95
home education: 220
home exchange holidays: 171–172
Home of Rest for Horses: 129, 155
homeless families: 21
HomeLink: 171–172
homeopathy: 30, 33–34
Honest Stationery: 175
Hopscotch: 92
horse riding: 188
horses: 134, 143, 155
horticultural events: 165
Horton hospital: 20
hospital, care after birth: 11
hospital, children in: 20
hospitals: 19–20
hospitals, cottage (outside city): 4
Hot Air Balloon Fiesta: 143, 166
hotels for families: 172
houseswap: 172
Housing Benefit: 41
Housing Rights Centre: 41
human milk bank, donating: 22
Humpty Dumpty music group: 195
Hunsdon House Nursery School: 216
hyperactivity: 34
I
ice cream: 117, 124, 146
ice hockey: 189
ice skating: 178, 181, 188–189
ice skating club: 189
Iceland: 78, 79
Iffley Church: 136
Iffley Church Hall: 191
Iffley Lock: 136

IMAX theatre: 161
immunisations: 18, 23–24, 183
Income Support: 41
incontinence: 14
independent schools: 219
Independent Schools Information Service: 219
Indian community: 21
Indian restaurants: 119, 121
indoor activity: 150–153
infant development group: 30
infant resuscitation: 17
Inland Revenue: 42, 203
Inner Bookshop: 31, 35, 83
instruments, musical: 194, 197
Integrated Dance: 190
Internet: 181
Internet access, free: 103
Internet shopping: 79
interpretation, for Asian families: 45
Irish dancing: 192
iron–on labels: 95
ISCis: 219
Isis Centre: 44
Isis Tavern: 127, 136
Islamic School: 69
Islamic study classes: 69
IVF (in vitro fertilisation): 2
J
Jack and Jill Club: 196
Jack Straws Lane Nursery: 208
Jacquie Bebbington's School of Dance: 192
Japanese restaurant: 120
Jardine's Club: 177
Jarn Mound: 147
jazz dancing: 191, 193
Jazz in the Parks: 166
Jazzmates: 191
Jehovah's Witnesses: 68
Jenners Pharmacy: 37
Jericho Family Lunch Club: 116
Jericho Health Centre: 51
Jeune Street Parent & Toddler Group: 58
Jewish Centre: 68
Jigsaw Day Nursery: 209

230

jigsaws: 92
Jo–Jo Maman Bebe: 89
Jobcentre: 43
John Allen Centre: 86
John Bunyan Baptist Church Hall: 192
John Bunyan Centre: 59
John Lewis: 87, 94
John Radcliffe Hospital: 1, 19
JR (see John Radcliffe Hospital):
Julia Durbin Day Nursery: 207
June events: 143
Just Fabrics: 94
K
Kaleidoscope Centre for Families: 117
Kaleidoscope Family Centre: 27, 51, 56
Kangaroo Club summer playscheme: 169
Kangaroo Craft Club: 198
karate: 189
Karate Academy: 191
Kazbar: 120
Kennington: 63, 67, 103, 104, 113, 196, 209, 216
Keycamp holidays: 170
Kiddies Korner: 208
Kidlington: 62, 67, 102, 109, 186
Kidlington & Gosford Sports Centre: 109, 151, 165, 177, 192
Kidlington Baptist Church: 67, 196
Kidlington Pre–school: 212
Kidlington swimming pool: 185
Kids' Art: 198
Kids Unlimited: 206, 207, 208, 209
Kidsplay: 193
Kinderkids: 152
King's Arms (Holywell & Broad Streets): 126
King's Arms (Sandford on Thames): 129
Kipper Foot Dance Co: 192
kites: 134, 148
knitting: 81

Knoll House Hotel: 172
kookaburras: 157
Kwiksave: 78
L
La Leche League: 14, 22
labels, iron–on: 95
labour rooms: 10
labour, pain relief: 10
Ladybird clothes: 86
Lake District: 173
Lake Street Playgroup: 212
lakes: 133, 134, 135, 146, 147, 153
lambing: 141, 154, 155
language development: 29
languages, foreign: 197–198, 219
Lark Rise Primary After School Club: 200
Lark Rise Primary School: 215
laser games: 153
Laserquest: 177–178
Launchpad: 163
laundry: 56
Lauvic Babysitters & Nanny Service: 205
Le Manoir aux Quat' Saisons: 121
Le Petit Blanc: 121
lead in water supply: 23
legal advice, free: 40
Legoland: 160
Leighton Buzzard Railway: 159
leisure centres with crèches: 109
leisure centres without crèches: 110
Let's Go with the Children: 145
Letterbox: 92
Letterbox Library: 93
Leys Community Church: 65
Leys Fair: 166
Liaison: 120
librarian, Children's Services: 101
libraries: 166
libraries, children's: 100–101
libraries, mobile: 103
libraries, toy: 100, 103–106
lice: 28

linoprinting: 198
literacy, adult: 111–112
literary festival: 114
Little Animals Activity Centre: 98
Little Music Group: 197
Little Scholars: 206, 209
Little Sharks: 60
Littlemore: 102
Littlemore Community Centre: 51, 56, 117
Littlemore Primary School: 215
Littlewoods: 123
Living Rainforest: 155
lizards: 157
loans, crisis: 41
Local Guide for Parents of Disabled Children and Young People and those with Special Needs: 29
lock: 136, 149
locomotives, see trains, steam engines:
Lollipop: 38
London: 130, 162–163
London Aquarium: 162
London by bus: 75
lone parents: 42–43
lone parents, holidays: 169
Long Bridges: 136
Long Hanborough Bus Museum: 158
Longleat Forest: 173
Lookout Discovery Centre: 161
loos: 84
Lord Mayor's Parade: 142
lunch–in–a–box: 123
lunches, cheap: 116–117
Lung Wah Choung Chinese Supermarket: 78, 140
M
Macclesfield House: 219
Maclaren buggies: 96
Magdalen College: 135, 142
magic: 176
Magic Café: 83, 84, 118
Magic Martin: 176

231

magic maze hire: 96, 175
Maize maze: 156
Mama Mia: 122
MAMA: Mothers and Children at Asylum Welcome: 54
Man Enough: 48
Mansion House nursery: 207
March events: 142
Mario's: 122
markets: 78, 86
Marks & Spencer: 81, 123–124
Marriage Care: 46
Marsh Gibbon: 180
Marston United Reformed Church: 66
martial arts: 189
Mary Colegrove Ballet School: 190
Mason's Arms: 144
massage: 34
massage for pregnancy & birth: 34
massage, baby: 17, 34
Matalan: 86
material: 82, 94
Maternity Allowance: 41
maternity clothes: 86, 89–90
maternity clothes, hiring: 90
maternity cushions: 90
maths puzzles: 137
May fly: 142, 166
May morning: 142
Maybush Inn: 130
mazagines, parenting: 97
maze, hedge: 135, 146
maze, maize: 156
McDonald's: 122
McDonald's, parties: 178
measles: 24
measles, German: 24
Meat Matters: 95
medicines, complementary: 10
Medina Mosque: 69
meeting people: 221–222
meningitis C: 24
Mesopotamia: 134
messy play: 55, 56, 58, 62
Methodist Church Hall,

Headington Quarry: 60
Michael Greenwood: 82, 86
Mid–Hants Railway: 159
midwife: 4
midwives, independent: 5
midwives, parent education: 6
milk delivery: 79
milk, free: 41
milking: 171
milking, by hand: 154
mill: 134, 135
Millets Pick Your Own Farm: 155
Milton Keynes: 153, 179
mime: 180
MIND: 45, 46
Mini Boden: 90
miniature steam railway (see also trains etc): 133
miniatures: 160, 161
minibus, accessible: 201
Ministagers: 187
Minster Lovell: 148
miscarriage: 3
mixed race: 43
ML Au Pairs: 205
MMR: 24
mobile crèche: 108
mobile home self–drive holidays: 170
mobile libraries: 103
model boat museum: 154
model railways: 160, 161
model village: 160, 161
models: 159–161
Modern Art Oxford: 84, 118, 138, 167, 199
modern dancing: 189–193
MOMA (see Modern Art Oxford): 118
Monkey Music: 195, 196
monkeys: 155, 157, 160
Monsoon: 81
Montessori nurseries: 216–217
Moonbase: 152, 178
Moonlight Tandoori: 121
Moreton in Marsh: 147
Mornese Centre: 59
Morris dancing: 142, 144

Mortimer Hall: 191, 193–194
Mortimer Hall Playgroup: 212
mosaic classes with crèche: 111
mosques: 69
Mothercare: 38, 72, 82, 86, 89
motor museum: 158
Moya: 121
multi–sport activity sessions: 168
multicultural books: 93, 106
multiple births: 9
mummers play: 144
mumps: 24
Mum's the Word: 205
Museum of Berkshire Aviation: 159
Museum of Oxford: 138, 166
museum, working: 154
museums: 137–139, 154, 157–159, 161–163, 166
mushroom hunt: 144
music: 180, 198, 194–197
Music & Fun for 0–4s: 196
music & movement: 189–193
Music at Oxford: 180
music groups, under 5s: 195–197
Music Service, Oxfordshire: 194
musical instruments: 91, 194, 197
Musical Tots: 196
Muslim groups: 53, 69
N
name tapes, stickers, labels: 94, 95
naming: 13
Nando's: 121
nannies: 204–205
nanny agencies: 205
nanny shares: 204, 205
Nan's Nearly New: 85
nappies: 35–38
nappies, disposables: 35
nappies, drying: 36
nappies, environmental impact: 35
nappies, home delivery services: 37, 38
nappies, laundry services: 38
nappies, real/cotton/washable: 36–38, 90

232

nappies, reusable swimming: 183–184
nappies, swimming: 183–184
nappies, washing: 36–37
nappy changing: 83–84, 86, 90
nappy liners: 35
nappy rash: 37
Nappy Tales: 38
National Association of Toy & Leisure Libraries: 103
National Asthma Campaign: 26
National Childbirth Trust: 7, 22, 25, 44, 48, 52, 57, 85, 89, 97, 172
National Childminding Association: 204
National Council for One-Parent Families: 42, 169
National Eczema Society: 27
National Gardens Scheme: 145
National Maritime Museum: 163
National Pre-school Learning Alliance: 211
National Rail Enquiries: 160
Natural History Museum, London: 162
Natural History, Oxford University Museum of: 139
nature: 202
nature reserves: 136–137, 148
NAWOCEC: 113
NAWOTOY: 105
NCT – see National Childbirth Trust:
NCT breastfeeding counsellor: 22
NCT Houseswap Register: 172
Neal's Yard Remedies: 35
nearly new sales: 52, 85
New Deal for Lone Parents: 43
New Hinksey Primary School: 104
New Marston Pre-school: 212
New Marston Primary School: 215
New Parent Network: ii, 48, 52, 57, 97
New Road Baptist Church: 64

New Road Baptist Church Coffee House: 118
New Start Adult Guidance Adviser: 111
New Theatre, Oxford: 181
New Year's Day: 149
newborn, sick: 12
Next Directory: 89
NHS card: 13
NHS Direct: 1, 21, 26
NHS treatment, free: 40, 41
NHS Trust staff, childcare for: 206, 207
Nigel the Clown: 176
nits: 28
non-smoking eating places: 116
noodle bar: 121
North Oxford Association: 1 78, 196
Northleigh Roman villa: 148
Northway Evangelical Church: 60
Nosebag & Saddlebag: 84
Notcutts Garden Centre: 124
Nuffield Orthopaedic Trust hospital: 20
Nuneham Courtenay: 147
nurseries, day: 205–209
nurseries, private: 208–209
nurseries, workplace: 206–208
nursery classes, state: 213–216, 218
nursery schools, private: 216–217
nursery schools, state: 213–214
Nursery, The: 208
nurses, school: 19
Nut Tree Inn: 130
nutrition: 22, 27, 34
O
Oak Farm Rare Breeds Park: 156
Oasis: 46
obstetric physiotherapists: 16
Odds Farm Park: 156, 180
ODEC: 106
OFSTED: 107, 203, 204, 205–206, 208, 211

Old Fire Station: 181
Old Manor House Riding School: 188
Old Marston: 102
Old Orleans: 121
Olde Leatherne Bottle: 130
One Parent Benefit: 41
open air market: 78
Open Learning Centre: 111
opera: 130
Orchard Meadow School: 215
Orchard Toys: 92
organic box scheme: 79, 95
organic cotton: 90
organic food suppliers: 79, 80, 83, 95
organic holidays: 171
Organics Direct: 95
orienteering: 202
Orinoco Scrap Store: 199
osteopaths: 30, 32–33, 34
osteopathy, cranial: 32–33
Otmoor: 146, 153
Our Lady's School: 215
Our Lady's School Playgroup: 212
Our Lady's Toddler Group: 59
out of hours health services: 21
outdoor clothes: 83
outdoor equipment shops: 83
outdoor play equipment: 87, 93, 94
outdoor pursuits: 201–202
outdoor swimming: 185–186
outreach workers: 50
oven cleaning service: 97
overseas adoption: 2
Owls Educational Direct: 92
Oxfam Workplace Nursery: 207
Oxford Academy of Dance: 190
Oxford Acupuncture Centre: 31
Oxford Airport: 109
Oxford Brookes Uni Nursery: 207
Oxford Brookes University: 119
Oxford Bus Company: 75, 76

233

Oxford Children's Book Group: 106
Oxford City Council: 182–183
Oxford City Ice Hockey Club: 189
Oxford College of Further Education: 111, 113
Oxford Community Church: 64
Oxford Complementary Medicine Group: 31
Oxford Dance Centre: 190
Oxford Development Education Centre: 106
Oxford Ice Rink: 178, 181, 188–189
Oxford Ice Skating Club: 189
Oxford International Women's Festival: 114
Oxford Karate Academy: 191
Oxford Literary Festival: 114, 142
Oxford Mobile Creche: 108
Oxford Montessori Nursery: 216, 217
Oxford Nursery: 209
Oxford Parent Infant Project (OXPIP): 44
Oxford Playhouse: 167, 181
Oxford Pram Centre: 72, 86, 96
Oxford Quaker Centre: 80, 82
Oxford Retail Park: 86
Oxford Riding School: 188
Oxford School of Martial Arts: 189
Oxford Silver Band Hall: 178
Oxford station, original: 158
Oxford Story: 140
Oxford Tube: 75, 162
Oxford Twins Club: 52
Oxford United Football Club: 187
Oxford University Dept of Continuing Education: 113
Oxford University Museum of Natural History: 139
Oxford University Press staff, childcare: 206
Oxford University staff/students; childcare for: 206

Oxford Women's Counselling Centre: 47
Oxford Women's Training Scheme: 112
Oxford Youth Choir: 195
Oxford Youth Dance: 191–192
Oxford, history of: 138, 140
Oxfordshire Active Sports: 188
Oxfordshire Children's Information Service: 29, 44, 57, 94, 107, 164, 169, 183, 187, 199, 204, 206, 210, 211, 217
Oxfordshire Education Department: 219
Oxfordshire Family Mediation Service: 44
Oxfordshire Mental Health Resource Centre: 47
Oxfordshire MIND (see MIND):
Oxfordshire Museum: 124–125
Oxfordshire Music Service: 194
Oxfordshire Parent Education Development Team: 221
Oxfordshire Parent Partnership: 28
Oxfordshire Parenting Forum: 48–49
Oxfordshire Playbus Association: 167, 201
Oxfordshire Pre-school Learning Alliance: 211
Oxfordshire Real Nappy Network: 37
Oxfordshire Women's Aid: 47
Oxkids After School Club: 200
OXPIP: 15
Oxsrad Sports & Leisure Centre: 110, 186
Oxsrad, hire: 178
P
paddling pools: 133, 134, 149, 150, 154, 161
paediatricians: 19
pain relief during labour: 10
pain, back: 30, 34
painting parties: 177

painting, face: 180
Pakistani community: 21
Palestrina Boys Choir: 194
panto: 192
Parasol: 169, 183
Parent–Teacher Association: 221–222
Parent Education Development Team: 49
parent education midwives: 6
parenthood classes: 6
Parenthood Web: 97
parenting education: 47–49, 52, 97
Parentline Plus: 27, 45
Parents Open Door (POD) Centre: 42
Parents with Disabilities Toddler Group: 58
parents, lone/single – see lone parents:
Park & Ride: 76
Park Sports Centre: 109
parking: 76
parks: 132–134, 141
Parks Office: 132
parties: 91–92, 96, 174–181
parties, farm: 179–180
parties, ideas for: 181
parties, items for hire: 175
parties, themes: 181
party entertainment: 174, 176
party food: 175, 176–179, 180–181
party games: 176, 178
party gifts/bags: 175
party invitations: 175
Party Pieces: 175
Party Plus: 175
party rooms for hire: 176–179
party stationery: 175
Party Works: 175
Partymania: 175
Partyworks: 92
Pass the Parcel: 85
pasta: 119
pastels: 198
patchwork: 95

Paulton's Park: 160–161
PE: 186
PEEP: 105, 220–221
PEEP groups: 52, 55, 221
Peers Early Education Partnership – see PEEP:
Peers Sports & Arts Centre: 178, 187, 192
Peers swimming pool: 184–185
Pegasus Primary School After School Club: 200
Pegasus School: 215
Pegasus Theatre: 191, 193
pelvic floor exercises: 16
pelvic pain: 9, 14
Pendon Museum of Miniature Landscape & Transport: 161
penguins: 157
Perch: 127, 136
performance: 192, 193–194
performing arts: 189–195
perineal clinic: 14
Persian restaurant: 120
petanque: 166
pets: 157, 165
pharmacists: 19, 21
Phoenix cinema: 181
Phoenix Day Nursery: 216
photography, family portrait: 94
physical education: 186
physiotherapists: 16
piano teachers: 197
Pick–Your–Own fruit and vegetables: 155, 156
picnic places: 131, 137, 147, 148, 154, 155, 163
pigs, free–range: 155
pilates: 109–110
pilates postnatal exercise: 16
piñata: 175, 181
pirate ship: 150
pitch & putt: 166
Pitt Rivers museum: 138, 166
pizza: 119
Pizza Express: 122
Pizza Hut: 122
places of worship: 64–69
Plasterer's Arms: 127

Play Day: 167
Play Development Team: 164, 183, 199
Play for All: 164, 168, 169, 200
play pen hire: 96
play projects: 199–201
play schemes: 143
Playbus: 167, 201
playdays: 183
playgrounds: 132–134, 146, 154
playgrounds, adventure: 164–165
playgroups: 210, 211–213
Playhouse, Oxford: 167, 181
playschemes: 165, 168–169
Plough (Garsington): 130
Plough (Long Wittenham): 130
Plough (Sutton Courtenay): 130
Plough (Wolvercote): 127
ploughing: 157
POD Centre: 42
podiatry: 28
poetry: 142
polio: 23–24
Polstead Playgroup: 212
Pomp in the Parks: 141
pond–dipping: 137
ponies: 155
Pooh sticks: 149
pool, birthing: 11
pools, adventure: 149–150
pools, indoor: 109–110, 149, 150, 165, 173, 179
pools, open air: 110, 134, 146, 149, 150, 185–186
pools, paddling – see paddling pools:
Port Mahon: 127
Port Meadow: 136, 143
portraits, photographic: 94
Post House Patchwork: 95
postnatal checkup: 13
postnatal classes: 17
postnatal depression: 15
postnatal exercises: 12, 16, 17
postnatal groups: 22, 44, 50, 51, 52
postnatal health: 14

postnatal illness: 15
pottery classes & workshops: 167, 199
pottery parties: 177
pram hire: 72, 96
pram repairs: 73, 96
prams: 71–72
prams, on buses: 75
prayer: 114
pre–eclampsia: 4
pre–school education: 205–209, 210
pre–school education, funding for: 210–211
Pre–school Learning Alliance: 211
pre–school teacher–counsellor: 221
pre–schools: 210, 211–213
pregnancy: 97
pregnancy tests: 3
pregnancy, planning a: 1
pregnancy, problems in: 4
prenatal problems: 4
prescriptions, free: 41
primary school: 218
Prince of Wales (Iffley): 127
Princes Risborough: 155, 159
private nurseries – see nurseries:
private schools: 219
private schools, summer playschemes: 169
psychotherapy: 44
PTA: 221–222
Public Health Service lab: 24
pubs: 125–131
pubs, in Central Oxford: 125–126
pubs, outside ring road: 128–131
pubs, outstanding: 126, 128, 129
pubs, within ring road: 126–128
Punch & Judy: 176
punting: 141
Pupil Services: 221
puppets: 91, 98, 160, 167, 176, 180
pushchairs: 71–72
puzzles: 91–92, 98

235

Q
Quainton: 157–158
Quaker Shop: 80
Quakers: 68
quiet time: 114
quizzes: 166
Quranic classes: 69

R
rabbits: 133
Radcliffe Infirmary: 19, 206
radio roadshow: 166
Radley School: 187
railway centres: 144, 157–159
railway timetables: 160
railway, steam (miniature) – see also trains: 133
Rainbow House: 56, 84, 116
Rainbows: 201
rainforest: 155, 161
Raleigh Park: 137
rash, nappy: 37
raspberry picking: 156
Read & Play packs: 105–106
reading: 222
reading, recommended: 101
Real Nappy Association: 37
rebound therapy: 186
reclaim schemes: 199
recorder teachers: 197
Rectory Farm Pick Your Own: 156
recycling: 199
red book: 18
Red Cross: 25
Red House Books: 86, 94
Red Lion: 130
Red Lion Hotel: 130
Red Star Noodle Bar: 121
reflection: 114
reflexology: 30, 35
refugees: 21, 46, 54, 112–113
Registrar of Births: 12
RELATE: 47
Religious Society of Friends: 68
Remnant Kings: 82
repairs, prams & buggies: 73, 96
Reptile House: 157
restaurant, Chinese: 120
restaurant, Eastern European: 121
restaurant, fish: 120
restaurant, Indian: 119, 121
restaurant, Japanese: 120
restaurant, Persian: 120
restaurant, Thai: 120
restaurant, training: 119
restaurant, Turkish: 119
restaurants, famous: 120, 121
restaurants, in shops: 123–124
restaurants, Italian: 122
restaurants, pizza & pasta: 122–123
RESTORE: 143
resuscitation, infant and child: 17
retreats: 114
return to learn: 111
Revival: 85
Rewley House: 113
RI Nursery: 206
Rice Box: 122
Risinghurst Community Centre: 61, 191, 193
river trips: 141
Road Safety Group: 76, 97
roads, crossing: 76
Roald Dahl Children's Gallery: 162
Robin Toddlers: 63
Rock Edge: 137
roller coasters: 160
Rollright Stones: 130
Roman villa: 148
roof box hire: 76, 170
Rookery Nursery: 207
room hire, for parties: 176–179
Rose Hill After School Club: 200
Rose Hill Community Centre: 192
Rose Hill Methodist Church: 66
Rose Hill Primary School: 59, 215
Rose Revived: 131
Round Table fireworks display: 144
roundabouts: 160
Rover Rompers Nursery: 208
Rowan: 81
Royal Oak Farm Tea Room: 125
RSPB Wildlife Explorers Club: 202
rubella: 1, 24
Rugbug: 91
ruins: 146, 148
Ruskin College: 111
Ruskin Learning Project: 111
Russell & Bromley: 82
Russian food suppliers: 78
Russian Orthodox church: 68

S
sailing: 147
Sainsbury: 78, 79
St Alban's Church Hall: 191
St Aldates Church Coffee House: 118
St Aldates Parish Church: 57, 64
St Aloysius: 67
St Andrew's Church Hall, Botley: 189
St Andrew's Church, Linton Road: 61, 67
St Andrew's Church, Old Headington: 66
St Andrews Morning/After School Club: 201
St Anne's Nursery: 206
St Antony of Padua: 66
St Barnabus After School Club: 201
St Barnabus Community Centre: 57
St Barnabus Mums & Prams: 57
St Barnabus School: 214
St Clements Church: 58, 65
St Clements Church Pre–School: 212–213
St Clements Family Centre: 51, 58, 195
St Ebbe's Church: 57, 64
St Ebbe's Primary School: 104
St Ebbe's Toddler Group: 57
St Francis: 65
St Francis C of E Primary School: 191, 201, 215
St Giles Fair: 143
St Gregory's Church: 67

St James Cowley: 65
St John Ambulance Badgers & Cadets: 201
St John Ambulance Brigade: 25
St John Fisher School: 215
St Luke's: 42, 59
St Margaret's Church: 61
St Margaret's Well: 136
St Mary & St John: 65
St Mary & St John Primary After School Club: 200
St Mary the Virgin, University Church of: 140
St Mary's, Iffley Village: 66
St Matthew's Church: 65
St Matthew's Church Hall: 58, 178, 192
St Michael & All Angels, Marston: 66
St Michael at the Northgate: 139
St Nicholas Church,: 67
St Nicholas School: 215
St Paul's Day Nursery: 208
St Peter & Paul Church Hall: 105
St Peter's Under 5s Group, Wolvercote: 61, 212
St Philip & St James After School Club: 201
St Philip & St James School: 85, 190
St Swithun's Primary School: 216
St Swithun's School: 104
St Thomas Day Nursery: 206
St Tiggywinkle's: 156
Salter's Steamers: 141
Samaritans: 47
Sandfield Day Nursery: 207
Sandford–on–Thames: 63, 67, 110, 129
Sandford lock: 129
Sandhills Pre–School Playgroup: 213
sandpit, giant: 137, 154, 155, 156
Sandy Lane Farm: 180
Santa Steaming: 158
Saturdads: 53, 59
Saturday clubs: 199–201
Save the Children: 92

Saxon Way Youth Centre: 190
Scallyways Mums & Toddlers: 60
scan, ultrasound: 4
SCBU: 11
Schmidt Natural Clothing: 90
school catchment areas: 218–219
school dinners, free: 41
school nurses: 19
school, participating in: 221–222
school, preparing for: 220–221
school, the system in Oxford: 218
school, when to start: 218
schools, independent: 219
schools, primary & secondary: 218–220
schools, Steiner–Waldorf: 219–220
schools, visiting: 219
schoolwear: 81, 85
science galleries: 137, 161–162, 163
science kits: 91–92
Science Museum, London: 163
Science Week: 142
science, family: 142
Scout Association: 201
Scouts, boy and girl: 201
sculpture trail: 147
seat belts: 76
second chance college: 111
secondary school: 218
secondhand baby equipment: 72
secondhand clothes: 55, 84–85
secondhand prams: 72
secondhand shops: 84–85
Select Nanny & Babysitting Service: 205
self–help groups for parents: 43–46
self–help groups, general: 46–47
self esteem: 48, 222
separation: 44
Seven Stars: 131
sewing: 81, 95, 112
sexual problems: 14
shearing: 154, 155

Shepherd & Woodward: 86
Shepherds Hill Playgroup: 213
Sheriffe of Oxford's Races: 143
Sherwood Forest: 173
Shillingford: 157, 185
shoe shops: 82, 86
shoes, labelling: 95
Shoo Raynor: 98
shops, discount: 86–87
Shotover Country Park: 131, 137, 144
shows for children: 180–181
shrunken heads: 139
Sightseeing Tour: 141
Silver Band Hall: 178
Silver Star team: 4
Silvertrek: 179
Simply Stuck: 95
Sing–along music group: 196
singing: 191, 194–195
single parents (see lone parents):
Sitting Tight: 97
Six Bells: 144
skating, ice: 178
skeletons: 162
ski wear: 83
skiing, indoor: 153, 179
Slade Nursery: 61
Slade Nursery School: 214
sledging: 148, 153
sleep: 28
sleep counsellor: 28
sleeping bags: 83, 90
Slice card: 183
slings: 70–71, 89
Small World Montessori: 209
Smiley–Miley Music: 197
smoke–free eating guide: 116
smoking: 6
snakes: 157
Snakes & Ladders: 152, 179
snakeshead fritillary: 136
snow: 179
snowboarding & snowbiking: 153, 179
Snozone at Xscape: 179
Social Security office: 42

237

soft play: 150–153, 176, 178, 179
software, educational: 99
solicitor, free: 40
Somerfields: 78
Somerset House: 128
Somerville College Nursery: 207
South Hinksey: 134
South Oxford Adventure
    Playground: 165
South Oxford Baptist Church:
    58, 65, 68
South Oxford Community
    Centre: 192
South Oxford Parent & Toddler
    Group: 58
South Oxfordshire Starter
    Choir: 195
South Parade Health Centre: 26
South Parks: 131, 134
Spanish: 198
Sparkle Stage Set: 193
Special Care Baby Unit: 11
Special Experiences Register: 15
special needs, children with:
    28–29, 183, 186, 190, 206–209,
    212, 213, 214–217, 221
spectacles, free: 41
speech: 29
speech problems: 213
speech therapy: 29
Spiceball Park: 157
spiders: 157
spina bifida: 1
Sport, Festival of: 166
sports: 109–110, 167–168, 173, 201
sports centres with crèches:
    109
sports centres without crèches:
    110
Sports Development Team: 167,
    168, 187
sports parties: 177, 178
Spotlight Stage School: 193
Spring events: 142
Springboard Family Project: 45
squash: 109–110
SSNAP: 12
stage schools: 193–194

Stagecoach: 75, 76
Stagecoach Theatre Arts
    School: 193–194
Standlake: 63
Stanton House: 114
Stanton St John: 63, 131, 156
Star Inn: 131
Starbucks: 118
stationery: 83, 86
Statutory Maternity Pay: 41
STEAM: 159
steam engines: 157–159
Steiner–Waldorf schools:
    219–220
Steiner Waldorf Schools
    Fellowship: 220
Stepping Stones: 61
Stepping Stones Day Nursery:
    209
stillbirth: 12
stitches, painful: 14
stocking fillers: 91–92
Stoke Mandeville: 153
Stoner, John: 96
stories: 142
story times: 101, 166
Stratford: 130
strawberry picking: 156
Summertown: 86, 102, 110
Summertown Baby & Toddler
    Group: 61
Summertown Health Centre: 51
Summertown Stars: 188
Sunday afternoons: 167
Sunningwell School of Art: 199
Supercamps: 168
supermarket, Chinese: 78, 140
supermarkets: 78
support groups for parents:
    43–46
support groups, general: 46–47
Sure-Start Family Centre: 42,
    45, 56, 117
Sure-Start programme: 21, 104
Sure-Start (crèche): 108
surnames: 13
Sustrans National Cycle
    Network: 73

Suzuki music teachers: 197
Swan: 131
swimming: 28, 109–110, 112, 131,
    134, 137, 146, 147, 149–150, 165,
    173, 183–186
swimming aids: 83, 90, 91
swimming courses: 165
swimming lessons: 165, 184–185
swimming pool parties: 177–179
swimming pools: 165
swimming, antenatal classes: 8, 9
swimming, babies: 183–185
swimming, postnatal exercise: 16
Swindon: 87, 159
Swindon & Cricklade Railway: 159
swings: 87
Swings & Things: 87
symphysis pubis dysfunction: 9
T
table tennis: 133, 134, 187
Tac au Tac Dance Theatre: 190,
    191, 192
TAMBA: 10
tandoori restaurant: 121
tap dancing: 189–193
tea in the country: 124–125
tea rooms: 125
tears: 14
teddy bear shops: 86
teeth, care of: 23
teething: 29, 94
Teletubbyland: 146
television, children's: 94
Templars Square: 86
Temple Cowley Health Centre:
    51
Temple Cowley Swimming
    Pool: 179, 184
Temple Cowley Toddler
    Group: 59
ten pin bowling: 177
tennis: 109–110, 133, 166
tennis, mini: 188
tennis, summer coaching: 168,
    188
Tesco: 78, 79, 86
tetanus: 23–24
Thai food suppliers: 78

Thai restaurant: 120
Thame: 86, 109, 175
Thame Show: 153
Theatre Express: 194
Theatre, Chipping Norton: 180
Theatre, Pegasus: 191
theatres: 180–181
theme parks: 159–161
therapies, alternative: 30–35
therapy: 44
Thomas the Tank Engine: 157, 158
Thorpe Park: 161
Thrangu House Buddhist Centre: 69
Three Horseshoes: 131
Tiddington: 180
Tinies Oxford: 205
tobogganing: 179
Toddle In: 57
toddler clubs: 170
toddler groups: 57–63
toddler gym: 187
toddler splash: 184
toddlers: 157, 160
toilets: 84
Tolkien: 136, 141
Tollhurst Organic Farm: 95
Tooley's Boatyard: 157
Torpids: 142
Tots R Us: 63
tours of Oxford: 140–141
Tower Playbase After School Club: 200
Tower Playbase, Northway: 60, 104, 190
towers: 139–140
toy libraries: 56, 100, 103–106
toy libraries, dormant: 105
toy shops: 82, 86
toys: 91
toys, secondhand: 84–85
toys, wooden: 82–83, 90, 91–92
Toytown: 160
tractor rides: 156, 179–180
tractors: 125, 154, 155, 156, 157
Trading Standards: 88
Traditional Chinese Medicine: 35

Traidcraft: 95
trailer bikes: 74–75, 93, 147
train information: 160
train rides: 160
train rides, miniature steam engines: 133
train rides, steam engines: 154, 157–159
train sets: 91–92
trains: 134, 146, 147, 154,
trampolines: 87, 178, 186, 187,
trams: 159
translation, for Asian families: 45
transport: 157–159
travel cots: 96
travel system, choosing a: 71–72
traveller community: 21, 106
treasure hunts: 179–180, 181
trees (see also woodland): 134, 147
tricycles, adult: 74–75
Tridias: 92
tropical plants: 135
Trout: 128, 137
Truly Scrumptious: 175
Tumble Tots: 186, 187
Tumble Towers: 152, 179
Turbo Ted's Nursery: 208
Turf Tavern: 126
Turkish restaurant: 119
TV programmes, children's recommended : 94
Twinkle Twinkle: 38
twins: 9, 52
Twins Clubs: 52
Two Foot Nothing: 81
U
Uhuru: 38, 80
UKParents: 97
ultrasound library: 97
ultrasound scan: 4
Uncle Wiggy: 176
Under 5s: 97
Unicef: 93
University boat races: 142
University Church of St Mary the Virgin: 140
University Museum: 134, 166

University Parks: 131, 134
updates to this edition: 182
Upstage Dance: 193
Urchin Mail Order: 93
Urdu classes: 53, 112
V
V–cushions: 90
vaccinations: 1, 23–24, 183
valley cushion hire: 96
Vera Legge School of Dancing: 191, 192
Vera Legge School of Performing Arts: 193–194
verruca: 28
Victoria & Albert Museum: 162–163
Victoria Arms: 128
videos: 93, 94, 106
views of Oxford: 134, 139–140
Village Bakery: 80, 95
village pub: 129
village, model: 160, 161
vintage transport: 157–159
violence, domestic: 47
violin & viola teachers: 197
vitamins, free: 41
vocational courses with crèche: 112
Volunteer Reading Help: 222
W
Waiting Room: 90
Waitrose: 79
walking: 134, 141
walking with babies and children: 70
Wallingford: 86, 157, 159, 185
Wallingford Castle: 148
Wallingford/Benson Twins Club: 52
Wantage Motorist Centre: 76, 170
Watch: 202
Water Babies: 184–185
Water Fowl Sanctuary & Children's Animal Centre: 156–157
water rides: 161
water slides: 149–150, 161, 173
water, lead in: 23

239

Waterman's Arms: 126
Watermill Theatre, Newbury: 180
Waterperry House Tea Room: 125
waterproof clothes: 91
Waterstones: 83
WEA (Workers Educational Association): 111, 113
weaning: 22
website, Oxford City Council: 182–183
websites for children: 98–99
websites for parents: 97
websites, educational: 99
weir: 134, 136
Welcome Holidays Ltd: 170
welfare rights and advice: 40–43
Wellplace Zoo: 157
Wesley Memorial Methodist Church: 65
West Oxford Community Centre: 62, 189, 196
West Oxford Fun Day: 166
West Oxford Primary School: 216
West Wycombe: 147
Westminster Leisure Centre: 185, 187
Westminster pier: 163
Westminster pool: 185
Westonbirt Arboretum: 148
wet weather: 150–153
wetting the bed: 26
Wheatley: 105, 109, 197
Wheatley Park Sports Centre: 179
wheelchair access: 206–209, 212–217
wheelchairs, on buses: 75
Whipsnade Wild Animal Park: 159
White Company: 90
White Hart: 131
White Horse: 148, 161
White Horse Leisure & Tennis Centre: 109, 185, 188

White House: 126
wholefoods: 80
whooping cough: 24
Wicken Activity Toys Centre: 87
Wiggy's World: 179
Wikki Stix: 91
wildlife: 147, 153–157, 159, 202
Wilkinet: 70, 89
Wilkinson's: 86
Windale School: 215
windmill: 146
Windsor Leisure Centre: 150, 160
Witney: 86, 152, 154, 179, 193,
Wittenham Clumps: 148
Wolfson College: 144
Wolfson College Day Nursery: 207
Wolvercote: 131
Wolvercote School: 214
Women of Colour: 47
women's activities: 114
Women's Centre: 7, 10
Women's Centre tours: 7
Women's Environmental Network: 37
women's festival: 114, 142
Women's Training Scheme: 112
Wooburn Common: 156, 180
wood carving: 198
Wood Farm Primary School: 60
Wood Green Leisure Centre, Banbury: 150
Woodcraft Folk: 201–202
woodland: 155
Woodley: 159
woods: 147
Woodstock: 75, 146, 185
Woodstock Road Baptist Church: 67
wool: 81
Woolworths: 86
Worcester College: 135
Working Tax Credit helpline: 42
workplace nurseries – see nurseries:
Works: 83

Worktrain: 47
wraparound care: 199–201
X
Xscape: 153
Y
yachting lake (models): 134
Yarnton: 63, 157, 196
Yarnton Nurseries Garden Centre: 157
yoga: 109–110
Yoga Garden: 110
yoga, parent & child: 189
yoga, postnatal: 16
yoga, prenatal: 8
Young Dads: 45, 53, 59
Young Explorers: 91
young mums: 53
Young Mums Pregnancy Club: 7
youth organisations: 201–202
Z
zoo animals: 154, 157, 159, 160
zoo, see Cotswold Wildlife Park

240

New Parent Network – Membership Form

Membership costs only £6.00 again this year. To join/renew, please send this form with a cheque/PO for £6.00 payable to *New Parent Network*, or the standing order form to: NPN, 69 Princes St, Oxford OX4 1DE.

Name: _____ Partner's Name: _____

Address: _____
_____
_____ Post Code: _____

Telephone: _____ Email: _____

Name and date of birth of each child:
_____
_____

Baby expected on: _____

Would you like to meet other parents if we are organising a group near you? Yes/No

Please give any suggestions you may have for future talks or activities:
_____
_____
_____

Where did you hear about NPN? (New members only) _____

Is there any kind of help you would like to contribute to the Network (eg, writing, photocopying, legal advice, helping organise events, entertainment at parties etc)? No/Yes (please specify)
_____
_____
_____

I am happy for New Parent Network to hold the details I have supplied for the purposes of producing labels to mail me magazines, organising contact with other local parents (if requested), informing me of and organising local activities, NPN administration (eg membership subscriptions). I understand that this information will be used only by members of the Committee and organisers of NPN events and will not be passed to any third parties outside New Parent Network without my consent

S.igned: _____ Dated: _____

New Parent Network
STANDING ORDER MANDATE

Please fill in the form below and send it to NPN, 69 Princes St, Oxford OX4 1DE and we will forward it to your bank.

To: The Manager,_____Bank/Building Society

Please set up the following Standing Order for the regular payment of £6.00 annually on 1 September from my account to New Parent Network.

MY BANK DETAILS:

Bank Branch name & address: _____

_____

_____ Postcode: _____

Sort code: __ __ - __ __ - __ __   Account No: __ __ __ __ __ __ __ __

Account Name: _____

NEW PARENT NETWORK BANK ACCOUNT DETAILS:

Lloyds Bank, Cowley Branch, Pound Way, Cowley
Sort code: 30-12-51
Account No: 0554826
Account Name: New Parent Network

PAYMENT DETAILS

Amount of 1st payment: £6.00
Date of 1st payment: on receipt of this letter
Amount of annual payment: £6.00
Date of annual payment: 1st September

Please debit my personal account annually until further notice:

Signed: _____   Dated: _____

Updates and Improvements

Let us know of anything that needs changing or that should be added to the next edition. Continue overleaf or on a separate sheet if necessary and return to: NPN, 64 Fernhill Road, Cowley, Oxford OX4 2JP.

Name:_____

Address:_____

Postcode:_____ Date: _____

☎ _____ email: _____

Please note the following change/addition: _____

_____

_____

_____

- - - ✂ -

Order Form

If you would like to order more copies of this book, please send this form and your cheque or postal order to:
      NPN, 59 James Street, Oxford, OX4 1EU

Please send me ___ copy/ies of 'Oxford for the Under-Eights' at £5.00 each plus p+p £1.20 each. I enclose a cheque/postal order for £_____ made payable to **'New Parent Network'**.

Name:_____

Address:_____

_____ Postcode:_____

For bulk discounted orders (724681

East Oxford - Refugee Resource
and other places working with refugees and asylum seekers

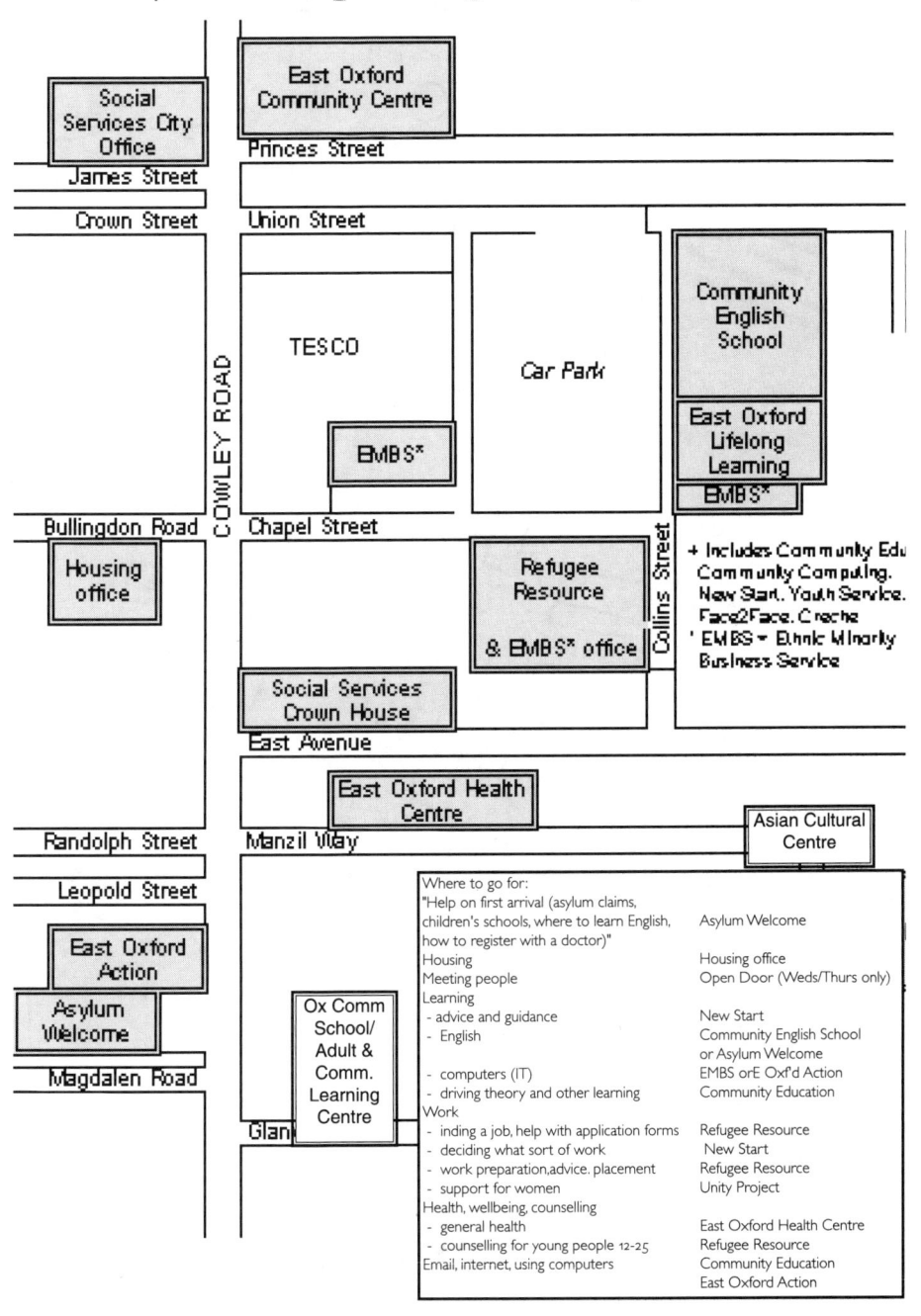

Map locations:
- Social Services City Office
- East Oxford Community Centre
- Princes Street
- James Street
- Crown Street
- Union Street
- TESCO
- Car Park
- Community English School
- EMBS*
- East Oxford Lifelong Learning
- EMBS*
- COWLEY ROAD
- Bullingdon Road
- Chapel Street
- Housing office
- Refugee Resource & EMBS* office
- Collins Street
- Social Services Crown House
- East Avenue
- East Oxford Health Centre
- Randolph Street
- Manzil Way
- Asian Cultural Centre
- Leopold Street
- East Oxford Action
- Asylum Welcome
- Magdalen Road
- Ox Comm School/ Adult & Comm. Learning Centre
- Glan[...]

+ Includes Community Edu, Community Computing, New Start, Youth Service, Face2Face, Creche
* EMBS = Ethnic Minority Business Service

Where to go for:
"Help on first arrival (asylum claims, children's schools, where to learn English, how to register with a doctor)"
Housing
Meeting people
Learning
 - advice and guidance
 - English

 - computers (IT)
 - driving theory and other learning
Work
 - finding a job, help with application forms
 - deciding what sort of work
 - work preparation, advice, placement
 - support for women
Health, wellbeing, counselling
 - general health
 - counselling for young people 12-25
Email, internet, using computers

Asylum Welcome

Housing office
Open Door (Weds/Thurs only)

New Start
Community English School
or Asylum Welcome
EMBS or E Oxf'd Action
Community Education

Refugee Resource
New Start
Refugee Resource
Unity Project

East Oxford Health Centre
Refugee Resource
Community Education
East Oxford Action

247

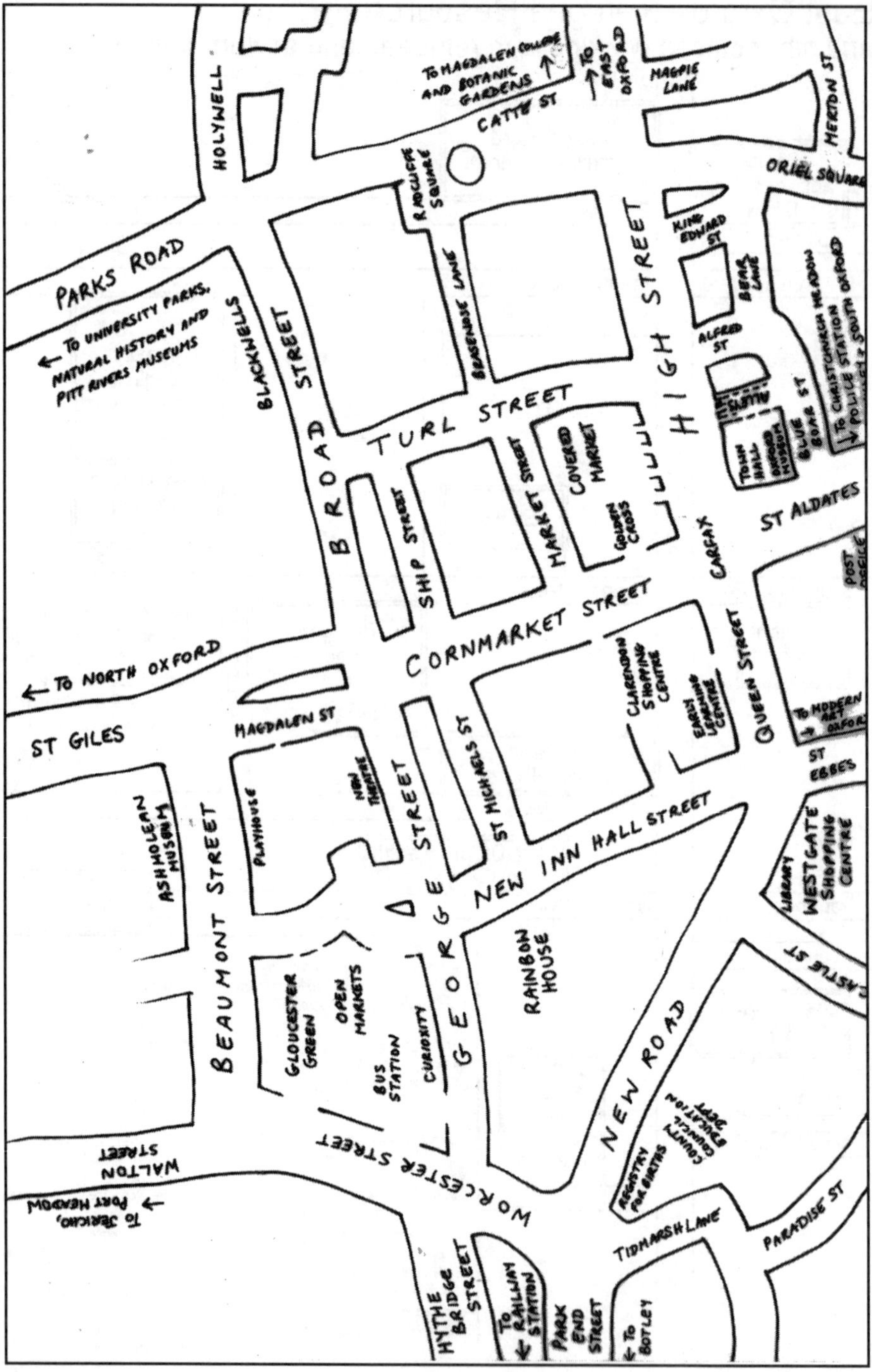
To Magdalen College and Botanic Gardens
To East Oxford
Magpie Lane
Merton St
Holywell
Catte St
Radcliffe Square
Oriel Square
King Edward St
Parks Road
To University Parks, Natural History and Pitt Rivers Museums
Blackwells
Broad Street
Brasenose Lane
High Street
Bear Lane
Alfred St
To Christchurch Meadow
Police Station
South Oxford
Turl Street
Town Hall
Oxford Museum
Blue Boar St
Covered Market
Market Street
Ship Street
Golden Cross
Carfax
St Aldates
Post Office
Cornmarket Street
To North Oxford
Clarendon Shopping Centre
Queen Street
To Modern Art Oxford
St Giles
Magdalen St
Playhouse
New Theatre
St Michaels St
St Ebbes
Ashmolean Museum
Beaumont Street
New Inn Hall Street
Library
Westgate Shopping Centre
George Street
Rainbow House
Castle St
Gloucester Green
Open Markets
Bus Station
Curioxity
New Road
County Council Education Dept
Walton Street
To Jericho, Port Meadow
Worcester Street
Registry for Births
Tidmarsh Lane
Paradise St
Hythe Bridge Street
To Railway Station
Park End Street
To Botley